FOR TONY

BE THE OCELOT,
MY FRIEND!

Christopher Foal
DEC, 2018
MAT 6:33

An Ocelot in an Underwear Drawer

Adventures of a Profoundly Imperfect and Intensely Happy Man

Christopher Scott Ford

WESTBOW
PRESS®
A DIVISION OF THOMAS NELSON
& ZONDERVAN

WestBow Press books may be ordered through booksellers or by contacting:

WestBow Press
A Division of Thomas Nelson & Zondervan
1663 Liberty Drive
Bloomington, IN 47403
www.westbowpress.com
1 (866) 928-1240

ISBN: 978-1-5127-7547-1 (sc)
ISBN: 978-1-5127-7548-8 (e)

Print information available on the last page.

WestBow Press rev. date: 02/21/2017

Contents

For those who call me Dad.

Author's Note

Welcome! I am so glad that you're here. You are holding something that took me over four years to make. It's funny to think that so much personal richness and so many profound moments can be boiled down into a five by eight rectangle of pressed wood pulp (or bits and bytes if you're doing the eBook thing.)

It was very important to me that the stories in this book not be in chronological order. This is not a biography. It is a collection of true adventures that just happen to be about a common central character; adventures that are arranged in an order that might seem random but are not. Much thought has gone into their order of appearance. These adventures, in most cases, can stand alone; but they, together, tell a greater story. It's the story of the Ocelot in the Underwear Drawer. Like individual bricks in a wall, or unique brush strokes of a painting, each adventure works together with the rest to form a larger creation.

The goal of this book is to entertain, plain and simple. If I can do that; if I can touch your heart a time or two, or make you laugh, or smile, or just tell you a story that you enjoy, I will have accomplished more than enough. But, deep down, there's more. If I can, with this series of adventures, build you a picture of what I've learned; if I can help you, even only one of you, to find something that you lacked before, then it was all worth my while.

As you experience each of these adventures, you might be able, little by little, to draw them into a single pile of pieces; which might then require some puzzling together. This is not a self-help book, providing some fail-safe path to happiness. This is simply a collection of adventures that one individual took to get there. Or, is it? Maybe it is a self-help book, in a manner of speaking. Maybe these adventures will remind you of some things; things that you'd forgotten; adventures of your own and what they've taught you. Maybe my adventures will work together with yours to help you draw a new path.

The stories held herein are written from memory, and with memories being what they are, I have had to creatively fill a few gaps, supplement a few shortfalls, and rely on some research, interviews and careful imagination to round some things out. Though it has been my goal to tell them as accurately as I can, some things have required a little bit of diligent tweaking. At times, I have needed to respectfully change some names, dates and locations, without losing the story. To make them readable, I have consolidated events and conversations a time or two.

By the way, if you don't like the first one or two, stick with it. These adventures are very different, one from another. I also, highly recommend that you have a look at the Notes section at the back of the book, a section that readers often skip. I know I do, sometimes. That portion of this book is filled with extra flavor and some background details that didn't render themselves well in the main body of the text. Some of my favorite passages are in the Notes.

Before you get started, I'll take this opportunity to just say thanks. It means a lot to me that my hard work is lying in your hands and I look forward to us spending some time together.

You ready? Let's do this.

On your mark, get set...

*"God has called you to live a
life of adventure"*

Donnie Thompson

"Mentsch Tracht, Gott Lacht."
(Man plans, God laughs)

Yiddish Proverb

1

Almond or Raspberry

Adrenaline surge to the gut.

There she is!

Cold needles shooting across my scalp. A strangely pleasant sick feeling all over. *Catch your breath and look away, quick! Before she sees. Too late! She's got me! Shot me, right through the eyes with her own big lovely brown weapons.*

Her name was Chelea. Isn't that a pretty name? She was working at the concessions counter, just outside the gym during a home basketball game. The concessions counter was in a wide indoor hall that connected the gymnasium to the cafeteria where our Friday night dance would begin shortly after the game.

The game had already started and my best bud Greg and I were late. The band played and the crowd cheered in the background, but it was only noise to me. I had just made eye contact with Chelea. She smiled at me and waved a dainty left-handed wave with her fingers, like she was playing a tiny piano up in the air. So cute!

Trying to be the very picture of cool, I gave her a slight head toss and a crooked half-smile and I immediately looked away, walking on by, toward the gym. *Just a normal Friday night, yes sir, all in a day's work. No love-struck eleventh grade boy here! Just a devoted Panthers fan, on my way to watch my team play basketball.* Not really. I couldn't care less who won that game. I had something far more important on my mind.

"Tonight's the night, Cwiffith," Greg said as he elbowed me in the ribs. "Go buy a Hershey bar from her. And chat a little. You can do it, man! And later, you'll ask her to dance. And then… you'll ask her to dance again. And again. And, if it looks like it's going okay, you'll ask her out."

"I know the plan, you jerk," I said with a nervous grin. "I'm the one that came up with it, remember?"

"So, go! Buy the stupid candy bar, pinhead!" Greg was a good friend. The best I've ever had. We would have died for each other. In fact, there was a time or two that we almost did. But that's another story. We're talking about Chelea right now. Try to stay on the subject, will ya?

If only I'd taken his advice and bought the Hershey bar, right then. Things might have turned out differently. Instead, I stood still, just out of view of the concessions counter, silent and sullen; my nervous stomach held a family of wrestling field mice.

Greg looked me in the eye for a long moment. "Plan B?"

"Plan B," I replied sadly, and I shook my head. Plan A had been a good plan, but it had to go. It seemed easy when we were talking about it beforehand but, now that the moment had come; it was just too direct. Too terrifying. Being a naturally shy boy with an added girl-anxiety was a lot like starving to death in a sea of food. There were pretty girls everywhere at Snohomish High School, 1985, and I wanted so badly to have one. For years it had been this way, but I hadn't taken the chance. I just couldn't. Too scared. Too insecure. Too stupid.

But this time was going to be different! No backing down! This was Chelea, after all! Had I set my sights too high? Yeah, pretty much. Was I reaching for the impossible? Probably. This was not just any girl. Chelea was a queen, a star, a diamond. She was way too popular and I was way too not. Probably not the right girl for me to choose at this point in my life. Maybe I should have aimed a little lower, but, The Crush is a fickle thing, and it chooses whom it will. I had no control. Roll with The Crush, or be crushed by it.

No, she wasn't perfect. Maybe she didn't have Kimberly's eyes or Dianne's hair or Lexie's bod. What Chelea had was special. She was an amalgam of all-that-Chris-wants. She had the intangibles. She was pretty, athletic, and smart. She was sweet, she was funny, she was kind. And when she smiled she made the person she was talking to feel important. At least, she did for me. She was what I wanted. And tonight, I was going to try. Pass or fail – sink or swim – win or lose; this was the night. But it was going to have to be Plan B.

There was a reason that Greg and I had arrived late to the game. Though I'd hoped that it wouldn't be so, I had known that Plan B would very likely come into play. So we'd made preparations. Now, I'm not assigning blame to anyone else. I am responsible for my own actions, but my dad was unknowingly partly involved in my Plan B decision and the unfortunate things that it would ultimately cause.

He too had had a shyness problem with girls when he was young. It's amazing that he and my mother had ever met. They wouldn't have, had it not been for Plan B. He didn't call it that. That was my name for it, but I took my Plan B right out of my Dad's playbook, based on stories that I'd heard him tell.

Well into his twenties, still dealing with the shyness, he went to a community dance one evening. I believe that they called them "mixers" in the mid-1960s. He was going to hang out with some buddies, have a good time and, if he was lucky, maybe meet a girl. But he wasn't going in unarmed. He was equipped with a secret weapon. When he tells the stories, he calls it, "Liquid Courage." It's that simple. A couple shots of something strong and a large percentage of that fear would go away. It worked! My mom was beautiful. The liquid courage was there for him and he danced with her all evening, and the rest is history. Way to go Dad!

Tonight, I would carry on the tradition. I would go to Plan B and employ the mystical properties of Liquid Courage, and dance with a beautiful girl. But there's a problem. Unlike my Dad on the night of the big mixer, I was well under twenty-one. I was only sixteen. So was Greg. Liquid courage can be a tough commodity to acquire at sixteen, not to mention that it's a really bad idea for about a dozen other reasons! Greg had somehow filched two bottles of cheap champagne from his parents. I remember laughing when Greg used the word 'filched.' Who talks like that? They were the kind of inexpensive champagne that came in brown bottles with metal twist-off caps. They were cheapos, but they were all we had. They were Plan B.

The bottles were hidden in the back of my pickup. I had my parents' red 1978 Toyota Long Bed. It was a great little truck that, a few years earlier, my parents had used to taxi our soccer teams all over creation. It was too small and cute to be called a 'truck,' so we called it a 'twuck.' The back end was set up perfectly for a band of dirt-covered, cleat-wearing soccer kids. There was an extra-tall shell on the back and a big foam rubber mattress inside. My parents had installed a pass-through boot in the window so the driver could talk with the people in the back. Tonight, the former soccer transport vehicle housed the supplies needed to execute Plan B.

Parked on a residential street, less than a block from the high school, Greg pulled up a corner of the mattress and removed the two bottles. He held one of them up to what little light was making it through the darkened side windows of the camper shell and read, "Raspberry Champagne. Hmmph. Sounds tasty." He rotated the second bottle into view. "Almond?! Ugh. That sounds gross."

We both curled our lips at the thought of almond champagne. "We'd better drink the raspberry first," he said. "Maybe the almond won't be so nasty if we're a little bit drunk."

"Okay." I didn't really care what it tasted like. I just needed the courage that was magically infused into the liquid.

He opened the raspberry bottle and he took a big drag on it. "Mmmm..," he smiled and handed the bottle to me. He was right. It was good. Less than three minutes later, after passing it back and forth numerous times, the bottle was empty.

"You take the first almond drink," he told me. "I don't know if I'm ready."

Prepared for the worst, I took a big gulp. Oh, it was so good! Better than the raspberry. I smiled and took another, even longer drink. I saw realization appear on Greg's face and he said, "gimme that, you jerk-weed!" I grinned and handed it over.

As we drank, passing the bottle back and forth, we tossed wise-cracks back and forth with it. Though I tried several times to change the subject, replacing it with trivial nonsense (which I was usually expert at), I couldn't shake the nervousness. Chelea loomed over me like a Sword of Damocles; fearful thoughts of what I was preparing to do and with whom I was preparing to do it.

Images and scenes came flooding in, uninvited and unwanted. They appeared for me in a Mind Movie, as I tipped the ugly brown bottle back in the dark. Mind Movie was a term that I had invented at about five years old, to describe the detailed clarity with which my memories, daydreams and fantasies sometimes appear for me. They play like movies. *"What are you laughing about over there, Christopher?" "Nuffin' Mama. Just havin' a Mind Movie."* For a five-year-old, it was a pretty descriptive term. I wouldn't know, until years later, that it's an uncommon ability. I have certainly experienced my share of them while writing this book; not all of them pleasant. In fact, without that unusual talent, this book would have been impossible to write.

This particular Mind Movie was a memory of Chelea from a month or so earlier. It was from Soccer class. I was taking Advanced Soccer to get a Physical Education credit. I usually enjoyed playing Goalie, but that day, I was a Power Forward. I had the ball on a break-away and I was making my scoring run. Only one person could stop me. It was the other team's excellent Goalie, Chelea. She was very good and I knew that I would need to make this shot count if I was going to score.

I went for a power crossing shot, up and in. The aim was to kick the ball into the upper corner of the goal to my left, her right. She read my body language like a book, as my kicking leg swung forward and a little to my left, and she started her move toward the very spot that I was aiming for. She was going to block my shot! But I missed! I got under the ball too much and it came off of my foot all wrong. Instead of going where it should, it bounded straight ahead, almost exactly to where Chelea had just been.

Seeing this, she stopped and tried to get back, but it was too late. She lost her balance and went down hard on her rear end. The ball planted itself in the net. She raised both hands to her face and she giggled. I stood there grinning like a knucklehead, mesmerized by her cuteness and her sweetness, and I watched her giggle. Coach Fowler roared with laughter at the sideline, yelling something about Chelea's gracefulness. I wanted to reach down and take her hand, helping her up. That's what a gentleman would do, right? I wanted to say something to her like, "Great try!" or "You'll get it next time." or "You're beautiful."

Instead, I ran away without a word; back to my position on the field. Secretly and silently I shouted at myself. *You Idiot! You blew it! That was your chance! You Dummy!*

I had missed the chance to touch her hand and feel the thrill shoot through me; to look her in the eye and laugh with her. From a distance, I watched another player help her to her feet. I saw him laughing with her as she dusted herself off.

From forty yards away, I saw her smile like I had a telephoto lens focused directly on her face. That smile, that seemed somehow to glow, could have been for me.

"Hey! You okay?" It was Greg. Suddenly, I was back in the twuck and knee deep in Plan B.

"Yeah."

It was time to go back to the school. Time for the magic. The Almond bottle was empty and it was time to dance with Chelea! *How can I dance with her if I couldn't even touch her hand?* Would the courage be there? It was going to have to be, because I was going through with this, by gum!

Bottles empty and bellies full, I lead as we climbed out the rear door of the camper shell. Suddenly, a bright light shined in my face. A deep male voice came from behind it, "What do you have under your jacket, son?"

Just below the blinding cone of light I saw two sets of creased black pant legs and four very shiny black boots. "Nothing," was my reply. It was, of course, the almond champagne bottle that was hidden in my Levis coat. I had the plain Levis on that night. Greg had his big one with the fake white fur. Levi's jackets were cool stuff in 1985.

I saw light reflect off of a utility belt that held a club, and a pistol. I hadn't seen their faces. I turned without a word and started walking down the sidewalk. I expected to hear a man's voice saying something like, "Stop!" or "Wait right there." Or "Freeze! You're under arrest." But nothing happened. I just kept walking. I heard Greg's footsteps just behind me. I also heard two sets of boots hitting the concrete a few yards farther back.

Maybe, if I can shove the bottle into this hedge up here real quick, I can hide the evidence. Pretty quick thinking. But my thinking was quicker than my champagne-dulled reflexes and a moment later there was an exaggeratedly loud crash and broken glass was all over the sidewalk. On went the handcuffs. One of the policemen mumbled something about "probable cause."

Wistfully, I looked toward the high school, just a half block away. *Chelea!* Someone else was going to dance with her tonight. Soon I would be on my way to the Snohomish City Police Station. Soon, my parents would be receiving a very unpleasant telephone call. Soon, I would experience punishment like I had never known.

As it would turn out, my restriction at home would last so long that I would never again have that golden opportunity with Chelea.

Once in a while, we get an opportunity to make a quick decision that changes everything; sometimes resulting in pain and loss, sometimes in blessings beyond measure. Oh, the trouble I could have saved with the purchase of one brown-wrapped Hershey's-with-Almonds. There it is again! Almonds! You know, I should probably hate almonds, but I don't. Strangely, I don't care much for raspberries.

2

To Be an Astronaut

"They didn't teach us about this," she told my parents. It was conference night at my school. Mom and Dad were there to meet my teacher and see my classroom. Miss Livingston was a good teacher, but she had so little experience. "I want to be the best first grade teacher that I can be, but I don't know what to do with Chris."

She explained that she had received training on how to handle all kinds of kids; the class clown, the quiet and shy, the learning disability, and so many others. "The cryer, the bully, the attention hound," she explained, "I think I'm ready for those."

This was her first job as a teacher and she was determined to get it right! "But, what do I do with Chris? They didn't teach us about him." She was so excited to be a teacher, to finally get into the real world and do all the things that she had been learning. My parents liked her instantly.

"What can I do with a child who finishes his assignments in half the time it takes everyone else? How do I motivate and challenge him when he breezes through his lessons like they're nothing? And how do I keep him from being a disruption to the others as he sits there, bored, watching them work? We've been having a bit of an issue with that."

A day or two later she took me aside. She knelt down to my level and said, "Chris, I have a question for you. Do you like the library?" I nodded my head shyly. "We went there last week as a class. It's kind of a special place for bigger kids." That got my attention! There were three kinds of people that I admired most and wanted to be; and those were cowboys, astronauts and big kids. I had a thing for pirates too, but they weren't on the same level as the other three. In my world, a fourth grader was just about the coolest and scariest person on the planet.

Someday, I was going to have a big cowboy hat and a star on my vest. Someday, I was going to fly through the stars in a flaming rocket and I was going to walk on the moon! And… best of all… someday, I was going to be *a Big Kid*!

"Would you like to go to the library all by yourself, like a big kid?" My eyes widened and my head nodded even more enthusiastically. "If you finish your work before everyone else does, like you did yesterday, I will let you go to the library all by yourself, just like the big kids do."

Later that day, I walked alone through the library. I had no idea what to do there. I didn't know how to read yet, so that took away a lot of my options. I looked at the globe for a while, pretending I was looking at the world through my spaceship portal. I looked at the phonograph records but I wasn't allowed to play them. *Hmmm… what do big kids do?*

I learned quickly that the library was a really boring place, but I wasn't about to tell that to Miss Livingston. Boring or not, that library was my ticket to Bigkidville! I went there every day for a week, looking for big kid things and trying to be big.

Being a big kid is tough! I thought. *Maybe the astronaut thing will be more interesting than this.*

Miss Livingston stood before the class, one morning, between us and the chalkboard. Sometimes she called it 'the blackboard' which I didn't understand because it was really a dark green, but I wasn't going to correct her. That would be bad manners.

"Billy! Chris!" she said sternly. "What's gotten into you two today? This behavior is not acceptable!" It's been a long time, and I don't have any memory of just what it was that we had done wrong. I do remember Billy pretty well though. He didn't like being called Billy. He wanted to be called "Bill," because "Bill" was a big kid name. I totally got that, so, to me, he was always "Bill." I also remember that his hair was so blonde that it was white. Mine was bright yellow. We were Miss Livingston's "two toe heads." I had no idea what that meant, but I figured that it must be a good thing, so I kinda liked it when she would call us that.

She wasn't calling us her anything today, though. She was mad. Whatever we had done must have been pretty bad.

"Today at lunchtime, I want you both to go to the cafeteria and eat your lunches. Then, I want you both to march yourselves straight back to this room. You will spend the rest of lunch recess in your seats with your heads on your desks. And, stay there, both of you. Do you understand? No moving from your desks."

A little later, tummies full and heads down, I whispered, "Bill… Hey Bill. Bill! Do you think we're allowed to talk?"

"I dunno," he whispered back.

A few seconds of silence.

"Hey Bill."

"What?"

"I need to pee."

"Okay."

We were silent for a while. The lights were off and we were the only people in the room. Sunlight was coming in through the windows. I noticed how the light shined brightly off of the shiny tile floor. *Hmm, I've never seen it do that before. Things sure look different when you're in trouble.*

"Bill!" I whispered.

"What."

"When do you think Miss Livingston is coming back?"

"Probably after recess," he whispered back.

Silence for a while.

"I really need to pee."

I knew that there was a boys' room right outside our class, in the main hallway, which Miss Livingston had always called "a corridor." I thought that that was strange because I knew for sure that it was a hallway.

My legs were doing the seated version of *the peepee dance* under my desk, which is a hard thing to do while keeping one's head firmly planted on a flat surface.

Bill whispered, "Just go. You know where the bathroom is. Just go in there, go pee, and come right back."

"Yeah, but she said we had to stay here! That's what she said, Bill!"

"I won't tell. Just go."

11

I knew that he was right, but Miss Livingston was the only person who knew my secret. Only she knew that I was actually a big kid. No one else knew about my special library privileges. No one else understood. I just couldn't let her down! She said that I had to stay at my desk until the end of recess. *Big Kids do what they're told!*

"I'll just let a tiny bit out." My whisper was getting more hoarse and urgent. "That'll help. Maybe I'll feel better if I just make the front of my underwear a little wet." Bill didn't reply.

My underwear was now wet in front and I was holding the rest back. It had been a bad plan! Once it had started, it had been so hard to stop it. Now, I felt like I was trying to hold the ocean back. I gritted my teeth together and used all of my will to hold on.

"Run!" This time Bill wasn't whispering. He heard my rough breathing and he saw my agonized face. He pointed out the open classroom door. "Go! I won't tell!"

I stayed. Strong, like a big kid.

The battle was a valiant one, but it was destined to fail. Eventually the dam broke and the flood came. Soon I was sitting in a puddle. There was a lake on the tile floor beneath me.

I don't know why, but as I type this just now, I'm remembering that I was wearing corduroy pants that day. What a strange thing to suddenly remember, after forty years.

"Bill." I was still whispering. "What do I do now?"

Minutes passed. Slowly my puddle became cold. It sloshed under my bottom on the smooth wooden seat. Suddenly, I sat upright. *I know!! Miss Livingston will come back soon, before anyone else does. She'll know what to do! She'll help me!*

I was so wet and so cold. The wait seemed to last forever.

The bell rang. No Miss Livingston. The students came. The lights were still off and the sun, coming through the windows lit my lake up like it does on a real lake. Some of my classmates looked at me aghast and shook their heads. Some pointed and laughed. Slowly the room filled with students returning to their seats and there was no Miss Livingston. The room got louder and louder with cruel taunts and laughing insults. Eventually, there was a chorus of singing first graders, belting it out in unison, "Chris peed his pants, Chris peed his pants, Chris peed his pants…"

There was one girl who was especially cruel. She was the class's token ugly girl, the one with the freckles and the missing front teeth, and the boy's haircut. She wouldn't even come into the room. "I'm not going in there with Potty Boy," she shouted, as she screamed with laughter. It was a gleeful laugh, but it was a scream. She had known her share of taunts and teases. She had always been on the receiving end. Now that she had a chance to be the giver, and though I had never been among her tormenters, she executed her righteous vengeance with enthusiastic venom. It must have felt good to her.

Soon, all but the screaming hallway girl were in their seats, and our laughing, singing classroom could be heard down the hall. This went on for what seemed an eternity, but it was probably just a few minutes. I saw her turn to look up the hallway and her screams increased. "Teacher! Teacher!" She pointing in through the doorway, "Chris Ford peed his pants!! Hah hah hah hah hah!!"

In walked Miss Livingston. She froze in the doorway and everyone stopped chanting. She looked at my lake. Then she looked into my eyes. At first she said nothing, but her eyes told me everything. They said, "Chris? You? Of all people?" For the second time that day, I had disappointed her. I wasn't crying. I wasn't defiant. I wasn't anything. What she encountered was blankness. I gave her nothing but a level stare. I looked into her eyes obediently, but there was no visible emotion for her to read. Behind my silent visage lurked a terror that my six-year-old mind could not have articulated, other than the repeating silent hope, *Please, tell me that I'm still a big kid. Please.*

A little while later, I sat beside the school nurse as she tried the telephone numbers on my student file. Finally, after several attempts, "Mr. Ford. You need to come pick up Christopher. He's had an accident at school." The nurse paused to listen as my father asked the obvious question. "Yes, he's alright." She replied. "He wet his pants. He needs to go home."

My dad left work and he came. He smiled, and he took me home. He was so kind. I was emotionally exhausted, and I slept for hours. Miss

Livingston and I never spoke about that day, but I was never sent to the library alone again. My Big Kid Club membership had been revoked.

"I kind of remember that," said Dad, thirty nine years later. "I remember getting that call at work," he said as he reached for the potato salad.

"Chris," said my brother, Shanon, over his paper plate. A light breeze blew across his back patio as we all dug into our barbecued dinner, enjoying the first time in years that his family and mine had been joined by our parents, now well into their seventies, visiting from retirement in Arizona. "I've never heard that story before. I am so sorry that that happened to you."

Conversation moved on to other things. Shanon's oldest daughter, Makenna was telling a story, and everyone was laughing. I stared into my glass of grape soda. In my forty five year old mind, I heard it again, *Chris peed his pants. Chris peed his pants. Chris peed his pants.* On it droned. I looked around the patio table. Makenna was just getting to the good part of her story. Grandma and Grandpa were listening and laughing. I glanced straight across the table, over my chicken leg and barbecued beans, and my wife was looking directly at me. I felt my bottom lip tremble and my eyes water. Her loving eyes softened even more, and she smiled.

I looked back into my grape soda. I saw the sunlight reflect off of the side of an ice cube; the same sun that had lit up my lake thirty nine years earlier, and, in the silence of my mind, I wondered; am I a big kid? That term meant something different to me at forty five than it had at six, but there it was.

I looked back up, and I saw a beautiful wife and a twenty-three-year marriage that is the envy of all of my friends, a smart and responsible sixteen-year-old son with my sense of humor, a confident and lovely eighteen-year-old daughter who had recently graduated top of her class, and would soon be moving into a dorm at Oregon State University; and I knew that they all loved me.

I got the reply to my silent grape soda question. And I liked the answer.

"Great story, Makenna!" I said happily, and I laughed.

"*Peter did not feel very brave; indeed, he felt he was going to be sick. But that made no difference to what he had to do*"

C.S. Lewis,
The Lion, the Witch and the Wardrobe

3

Sorry for the Visual

I nervously walked through the main entrance of the Parkway Nursing Home. The first thing that hit me was the smell. I can't explain it except that it was sour. My newspaper bags were heavily loaded and they hurt my shoulders a little. My brother, Shanon, was going to be busy and he had asked me to sub for him on his paper route.

I walked through the large central room with the book shelves, the colorful aquarium, the comfy looking couches and the bored looking white haired people. I turned toward the hall to my right, down which most of my deliveries would be made, looking forward to getting done with this uncomfortable portion of the paper route, wanting to get back on my bike and on to the next neighborhood.

I was fifteen years old and, in the mid 1980s, being a paperboy was a great job. Today I was delivering on both my brother's route and on my own. It would be a long afternoon. We both delivered papers for The Everett Herald. Herald routes were huge compared to some of the other local newspapers. We both had over seventy customers. When my best buddies, Jeff, Brad and Greg, would mention their own paper routes, on the other side of town, for papers like The Seattle Times and the Seattle Post Intelligencer, I had to laugh. My route had more papers than all three of theirs combined. Today I would be delivering over a hundred fifty newspapers.

This Nursing Home was the part of today's job that I had been dreading. I was a very shy fifteen-year-old and I felt very out of place there, knowing that I was the only kid in the building. Though I knew that I had permission to be there, walking the halls unsupervised, I felt as though I was trespassing. I worried that others would think so too. I felt so conspicuous and out of place. *Please, just let me get through this... let no one talk to me or look at me.*

I was almost to the south hallway when I heard a high pitched screech, "Paperboy!" *Did I just hear that? No, keep walking... it'll be okay.*

"Oh, Paperboy!" There it was again, no mistake. I had the urge to ignore the voice, but I knew that I couldn't do that. Shy though I was, I was raised to have good manners. I took a deep breath. I turned around with a smile, and I looked out over the room. On the far side, near the shelves of Reader's Digest Condensed Classics, sat a tiny gray-haired woman in a wheelchair, waving at me.

"Paperboy!" she shrieked again. Then she smiled and beckoned to me like she was trying to pull me to her with an invisible rope. Through my already mounting discomfort and my timidity with strangers, I couldn't help but chuckle at how cute that was.

A moment later, I found myself, at her request, pushing her aluminum chariot down the south hall, cursing my good manners. *I should've kept walking... dummy!*

She rode along with a big look-at-me smile as one ancient gentleman shouted, "you're choosing your men kinda young, aren't you Agnes?" A woman in a chair lowered her knitting and shouted, "Oh, Agnes, he's supposed to deliver papers, not old women!" and she cackled with laughter. "Hey, kid!" someone yelled. "No kissing on the first date!" A room full of one-thousand-year-olds howled with laughter. *So much for getting in and out unnoticed.*

I turned red as I silently pushed Agnes down the hall. Agnes, on the other hand, was having a grand time, waving to everyone we passed like she was a pageant princess on a parade float – the newly crowned Miss Wrinkles.

As we neared the end of the hall, where we would be turning left at the tee, Agnes threw her arms up in the air and shouted "Weeeeeee!" Had I been pushing her too fast? I was fifteen, what did I know about octogenarian wheelchair etiquette?

After leaving an appreciative grinning Agnes at her destination, I moved on down the hall toward my first customer.

When Shanon had given me the list of room numbers and a hand-drawn map of the building the day before, he had also given me some delivery instructions. "Now, don't leave the papers outside their rooms," he said. "The other old folks will just steal it. And don't knock on their doors 'cause they might not be there, and half of them can't hear you knocking anyway. Just walk in and lay the paper on their bed."

"What?! Just walk in?" I was very reluctant to do that. That would be bad manners. It would be intruding. That's just a tough thing to ask of a very shy fifteen year-old. I'm not sure why I thought that, since my brother was only thirteen, and he'd been doing it for weeks.

So, here I was, opening doors and laying newspapers on beds. After that first one, which had only happened after a full minute of standing outside, I was starting to get the hang of it. Almost done, I looked at my list of room numbers, and boldly launched into room 117. *Good, another empty room.*

"Well, hello there young man!" *Not so empty!*

I froze. The voice had come from my left. I slowly turned and looked in that direction. I saw something that, no matter how hard I tried, could never be unseen. There stood a smiling taller-than-average senior lady wearing curlers. Oh, and slippers. Yeah, that was pretty much it. It took me a moment to understand what I was looking at. *Is she wearing curtains? No, that's just giant folds of sagging skin.*

She stood in a shadowy area of the room. The sun streamed in through the window blinds, casting stripes across her, so it's no wonder that I didn't immediately understand what I was seeing. It looked like she had a pair of softballs at the ends of two stretched out tube socks somehow attached to the front of her upper torso.

Oh my goodness, those are her… those are her… (gulp!)

"How are you today?" she asked me with a happy smile. "Isn't the weather just lovely?"

"Uh… Yes ma'am," was what squeaked out of my mouth, while my mind erupted with thoughts like, *Would it be bad manners to scream and run with arms flailing over my head and crash through that window to my death on the street below? Yeah, I might need to do that.*

"I just adore the flowers this time of year," she said as she took a step toward me. I backed up and my heavily packed back newspaper pouch pressed against the wall. Trapped! Nowhere to go! And she kept coming closer! *What do I do?!*

Doesn't she know that she's naked? Doesn't she care?

"And the sounds of the birds outside my window," she said as she clapped her hands together with delight, a motion that caused waves to roll across her many folds and dimples. I didn't want to, but I stared. I stared at all of that cottage cheese rolling and rippling across her massive front. I couldn't pull my eyes away. I was a deer, helplessly staring into the headlights of impending death, as she took another step toward me. *Oh no! What if she wants a hug?*

Suddenly, the door opened and in walked a nurse. *Noooo!!!* What couldn't have possibly gotten any more awkward and uncomfortable, just got more awkward and uncomfortable. Someone has now seen me at the most awkward moment of my life. I'm probably going to be in trouble now. I looked up at her, my face beet red and my eyes twice their normal diameter.

The nurse stood still. She looked at me. She looked at the woman. She looked back at me. Suddenly, she laughed. It was a single laugh, like a soft dog bark, and then, just as quickly, she composed herself and told me with a smile, "You can go, and wait for me in the hall."

Now, I was sure that I was in trouble. *Should I run? Yes! No! That would be bad manners.*

A moment later, out in the hall, the nurse laughed again and said, "I am so sorry. That's Helen. She doesn't know any better."

From that day on, no paperboy would ever have to open another door at the Parkway Nursing Home. All he had to do was leave a stack of newspapers at the nurse's station with a list of room numbers. And I had nightmares for the next week. Oh, who am I kidding? I've had nightmares for the last thirty years!

"Proportional Limit: The greatest stress at which a material is capable of sustaining the applied load without deviating from the proportionality of stress to strain"

Engineer's Edge

4

Sequins and Safety Pins

The view here was amazing! I had timed our dinner reservation so we could see the mountains and the water, watch the sunset and then see the city lights before we had to go. The Space Needle Restaurant stands five hundred feet above Seattle. It's another one-hundred-five feet to the top of the spire. It was built for the 1962 World's Fair, and here we were twenty-four years later, enjoying a delicious meal.

It was a strange sensation stepping from the waiting area in the stationary center portion of the restaurant onto the rotating outer ring where the tables and customers make exactly one full revolution per hour, affording a peerless view of Puget Sound, the Cascade and Olympic mountain ranges and one of America's most beautiful cities.

Over a year had gone by since the "Chelea Plan B" debacle, of which she was, thankfully, completely unaware. I still thought very highly of her, and I still entertained the occasional Chelea daydream, but I had, for the most part, moved on.

Tonight I dined with Laura, the first girl I had ever asked out. Though still difficult enough, this had been much easier to arrange, and had not required Plan B or any other mood-altering gimmick. I had gotten to know Laura on the ski bus earlier that school year, and we had struck up a friendship. We were both Seniors and we both wanted to go to our prom. Pretty simple. I would have gladly welcomed a boy-girl relationship with her, but it was pretty apparent that this one was going to stay in "the friend zone." No pressure then, and no real reason to be afraid. I had asked her, as a friend, to the Snohomish High School Senior Ball, and that friend had agreed.

I was wearing a tuxedo for the first time in my life and feeling rather grown up. We were laughing together over a yummy seafood gumbo that had some kind of fancy French name. "I can't believe you did that!" she giggled. "I think they believed you!"

She was laughing about the older couple who had ridden the Space Needle's glass elevator with us a little earlier. We had gotten off at the restaurant level and they had continued up to the observation deck. The lady had remarked at what an attractive young couple we were, in all of our formal finery. I told her that we had just gotten married, which had caused the woman's expression to change to a mix of congratulatory delight and a very noticeable aren't-they-awfully-young look of concern.

As we laughed about that, Laura looked over my right shoulder, back toward the waiting area behind me. Her eyes widened and she whispered, "Wow." I turned to look. There, in the waiting area, seated with her back to us, was a vision of bright blue perfection. There was a woman in the most spectacular gown that either of us had ever seen. It was a skin tight strapless dress, the entire upper portion of which was covered in dazzling blue sequins. The dress scooped very low behind her, revealing a beautiful back of perfect skin, a tiny waist, a lovely v-shaped upper torso and a voluminous mane of light brown hair arranged like a movie star on a Hollywood red carpet might wear it.

Involuntarily, I repeated what Laura had said. "Wow," I whispered.

I collected my wits and turned back, reluctantly pulling my eyes from those beautiful shoulder blades, and I gave my attention back to Laura. After all, what was Laura, chopped liver? Of course not! She looked terrific in her pink prom dress, with the corsage that I had bought her. We smiled at each other, unable to remember what we'd been talking about.

Laura's eyes shot back over my shoulder and she audibly gasped, then she pointed. I looked. The mysterious woman with the perfect back had stood and turned toward us so we could see her front. It was our very own high school classmate Lisa Elliott! It was my turn to gasp.

Lisa had, less than a year before, been crowned winner of a prestigious teen beauty pageant. She had ridden in Seattle's 1985 Torchlight Parade wearing a tiara and a sash, and she had even gotten to compete in the national pageant, representing the state of Washington. She was the kind of beautiful that is rare at such a young age.

Now, here she was at the Space Needle Restaurant, prom night, Spring of 1986. I had seen her almost every day at school, but I had never seen her like this. And, I had never seen this much of her! This was a very well-built girl, and I had to wonder what was holding her in that little dress. There was a lot of Lisa on display.

She and Ken, her handsome "friend zone" prom date, were led away from us to their table. They hadn't noticed us. Like everyone else on that side of the Needle, we watched them walk until they were out of sight. "Wow."

Fast forward an hour or two and here we were at the Snohomish High School Senior Ball. Our theme that year was, "On the Edge of a Dream." What in the world did that mean?

Shortly after we had posed for our obligatory prom photo, Laura and I parted for a few minutes as I went to get us both some punch. My friend Tim found me. "Mondo!" he cried with delight.

"Rat Face!" I grinned and shook his hand. He looked better in a tux than I did.

"Who are you here with?" he asked me.

"Laura Cruger."

"Cool. Way to go," he replied.

"How 'bout you?" I asked.

"My girlfriend. You don't know her. She goes to Bothell." The town of Bothell was about a half-hour south of Snohomish. "Hey, I'll bet my date's prettier than yours!"

"Maybe," I replied with a smile. "My date's pretty cute." I never did see her that night. I would have never guessed that Tim's 'prettier-than-my-date' mystery girl from Bothell would someday be my wife and the mother of my children. Ah, but that's a different story – and a good one.

Between the cafeteria, where the Senior Ball was being held, and the gym, where our basketball team played its games, was a wide indoor hall with a concessions window built into the east wall. It was the same concessions window from which Chelea had waved to me, about fourteen months earlier, and it was the same wide hall where I had made the fateful Plan B decision.

Tonight that concessions window was closed, and the almond champagne fiasco was a painful but distant memory. My teenage police record, though, was still all too real.

It was in that wide hall that we had set up a really nice coat check area for our prom patrons to leave their coats and wraps. There were racks and racks of coats on hangers. The two coat check attendants were none other than my tenth-grade brother, Shanon, and his best friend Brad.

Brad was an interesting fellow. His family ran the local hardware store there in Snohomish. Through the years, my dad had bought a lot of nails and paint, a lot of thinga-ma-jigs and a lot of whatz-its from Brad's dad Bob.

Brad was a handsome kid, a little too tall for his age, and he may have had the largest head I've ever seen. The cat had an impressive melon!

They had a good friendship, Shanon and Brad; a lot like mine with Greg. They even looked a bit alike, in that they were both handsome and both really tall. I don't know how tall they were at fifteen but they would eventually grow to six-foot-four and six-foot-seven, respectively. It's a rare thing to be a teenage boy whose younger brother is bigger than you are, but that's been my lot since before our voices changed. I never did make 6'4" like Shanon did. I topped out at a little under 6'2"; the runt of the litter.

Brad's sister was in my grade and was there at the Ball that night, somewhere in the throbbing dance crowd; on the edge of a dream, no doubt.

Shanon and Brad were having the time of their lives, working that coat room. These were a couple of healthy red-blooded young men who, being only fifteen, had not seen much yet in their few short years. They were helping all of these dolled-up older prom girls out of their wraps and shawls and thoroughly enjoying themselves. They'd never seen so much cleavage in all of their lives!

Just like at the Space Needle, everywhere that Lisa went, heads turned. She glided through the room in sparkling blue elegance. The greatest thing about Lisa was that, though she was beautiful and smart and wealthy, she never acted like it was a big deal. She was very sweet and I respected her. I couldn't help but think it again, what's holding her in that thing? I also wondered a little if she was going to be in trouble for showing that much of herself at a school function. Being as sweet as she was, I'm not sure that she even understood just how provocative that plunging neckline was. I'll bet that she saw it as "cute." The truth was, it was jaw-dropping.

Laura and I mingled, we drank punch, and we danced a bit. One of us was pretty good at that. We chatted with some of the teacher chaperones. It was fun to learn that she and I had the same favorite teacher in Mr. Mike Jenson. Mike was one of the few teachers that didn't mind whether you called him by his Mr. Jenson title or just Mike. He'd had his finger shot off in Vietnam. I think it was his left ring finger. I don't know if it's true, but the story goes that, every year, shortly after the beginning of the school year, Mike would go up to the Audio Visual room above our school library, where the really big paper cutter was. It was one of those old guillotine-type cutters that could do multiple sheets at a time. He would wait until there was a sweet little Sophomore girl nearby, and then chomp! "Oh, my finger!" he would yelp as he held up his four-digit hand, his other hand holding a fake rubber finger. Then he would stand back and enjoy the predictable high-pitched squeaks from the young prank victim.

We all loved the guy.

We walked away from the chaperones together to enjoy some more punch. "I wonder why this punch is so good," said Laura.

"Did you ever see *Hollywood Knights*?" I asked. Her blank look was all the answer I needed. "Never mind." (grin).

I don't know where I was when it happened, but it happened – the inevitable. That poor little blue dress of Lisa's had done the best that it could but, alas, the laws of physics ultimately prevailed and out she came. Her dress had suffered what my later professional colleagues and I, when computing structural load calculations, would call a "critical failure." The inertial characteristics of the load had exceeded the capabilities of the load carrier.

I was not in the immediate vicinity at the moment of the disaster, a fact that I would lament bitterly when I heard about it later. It was to Shanon and Brad that she and her noble Ken would turn for rescue.

"Quick! We need help!" The boys turned to see two embarrassed twelfth graders standing before them in the coat room, Ken behind her doing what he could to hold the dress' back together, and Lisa, arms crossed in front of her failed dress, doing her best to contain her ample endowment, and almost succeeding.

"Safety pins!" Ken yelled.

Brad looked around and suddenly, there they were! A small box of safety pins! Had they been there the whole time? It's likely that some very wise faculty member, most likely a lady, had left that box of pins there for just such an event. Shanon and Brad, I think, probably saw them as more of a miraculous gift from God.

When the boys magically presented that box of safety pins, hope returned to Lisa. At that moment those two boys were, quite literally, her heroes. Hidden behind numerous rows of coat racks, it took all three boys, the better part of a box of pins, and a few rather intimate moments, to put her back together. It was a bit of a bonding experience.

As the couple walked back to the dance, two taller-than-average high school sophomore boys stood silent and still, watching them go; each lost in dreamy memories of sequins and safety pins.

Slowly, Brad turned to Shanon, took a deep breath and softly said, "That just made my life."

"Life isn't a matter of milestones, but of moments."

Rose Kennedy

5

The Summer Blockbuster

It was going to be a great night. To a ten-year-old boy, this was some exciting stuff! We weren't exactly poor but we sure weren't wealthy, so we spent a lot of time at home. We didn't go into town for shopping and other things very often because we just didn't have the extra cash. We found ways of entertaining ourselves at home and we made do with what we had.

Because of that, we really appreciated it when we got to go somewhere and do something special. Tonight would be one of those times. In fact, tonight we were going to do one of my very favorite things. To me, movie night was magical. We had probably been to five or six drive-in movies in my short life, in various cities as we'd moved around the country, and I just loved them. It was a hot summer night in 1978, and I was so excited.

It was sort of the tail-end of the drive-in theater era in America, though we didn't know it at the time. The big indoor theater complexes would completely take over less than a decade later.

I can remember several specific drive-in movies, dating back to when I was very small. *The Poseidon Adventure*, starring Gene Hackman, was probably the first one that I can remember. I was only four and I slept through the entire second half, but I can vividly remember that guy in the tuxedo falling into the big skylight, as the huge luxury ship rolled onto its back.

My brother and I slept through big portions of all of our early drive-in experiences, but I still thought that they were great times.

Right under the enormous movie screen, in almost every drive-in we visited, there was a small playground. We always got to the theater quite a while before the film, so there was plenty of daylight and, for some reason, those playgrounds were extra special to play on – a rare treat! No sooner had we nestled our car into some carefully selected parking spot, then we would start begging, "Can we go to the playground? Can we, can we? Huh? Can we? Pleeeeease??? Can we go? Can we go?" We'd wait for that smile-and-nod from one of our parents and off we'd tear. "Yaaaaaaaayyyy!!!"

Then, after playing for a while, as daylight was fading, an even better part of the evening would begin; the pre-movie cartoons! The Theater Manager would use this time to keep us all interested during the fuzzy twilight moments before it was dark enough to start the movie. The cartoon picture quality was usually a little bleached in the evening light, but we didn't care. I can remember Porky Pig, and Popeye the Sailor, and Heckle And Jeckle, and Tom And Jerry. More often than not, they would play Pink Panther Cartoons. I loved those! But best of all was Mr. Magoo! I would laugh and laugh and laugh! For days afterward, I would run around the house, purposely bumping into things, yelling, "Road Hog!" I'm sure my mother loved it.

Sometimes, after the cartoons, a little before the main feature came on, a circle of light would appear and shoot across the dark movie screen. Then it would stop in the middle, daring another light to appear. And it would! Every time! The new light would chase the first light around the screen, playing tag. The lights would shoot and spin around, and we would laugh at the funny zig-zags and cheer when one light caught another.

It wasn't until I was older, maybe seven, that I learned that those funny lights had been door-mounted spotlights on pick-up trucks. Some daddy who had a spotlight would take those few minutes after the cartoons to play spotlight tag with another daddy somewhere else in the Drive-in. How fun!

"Yum, yum!" A familiar voice would suddenly say from the metal speaker box that hung on our driver's side window, just as the screen would light up. "It's time for a refreshing snack." Happy background music would bounce along as cartoon images of smiling hot dogs and soda cups would dance around on the big screen. An enormous smiling over-filled popcorn bag would juggle and popsicles and ice cream sandwiches walked on a circus tightrope. "We promise to satisfy your hunger… your thirst… your sweet tooth." It seemed like the same guy narrated everything back then. "So go visit our refreshment center now… let's go! The show will begin in seven minutes."

I remember one particular drive-in visit in Southern California. There was a long line of cars, three cars wide, moving slowly forward a few feet at a time, working our way into the theater.

"Daddy, why are so many people looking at us?"

"Well, Chris," he replied. "It's because they like our car." I knew that Dad was excited about the used car that he had recently bought, but I was surprised to learn, at seven years old, that everyone else would be too. I had no idea that a 1958 Edsel was something special. Oh, but it was! I felt like we were celebrities with all of those people pointing and smiling.

I fell asleep again, partway through the movie that night; thankful that the Edsel had such a large comfy backseat. I had no way of knowing that history was being made and that the movie industry was being revolutionized before my eyes. The movie that I saw the first half of that night, sleeping through the rest, was the 1975 summer sensation, *Jaws*, directed by a young then-unknown Steven Spielberg. It was the birth of the Summer Blockbuster. *Jaws* shattered all previous box office records and launched a revolution in poster and t-shirt sales.

Just two years later, the blockbuster of 1977 would eclipse the massive numbers of *Jaws* by orders of magnitude. *Star Wars*, written and directed by a young then-unknown George Lucas, would pound *Jaws* and all others in ticket sales and merchandise, forever solidifying the box office legitimacy of the Summer Blockbuster.

Fast-forward a year, to the setting with which we began this chapter; back to that hot summer night of 1978 and one very excited ten-year-old boy. Tonight we would do things a little bit differently. Instead of nosing into our theater parking spot in a classic collector car, we were backed in, in a yellow 1974 Chevy pickup. In the truck bed, my parents reclined side-by-side in folding outdoor lounge chairs. My brother and I sat on the truck bed beside them, in the little areas between the wheel wells and the cab. Thinking back on it now, it must have been uncomfortable for us, but I don't remember anything about that. We might have been kneeling on folded blankets.

We were there to see the Summer Blockbuster of 1978, the Burt Reynolds smash hit, *Smokey and The Bandit.* The first movie of the double feature was a serious car chase drama called, *Gone in Sixty Seconds.* It was fine but it wasn't the movie that we had come to see, though it would go on to become a *cult classic* to Mustang lovers. It had some cool car chase scenes, which were pretty neat.

Between the movies, there was the familiar intermission filmstrip, probably the same one they'd been using since 1965. "Come visit our snack stand…"

"Well," said Dad happily. "I'm going to go get us some dinner. Chris, would you come along and give me a hand?"

Walk alone with my dad in the dark? Hours after my regular bedtime? To help him provide for the family? You bet I'd like to come! This is Dad-and-oldest-son kind of stuff! Big Kid stuff! You bet'cha Dad! Let's go rustle up some grub for the family, just us two men! Yes!

"Sure."

A few minutes later, after a visit to an unusually nasty restroom, Dad was ordering a big bunch of yummy stuff from the snack counter. "And five hot dogs please. Wait!... Chris, would you like to have two hot dogs?"

Gasp!! Two? For me? Did he really just ask me that? He's offering me TWO hot dogs? Oh my goodness! I get to have two? Just like Dad does? I must really be a Big Boy now! I LOVE being ten!

"Yeah, two sounds nice."

"Make it six hot dogs please," he told the man, as he reached over and tousled my hair.

Two hot dogs! This is a first-ever!

The lights dimmed and the pre-movie credits began before we made it back to the truck. It was so dark that it was difficult to walk back, stumbling along - our arms loaded with food and drinks.

The main feature started pleasantly and it got better and better. The theme song was really catchy. What a great movie! What a great night!

"Westbound and down, eighteen wheels a'rollin'." I had never heard anyone speak in CB lingo. It was so funny and so different.

Wow! This is the worst hot dog I have ever tasted!

What was I going to do? My dad had, for the first time ever, bought me a Big-Boy-portion of two hot dogs. I couldn't let him down! The moment that he ordered that second dog, I was a bigger boy than I had been before! It had been a special moment between Dad and me! I knew that I had to eat them both, but, oh my! This hot dog was terrible! Absolutely terrible – maybe the worst thing I had ever eaten. I think I would rather lick an ashtray.

I chewed and I chewed in the dark, my eyes riveted to the big screen, rolling the dry chewy mess around in my mouth, forcing down every swallow. Burt Reynolds and his beautiful black Trans-Am screeched across the screen. "Ha'-haaah…" Ol' Burt did his now-famous Bandit laugh. "Breaker, breaker - I'm puttin' the pedal to the metal…"

Gulp. Down went the last of hot dog number one.

Bleh!

My expression was stretched into what could easily be described as an "icky icky" face. I stared at the long dark foil-wrapped hot dog in my left hand. It seemed to grow as I looked at it. It laughed at me. "I dare ya'!" it seemed to say, in the pale flickering light from the movie screen.

How am I going to eat another one of those?

Slowly, I opened the foil package that contained the ominous hot dog number two, and I pulled it out. I then unwrapped the paper towel that was wound tightly around the dog. I sighed and reluctantly confronted my opponent head-on, taking a cautious bite. Warm juicy flavor exploded upon my palate like a tropical storm.

Wow! This is delicious!

I bit again. It was wonderful! I swallowed the moist delicious mouthful, wanting more.

This might be the best hot dog I have ever eaten! What's going on here?

I looked at the foil wrapper and the paper towel from which the second hot dog had come. I picked up the foil wrapper from the first hot dog and looked around for the corresponding paper towel. It was nowhere to be found.

What the…

I looked everywhere, feeling around in the dark. I took another delicious bite of hot dog number two. *Yum!* Then realization smacked me in the forehead.

Oh my goodness! I know where the first paper towel is! It's in my stomach, in tiny individually chewed morsels. That's why the first hot dog was so bad! So dark was it that I had eaten an entire paper towel along with the hot dog that had worn it.

"Ha ha ha ha!!" A loud barking laugh ripped forth from me like a gunshot, during a quiet non-joking part of the movie.

Dad turned toward me with a quizzical look, and a raised eyebrow – serious yet not unfriendly.

"Ha, ha… er… um…" and I cleared my throat, looking back at the screen. I smiled as I tossed the last bite of hot dog number two into my mouth. *Mmmmmmmm…*

I should probably dab that little trace of mustard off of my lip. I could really use a paper towel right now. Well, by George, I happen to have one of those! -- One, that is.

"A man's got to do what a man's got to do."
John Wayne
(and a lifelong Troy Ford-ism)

6

The New Kid, Part One: "Boy, You're Gonna Carry That Weight"

I was a Hillcrest kid, so I lined up against the wall with the other Hillcrests. Mrs. Swanson would dismiss us from class each afternoon in groups. If we wanted to be the first group released for the day, my Hillcrest compatriots and I would need to be the very best group in the class. We were quiet and orderly, and we stood straight up, with our heels against the wall.

"Parkway, you can go." A small group of students to our left quietly grabbed their things and walked calmly toward the classroom door with silent smiles of triumph on their faces. They were quiet because they knew that, if they weren't, they might get chosen last tomorrow.

Why do the Parkway kids get to go before we do? Maybe we'll be next. Oh, please please please please. It was so important that our kindergarten teacher not pick us last. I'm not sure why it was so important, but, at the end of each day, that was all I could think about. It was very competitive.

"Good job Hillcrest. You're next."

Yaay! At least we beat the Maples! We walked slowly and purposefully to the door, remembering to be very quiet in the corridor until we got outside. The moment we stepped out into the cool Autumn air, the screams of glee and the sounds of stomping running feet would shatter the silence. I don't know why we did that either, but we did.

39

Then the magic spell would vanish and come crashing down. My favorite part of the day was over. For a moment, I had been someone. I had been a contributing member of the Hillcrest team, and I had helped my team to be chosen. I had belonged. I had screamed with them, and I had thrown my hands in the air and run with the rest of the Hillcrests, just like I had the day before and the day before that.

As always, the running soon became a walk. The joyful screams became quiet conversations, and the familiar weight came down on me as we all slipped into our standard drawn-out serpentine convoy of kids walking quietly home from Emerson Elementary School, in groups of twos and threes, chatting and laughing. There was one lone figure among those couples and trios of kindergartners walking North toward the crosswalk. That one boy, with the super-blonde hair and the homemade clothes, was The New Kid.

We all walked the same direction. We would go North up Pine Street, and we would turn West on 13th Avenue, a street that would eventually lead to the Hillcrest neighborhood, which was kind of an ironic neighborhood name since it wasn't on a hill at all, let alone the crest of a hill. I could see the Parkway kids walking a little ahead of us. That was the other group that went North up Pine every day. Now that I think about it, unlike Hillcrest Drive, Pine Street actually was at the crest of hill, and though there were fir trees everywhere, there were no pines. I wonder who came up with these names. The Parkway kids would also turn West and go down 13th Avenue, but they would all turn right at Park Street (which did have a park) and walk out of our sight, toward the Parkway neighborhood to the North, as we continued West. They walked a little farther than we did.

Emerson Elementary was so different than my other school had been, just a few miles North, in the tiny town of Lake Stevens, Washington. I liked my new house and my new yard a lot, but I missed my old school friends and my old neighbors. I hadn't known them very long, because we had only lived in Lake Stevens for a little while, having moved there recently from New Mexico; but I missed them. I had finally gotten past being The New Kid at Lake Stevens.

"You'll get used to this place, honey," my mother told me. "You just watch, it won't take long before you have some new friends." My mother was very encouraging.

I remember one day, Mrs. Swanson was helping Denise with something. Denise was a quiet girl who wore skirts and knit stockings a lot. She wasn't a Hillcrest, she was in a different group. She lived in a different neighborhood than I did. I thought she was pretty, but I could never talk to her. That would be so scary!

"Hey, new kid! Chris… or Eric, whatever your name is. Hey!" It was Jeff. I knew his name. I knew everyone's name. Why didn't they all know mine? But, I knew why they didn't. It was because I was just 'The New Kid' to them.

"Hey, watch this!" Jeff had a handful of crayons. He made a big toothy grin, stuck the crayon tips between his grimacing lips and then ran his hand side to side, over and over. The crayons made a funny clicking sound as they raced, back and forth, across the fronts of his teeth. Then he lowered his hand and his moist bouquet of standard issue kindergarten crayons, and he smiled as wide as he could. What a colorful mess!

"You're funny," I laughed. Someone had finally talked to me. *Maybe I could be friends with Jeff. Jeff's funny. I wish Jeff was a Hillcrest.* But he wasn't. He was a bus kid.

"What's Connecticut going to be like, Mom?"

"You'll like it, Christopher. It's very pretty there. You'll make some good friends, just like you did at Emerson and at Lake Stevens. It'll be great."

The big U-Haul truck roared Eastward. I thought it was neat that we were in such a big truck. "Will it take long to get to Connecticut, Momma?"

"Just a few days, honey. You relax now. Everything will be fine."

A few days later, I was in a big pretty school in Manchester, Connecticut, a little outside of Hartford, standing in front of my new Kindergarten class. "This is our new student, everyone," my new teacher said with a friendly smiling voice. "His name is Chris." I looked out at my new classmates, who were all looking at the floor. For the third time as a kindergartner, I was 'The New Kid.' For the third time that school year, I ate lunch and walked the playground alone. Different cafeteria, different playground, same feeling; same heavy weight.

"You'll make lots of new friends, honey. It'll be good. You'll see."

First Grade was going to be great! I was still at that nice school in Manchester, but I wasn't a kindergartner anymore. I was a "first grader!" I was in a real classroom in the big-kid part of the school. It was so very exciting! I made sure that I would sit next to my buddy Bill. I hadn't seen him all Summer, so I was really glad to see him in Miss Livingston's classroom.

It had been a wonderful Northern Connecticut Summer, with hiking and camping, and lots of time in the sand box at our apartment complex. I had even taken my first set of swimming lessons at a big lake. It was probably a small lake, but, to a six year-old, it was huge. What a summer!

And now I was a big first grader! Miss Livingston gave us real assignments to do. We were learning how to read! I was excited about that!

I was riding a school bus to and from school. I loved riding in the very back seat and bouncing high when the bus drove over the bumps.

It was a warm Spring day. The big kids on the sidewalk near the apartment playground, shouted and yelled words like, "Cool!" and "Whoa, man!" and other big-kid sayings that I quietly mimicked as my metal toy Tonka truck rumbled over my sand piles. "Whoa, man."

The hot new toy in 1974 was the pump-up Evel Knievel Stunt Cycle. It came complete with a sturdy red white and blue motorcycle, a crank handle starter stand, a life-like Evel in a swanky white jumpsuit and plastic ramps for him to jump off of. One of those bigger boys was a proud new owner. Oh, how I wanted one!

I didn't walk over there or try to join in. I already knew that, if I did, I would get the standard "What do you want, kid?" Just a lowly first grader, I didn't stand a chance of even getting a *Hello* from those scary big kids.

I couldn't see the boys from where I was in the familiar safety of my playground sandpit refuge, but I didn't need to. I could hear them. In my mind, a movie played. I saw myself cranking that handle around and around, with a look of determination - my imaginary movements perfectly timed with the real sounds that I was hearing. I could hear Mr. Knievel's little motor spooling up; screaming out higher and higher

RPMs with every hand crank, until I was sure that it was just about to burst. I was on my knees, on that sidewalk, surrounded by my cool friends. I felt my arm muscles tightening as my upper body bobbed up and down above that wonderful colorful machine. And, just when I thought that the little motorcycle could take no more, I saw my left hand as it reached down to the stand and pressed the release button. Off he flew, like a streak of lightning, tiny wheels spinning, down the sidewalk and up the plastic ramp, into the air and over an impressive field of molten lava (lava monster included) and upturned spear tips.

"Alright!"

"Whoa!!"

"Cool, Man!!"

I heard the boys all yell at the same time. I pumped my fists in the air triumphantly, as they rushed toward me to congratulate me for the best jump of the day. I heard them shout, "Way to go, Roger!!"

Roger?!

There was a silent shattering as my daydream imploded.

Suddenly, I was back in my sand pit with my Tonka. Nearby, I could hear the well-deserved adulation that my big kid neighbor, Roger, was receiving from his friends. With a sad smile, I allowed my Evel Knievel fantasy to fade, as it was slowly replaced by the familiar feeling of being alone. *Someday, I'll be a cool big kid... just like Roger.*

"Mom!! Mom!!" Look what I found!" I burst through the front door, waving my hand over my head. I had been digging and playing in the sandbox again. I had been all alone, but I had been pretending that I wasn't. Looking back now, I wish I could listen to a recording of some of those self-orchestrated, but by no means one-sided, sandbox conversations.

This afternoon, something had possessed me to dig deeper in that sandbox than I ever had before. Today, I was a pirate. My flat blue plastic hand shovel was a giant metal spade. My play-worn Keds had transformed into tall shiny brown boots of the finest leather. My red-and-blue-striped t-shirt was suddenly a fancy pirate's tunic. My left eye had been closed throughout the dig, because, as everyone knew, all pirates had an eye patch!

"Yarr, laddies..." I dug deeper and deeper, because that's where the big X was on my worn blood-stained map that many men had given their lives for, and others would kill for.

Wait… which eye has the patch? Oh, yea," I thought, as my right eye clamped shut.

"Mom! Mom!" Look what I found!"

"Chris! Stop. You're getting sand everywhere!"

"It's buried treasure, Mom!!" I shouted with joy. "I found it! I dug it up! We're rich, Mom!"

I hadn't been able to believe my eyes as I had found more and more bills of cash in that sandbox. There was a bunch of it. I wondered who would have buried it here. How long had it been here? Had I been sitting over it all those weeks that I had played here with my Tonka?

I didn't care about the sand that I was tracking into the apartment. I had treasure in my hands! It was the best day ever!

Mom looked at me and smiled as I stood in the entryway excitedly panting from my top speed downhill sprint from the playground. "Honey, that's Monopoly money." She paused and saw the confused look on my face. "Sweetheart, it's not real… it's from a game. It's just Monopoly money."

I had no idea what she was talking about. "Oh," I said smiling. "Okay."

Mom did that special laugh that she always did when my brother or I had one of those *isn't-that-just-the-cutest-thing-in-the-world* moments. I tried my best to hide my disappointment and I took my Monopoly money (whatever that meant) upstairs to the bedroom that I shared with my younger brother, Shanon, and I buried it under my bed.

Aye, ye skallywags! Here be me treasure. Safe and sound! A plague on any who disturb it. Arr!"

What's California going to be like, Mom? Will I still be in first grade when we get there?"

"I think you'll like it, Christopher. And, I bet you'll make lots of wonderful new friends there."

I didn't know what to call my California first grade teacher. Unlike my Connecticut first grade teacher, Miss Livingston, who was young and sweet; my California first grade teacher was a savvy veteran with many years under her belt. Is that a nice way of saying that she wasn't young? Happily, though, she was also very sweet.

Should I call her Mrs. Ford? Probably, but that felt weird since she was my Aunt Neva. I knew I could not call her Neva at school, like I did at home, because no one else was allowed to. So, I just didn't call her anything – ever – the entire rest of that year. I would just silently raise my hand if I needed to talk to her, and I would hold it up there no matter how long it might have taken.

We were living in an apartment in Newbury Park, California, about an hour Northwest of Los Angeles. It was nice. The weather was great and we had a swimming pool. The apartment complex was covered with kids.

My parents had chosen Newbury Park for a number of reasons. In the mid-1970s, Southern California was a land of plenty, and was growing at a record rate. They figured that it wouldn't take long for Dad to find a good job. More importantly, Dad's older brother, Howard, and his family were there. That was how I came to be in my Aunt Neva's first grade class.

I was The New Kid at Manzanita Elementary School, and I was starting over. I needed to make friends like Mom had told me I would, and it was working. The business of friend making went unusually well there at Manzanita. My transition there was quicker and more comfortable. I learned how to read in that class. I still have very fond memories of the reading book, *Fun With Dick And Jane*. "See Dick. See Dick run. Dick can run fast." I ordered a used copy of it from *Amazon. com* decades later, just because of the good memories and feelings that I associated with it, from those wonderful few months in Neva Ford's first grade class at Manzanita Elementary School, 1975.

"Do you know what Chris did?" Aunt Neva exclaimed through her laughter. She and Uncle Howard were visiting us at our apartment. She was the kind of lady that laughed a lot. "I was walking around the classroom, and I saw Chris' hand up, so I went to him. He wanted to know how to spell toe-fer!!"

It's funny as I look back on it now, but it wasn't very funny at the time. I remember thinking that it was a perfectly logical question, and I was frustrated by my teacher-aunt's inability to answer it. I actually was pronouncing it more like "t'fer," but, when Neva told the story to my parents some time later, she was pronouncing it "toe-fer." Who was I to correct her? That would have been bad manners. Plus, she was having so much fun telling the story.

"Just, how do you spell it?"

"I don't know, honey. I don't know that word," she replied patiently.

"It's t'fer! It's not a word. Just t'fer! That's all. How do you spell it?"

"Do you mean fur, like on a beaver pelt?"

"No! Just t'fer!" *Why isn't she getting this?*

"I'm sorry Chris, I don't know how to spell that. Can you use the word in a sentence?"

Why should I need to do that? I thought to myself. I thought teachers were smarter than anyone in the world. She should be able to spell anything! "Well, I know how to spell Chris, but I don't know how to spell t'fer."

"He wanted to write his full name on an assignment!" she told my parents. "He was trying to spell Christopher!!" All four of the grown-ups in our little apartment roared with laughter at the end of Neva's story. My Dad has called me Topher, off and on, (using Neva's 'Toe-fer' pronunciation) ever since then. I've had a lot of nicknames in my life, but I think I might like that one best.

"You'll like it in Thousand Oaks," Mom told me. "No more apartment. You'll have your own bedroom, and a yard to play in."

"Will we have a swimming pool there, Mom?"

"No, sweetie."

"Will I be going to a new school?"

"Yes, you will be starting the second grade at a school in Thousand Oaks. It'll be nice. Think of all the new friends you'll make there."

Long pause…

"Oh."

"And forgive us our trespasses as we forgive those who trespass against us."

Jesus Christ

7

The New Kid, Part two: Mighty Mouse and his Reign of Terror

There was something cool about living in Gold Rush country in Northern California. Placerville was a small town in the foothills of the Sierra Mountains, about halfway between Sacramento and Tahoe. The city was named after the tiny flaky placer gold that was mined in that area in the early 1850s.

Tradition holds that the area was originally known as "Dry Diggins," due to the almost rocklike hardpan earth that we still had to deal with years later. During the boom times of the Gold Rush, the city was called "Hangtown." In school, we learned that the city was given that name because of the large number of hangings that took place there, due to claim jumping, theft and murder.

I remember my Placerville years with a smile. As I look back on my life, I recall those times as the happiest of my childhood. It was a wonderful place to grow up in the 1970s. We lived a little over three miles outside of town on some acreage. We had a beautiful border collie with Lassie's markings. Her name was Buttons, and she was smarter than most people. We had a tough-as-nails female orange tabby cat, imaginatively named "Kitty," who sometimes chased dogs out of the yard. We raised honey bees and goats and we heated our house with wood. We had some serious chores – the kind that a city kid or a suburbanite kid would not understand. We had plumb trees and pear trees all around us, and a giant oak with a huge rope swing. Shanon and I tore trails into our parents' land with our minibikes and BMX bicycles, and we were surrounded by miles and miles of hills covered in oak and pine that we and our best buds, the Harwell brothers, roamed freely with our dog and our BB guns. We enjoyed hundreds of wrestling matches and one-on-one or two-on-two football games in the front yard – a yard that sometimes sparkled a bit when it was wet, and when the sun was just right, as countless tiny golden placer flakes had risen from the ground with the grass and caught the light, as though someone had shaken a big box of glitter over the yard. We worked hard and we played hard. We were country boys.

Life had a sort of pioneer-cowboy feel there in the Sierras. Boots, hats and big belt buckles were a common sight. Even the area businesses and city places helped to perpetuate the Western mood simply with their names. There was the Pioneer Savings and Loan, Hangtown Bowling Lanes, El Dorado Hardware, Gold Bug Park, Outlaw Barbecue, Gold Hill Vineyard, Mother Lode Motel and so many more. Our two local high schools had names and mascots that were about as Western-America as it got. They were the El Dorado Cougars and the Ponderosa Bruins. I was right in the middle of it. I went to Gold Trail Elementary school and I played baseball for Hangtown Little League. Though it might sound strange to an outsider, it seemed perfectly normal to see a local business using a hangman's noose as a decoration outside their office door. Our McDonalds, brand new at that time, had four tables where you could sit on saddles instead of chairs. It was such an exciting event, when we finally got a McDonalds in town.

I had the best times of my young life in that house and at that school. Shanon and I played soccer and baseball and we did chores and we helped our dad run his parking lot striping and cleaning business – pretty tough work for young boys. I met some of the greatest friends that I will ever know. My family was the closest there that I can remember.

"Boys!! Stop that! Kittens are not to be thrown!" My brother and I had been carefully tossing kittens back and forth and giggling at their funny meow-scream noises and the panicked way they would spread their four little legs out in every direction as they somersaulted and cartwheeled through the air, end over end. Mom pointed her finger at us and continued, "Do not throw the kittens anymore!" But it had been so much fun! *Well, what'll we do with them now? Hey! If we each hold opposite ends of a big bath towel and put a kitten on the towel, we can launch the kitten into the air and catch her in the towel when she comes back down. That's not throwing, so that must be okay!* It's amazing how boy-brain works, and we both had an abundant amount of boy-brain!

If someone had been listening to us, playing together and giggling in the side yard, they might have thought, "Isn't that sweet? What a delightful pair of brothers, playing and laughing so nicely together. How precious," that is, right up until they heard the panicked screams of "Meeeeooooooww! "Meeeeooooooww!" *giggle, giggle, giggle.* That game stopped being fun when one of the kittens ended up on the roof.

We had been in Placerville since just before I started fourth grade. We had moved there from our home in Thousand Oaks, which was in Southern California, a little north of L.A. Thousand Oaks was where I had spent my second and third grade school years with a teacher named Mrs. Charles.

Mrs. Charles was a very different character than my previous teachers had been. In my first two years of school, Kindergarten and first grade, I had worked under five different teachers in three different states. They had varied in ages from right out of college to almost retiring, but they all had one thing in common, other than being female, and that was sweetness. I had truly felt that all five had liked me – even loved me. That ended in second grade.

Mrs. Charles' permanent frown lines extended from the corners of her mouth, all the way to her generous double chin. When she spoke, her chin seemed to move up and down, independent of the rest of her face like a wooden Howdy Doody puppet, but without Howdy's ubiquitous smile.

She ruled her class with fear. This was the way that it seemed to my small boy sensibilities, and this is the way that I remember her. To be fair, if I was able to go back forty years and watch it now, I might look upon her teaching style with a little more charity, but I doubt it.

She taught a second and third grade split class, so I was with her for two full years. It's ironic that I finally got to live in one place and stay at one school for more than just a few months, and that it was with my least favorite teacher of my entire life. I did have a couple of teachers later in high school that made a valiant run for that title, but, in the final analysis, Mrs. Charles was the worst.

During those two years, I did make some friends, and I did have some good times. It had taken me a long time to fit in there at Park Oaks Elementary School – to get past the aloneness of being The New Kid. My time there with Mrs. Charles was less than ideal, even requiring one very unpleasant meeting that involved her, my parents and the school's principal. I would rather not rehash the unpleasantness of that time, but I was not unhappy when I heard that we would be moving away.

A short time later, there I was, a brand new fourth grader at Gold Trail Elementary School, in the rolling hills outside of Placerville, California; eating my lunch alone, wandering the playground alone, riding the bus home alone. This again, huh?

The weight was heavy on me at Gold Trail. This was worse than I had felt it before. I was more alone here; more The New Kid than I had ever felt. I've heard some people describe being alone as though there is a bright spotlight on them that draws attention to their plight, that embarrassingly shouts "Lonely! Loser! Alone! Outcast!" For me, the beginning of fourth grade felt like just the opposite of that. It was as if my spotlight shined only black. No one could see me through it. I was a rock in a stream that was surrounded by noise and movement, but it all separated and passed me by, paying me no mind. This was how fourth grade went for a long time.

Then a miracle happened, a bright blonde miracle named Mike Vogan. I was found, and I was rescued. I now had a friend, one who didn't look at me as just The New Kid. I now had someone to eat lunch with and play with during recess – someone who wanted to talk with me and cared about what I thought. Through Mike, I got to know Steve and Bruce and Pickle, and the others.

One year after my awkward and lonely introduction to Gold Trail Elementary, a new boy named Frank moved there from San Jose and went through The New Kid experience. Frank and I would eventually become friends. We later shared stories about our respective first days and weeks there, and he told me of how Mike Vogan had helped him – about how hard it had been for him when he'd first come to Gold Trail, and about what a difference Mike had made. Frank would go on to die in a tragic falling accident in high school.

Mike Vogan, you're all grown up now with kids of your own, and I speak for myself and for Frank who can't. I hope it's not too late to tell you *THANKS!*

One of the saddest things I've ever seen was Placerville, California in the rear view mirror of a big moving truck.

We were there for a little over three years. I went through fourth, fifth and sixth grade at Gold Trail. Seventh grade had been shaping up great. It was Fall of 1980, the tail end of the Disco era and the beginning of what the music industry would later call "New Wave." Devo had a huge hit with "Whip It!" and The Knack's song "My Sharona" was playing everywhere. My favorite was "Cars" by Gary Numan. Music was changing, and I was changing. My friends and I were starting to get a bit greasy, pimply and funny smelling. Some of the boys were having odd things happen to their voices, though that wouldn't happen to me for another couple of years. I kept the prepubescent soprano a bit longer than most boys did. We were all starting to really notice girls.

I was popular and well liked, one of the better athletes in the school. I kind of liked a girl, and I thought that she was kind of liking me, but it's hard to know for sure. I got in a little bit of trouble, once, for letting her copy from my Science test. I was playing in a youth soccer league with my Gold Trail friends, a team coached by my mother, and really having a great time. Yup, seventh grade had been shaping up real well.

But, there I was, late fall of 1980, heading out of town, sitting in the passenger side of a big yellow rented International Harvester with Ryder Trucks printed on the side. My mom and brother were following us in the family pickup, and Dad was in the position that I had seen him in so many times before – sitting at the wheel of a really big truck, moving his family to their next big adventure, doing what he thought was best for the ones that he loved.

I stared silently out the window, remembering the words that my mother had told me the night before, "You'll like it in Washington. You'll make lots and lots of wonderful new friends. You'll see. It'll be great."

Thus began the worst year-and-a-half of my life, and my introduction to Mighty Mouse and his reign of terror.

"I wonder why it sometimes takes you so long to walk home from school," Mom asked one afternoon. "Didn't school end over an hour ago?" My normal technique was to simply go silent and hope that tough questions weren't asked twice. It usually worked pretty well.

We were back at the Hillcrest house, where I had lived for a brief stint in Kindergarten. My parents had been renting that house out to various tenants during our Connecticut and California years. I was now a seventh grader at Snohomish Junior High School. A few of my old Kindergarten classmates were there. None of them recognized me. Why would they? Denise had really changed. Wow.

I was The New Kid again. I was alone, but, unlike my New Kid days at Gold Trail three years earlier, I wasn't unseen or unnoticed. How I wished I was. Now, instead of feeling like I was in a dark lonesome hole, I seemed to have a big target on me.

I heard words like "dork, nerd, stupid, dummy and loser" on a daily basis. I heard some pretty profane words directed toward me as well.

"Waste ya" was a new phrase that I quickly learned at Snohomish Junior High School. I had never heard those words used together before. "Shut up, or I'll waste ya!"

It seemed that I was somehow particularly good at getting myself into situations where someone was about to "waste" me, or, at the very least, call me some cleverly constructed phrase that held multiple cuss words artistically welded together.

Ah, the flat tire! Do you know what the flat tire is, my friend The Reader? That's where I'm walking down a crowded hall and someone steps on the back of my shoe, pulling it nearly off and leaving a small tender abrasion on my heel. The Flat Tire was a favorite among my tormentors, as was the push-trip. Rather than reaching out and hooking your foot with their own in an attempt to trip you, these clever youngsters employed something that I will call the "push trip." The push trip is far more subtle and elegant than the old-fashioned hook trip, and was therefore far better, I suppose. This particular form of cruelty was done by simply using one's foot to push my own foot inward as I walked, causing me to hook said foot behind my other foot, resulting in me virtually tripping myself. Very clever! This technique is especially useful when the victim is carrying a large stack of books and folders. To keep one's self from falling flat, one must forsake his aforementioned pile of cargo in favor of putting his hands down on the ground to break his fall, resulting in a loud and very visible mess of books and papers dropping and spreading out across a hallway floor. This always brought on a chorus of laughter from anyone who might be nearby. If done correctly, the victim might not ever see the perpetrator. I suppose that was worth bonus points.

The beautiful girls and the nerdy boys were the safest for me, because they simply left me alone. Most nerdy boys, themselves likely victims of these same terrors, would have been more afraid of me than I of them, and were therefore not a threat. The beautiful girls left me alone because I simply did not exist, as far as they were concerned. However, I seemed to be open game to all other demographic groupings.

My next class is down at the end of this really long crowded hall. I wonder if I can make it all the way there without something…

Ear flick.

Spit Wad.

"Loser!"

A derisive scowl.

A Flat Tire.

"Dork."

Book flipped out of my hands from behind.

No, it didn't happen every time I walked down a hall. But it happened a lot – so often that I expected it.

"Hey there, you're really cute!" she said with a provocative smile. "Where can I get some pants like those? Those are really sexy," wink, wink. Four girls all fly into a high-pitched giggle and run off. "Dork," I hear one of them say as they disappear into the crowded hall. I don't know why, but I know that I will never forget that one. That one hurt.

Why do you all hate me? You don't even know me! What have I ever done to you? I repeatedly screamed these words at the top of my imagination, but I remained silent. I wanted to run away, to just leave. I wanted to run all the way back to Placerville, California.

At Gold Trail, I had been a leader, a catalyst, a person around whom things moved and happened. I had been popular – well liked. Now, I was a loser. I was a nerd. A target. Sometimes, I was even a stupid… (*insert a nasty string of cuss words here.*)

Worst of all, I had become Mighty Mouse's play thing. I don't remember all of their names, but I do know that my first Mighty Mouse was an eighth grader named Danny. Danny had a small gang of boys that always hung around him. He was a year older and several inches shorter than I was. I was terrified of him, and he knew it. He relished that fact, and he reveled in it. He rarely put a hand on me, though I do remember one vicious blow to my right cheek. He must have been left handed. Most of his bullying came in the form of angry-sounding profanity-laced threats of violence - threats that I believed.

"Hey, tall guy. You think you're pretty big, do ya? Well, you won't be so fu#%ing tough with my fist buried in your face now will ya? Huh? Hey, I'm talkin' to you!"

Danny's friends would circle around me, casting taunts and jeers.

"C'mon New Kid! Do something about it!"

"C'mon big guy!! Can't you talk? What's the matter? You too Chicken! Bock-bock-bock-bock-bock-bock."

"Hey Danny, I think he's going to cry! C'mon, Cry Baby! Cry for us!"

Danny moves in, trying to go nose-to-nose with me, but his eyes are only as high as my chin. He's so close now that I can smell his breath. Suddenly his two hands are on my chest, pushing me backward violently. I try to step back, but there's a boy - one of Danny's devoted minions - on his hands and knees behind me. I trip over the boy backward and bang my head in the dirt. The boy stands up and shouts at me, "Don't touch me! Did I say you could touch me?" They all laugh louder.

Aside from Danny and his *Dannyettes*, there was Mike, there was Troy, there was Shawn, and there were others whose names I can't remember. They didn't know each other, as far as I could tell. But, they all had their own little gangs and the spirit of Mighty Mouse indwelled them all, and I was one of their favorite marks. If it wasn't one of them, on any given day, it would be another. Mighty Mouse was everywhere.

I've heard it called "Little Guy Syndrome," or a "Napoleon Complex." Call it what you want. I call it Mighty Mouse.

Looking back on it now, I can see that I was a prime target. You see, Mighty Mouse usually isn't going to get his needed manly feeling from beating up another little guy. No, he's got to have a big guy. Mighty Mouse hates big guys! He doesn't need to know anything else about you, he just hates you – simply because he's little and you're not. Oh, but Mighty Mouse is smart. He's a cagy character. Like a predator in the wild, he'll watch the herd for a while, licking his lips, looking for the easy prey. When he finds his patsy, he zeroes in.

I was a new kid, so I had no friends to back me up. I was a country boy, badly out-of-style with the fashion of this city school, so I provided plenty to make fun of. I was shy and insecure looking. But, best of all, I was skinny. Every Mighty Mouse knows that there is a certain amount of risk, doing what they do. It may be great fun to bully a big guy, but you don't want to pick a target who might squash you. The bravest of them might, the ones for whom their own need for conquest has reached such proportions that they no longer get the same rush by picking on just anyone. Those guys might try a tall muscle guy. But, most Mighty Mice lack that kind of courage. Most will go after the thin guy.

But all of them have one thing in common. They're insecure. When he has cowed a larger boy, and he has that larger boy scared, Mighty Mouse can almost feel himself grow taller, if only for a few moments. It is a temporary salve for his inner wounds. Though they won't understand it for years, or ever for some of them; what they're doing is a glowing outward admission of weakness; an inability to handle their insecurity; a weakness every bit as bad as the weakness shown by the tall thin worm that they torment – the worm who lacks the security to take a chance and defend himself, a worm whose self-doubt and self-loathing grows with every Mighty Mouse encounter.

For Mighty Mouse's victim, the shame can take a long time to go away. In fact, I can tell you that the very act of writing about it, all these decades later, has been rather cathartic for me. I've had to get up from my computer and walk outside more than once. Through the years, I have barely talked about it. My immediate family members know that I got bullied some, but I have never described it to anyone in detail. My mom and dad have been excellent parents all through my life, and they have always tried to be there for me when I needed them, but reading this chapter will be the first time that they will learn many of these things. I was kept quiet by my shame, and by my reluctance to be a bother. After all, who was I to trouble others about my issues? I was just a worm. In fact, there was a group of boys and girls in my P.E. class that called me "Worm."

For years afterward the memories made me angry, and it took a long time for me to forgive. I used to fantasize various forms of violent humiliating revenge. Now, I hold no anger about seventh and eighth grade - only a profound sense of sadness. I'm sad for that terrified boy; 'Young Chris,' who suffered secretly, sometimes quietly crying himself to sleep, the familiar tickle of tears welling in his ears as he lay on his pillow. But I'm not sad for myself. It was a long time ago, and I like who I've become. That terrible experience helped to form me into the man that I am now. I like to think that, if I were to meet face-to-face with one of my old Mighty Mice, I could be friends with him now. I hope I could.

Well, let's get back to the story, shall we? And a few more of those details that were so hard to write about.

Mighty Shawn Mouse was especially cruel. Unlike a lot of the others, he would actually throw punches. Sometimes he would be satisfied with grabbing me by the throat, squeezing until I cough, and faking a punch, coming up just inches from my face, then laughing at the terror in my eyes. Other times, he would go ahead and deliver a vicious blow or two (or more) to the arm, the shoulder, the chest – a knee to the thigh - carefully selected locations where a victim can endure a lot of pain without receiving any noticeable injuries. All the while, a never-ending flow of hate-filled speech would pour forth from him. "You scared? Yeah, you know you are! C'mon! Why don't you fight back? Defend yourself. C'mon, wimp! Do you want your mommy?"

That was the worst. "Do you want your mommy?" The simple truth was, yes; I did want my mommy. At those times, when I stood alone, facing Mighty Mouse and his gaggle of devoted wanna-be's, yes; I wanted my mommy very badly! And that made me feel even smaller. I was a wimp who was afraid to fight, who couldn't stand up for himself, who wanted his mommy! *Will I never be a big boy?*

I know what shame and fear taste like. A taste similar to copper, but that's not quite it. Blood. Salt. No, not salt - dirt maybe. Hard to describe. Dry. Thin. Hot. Sour but faint. Vague but there. Very much there.

I eventually found a lunchtime refuge in the study area of the school library. There were small individual study desks with sidewalls. I was safe there, so that's where I went every day after eating. It was there that I would stay until the lunch bell would ring, sending us all to fifth period. It was there that I hid - every day.

"What are you doing in here?" asked Rudy, a classmate from one of my morning classes. Rudy had never treated me badly, but we weren't friends either. "What're you doing in the library? Man, why aren't you out cruisin' the halls, meetin' girls… shootin' hoops in the gym? This place is lame."

What could I say? *This is the only place where I'm safe! I'm afraid, Rudy!! I'm scared to death to go out there!* They *are out there! Pain and fear and shame are out there, Rudy!*

"I like to read." I smiled, looking up at him from my book.

"Okay, man…" Rudy rolled his eyes as he left. He had some serious hall-cruisin' to do and he wasn't going to waste any more time on the skinny bookworm.

I started reading books there in that study area, not because I liked to, but because that was the only way that the librarians would allow students to stay there. It was during those times of hiding from Mighty Mouse that I slowly developed my love for reading. The stories would take me to some faraway place and time, where Shawn and Danny and the others would not be. I especially remember *The Count of Monte Cristo*, by Alexandre Dumas, and *A Day No Pigs Would Die*, by Robert Newton Peck. So good! I know why I remember those two above all of the others. In the first, the main character went from being the victim of unjust persecution to the master of all, one-by-one avenging himself on his tormentors. That can be a very attractive idea to a boy in my situation. The second was about a young boy who dealt with troubles worse than mine, and he powered through them with the strength and courage that I knew I lacked. More than tickling my imagination and my desire for justice, as Monte Cristo had done, this second one inspired me to be better than I was - or at least to want that, though I had no idea how to. Robert, the character in that book, was strong and resourceful. I was not. I loved him. I envied him. Though he endured some terrible and tragic things in that book, I wanted to be him.

To this day, I have not been without at least one partially read book - sometimes many - in my handy gym bag or, nowadays, my brief case. And, as an adult, I have reread and treasured both of those excellent and extra-memorable books.

"I wonder why it sometimes takes you so long to walk home from school," Mom asked. It was because I had been hiding. I was hiding from Mighty Mouse, whatever form he chose to take that day. Danny, Mike, Troy? It didn't matter which. They were all out there – somewhere. They couldn't hurt me if they couldn't find me. I hid in bushes, empty classrooms, dark hallway corners, between parked cars. Some-times it worked. Sometimes they found me.

"I don't know, Mom. Sometimes it just takes a while to get home."

Parents often have a way of finding things out. Eventually, they learned that I had been getting picked on. My brother had been through some bullying as well, though not to the extent that I had. Some phone calls were made and we were both enrolled in a local Judo class that was being taught by a former Marine Corps. Drill Instructor. Top Sergeant Dick Daly was quite a guy. He was Brooklyn-tough and had been wounded on Iwo Jima, late in World War II. After the war, he had been a Basic Training Drill Instructor. He now taught Marine Corps. Junior ROTC at the High School and he coached the High School Judo team. We attended his Karate class Mondays and his Judo class on Tuesdays and Thursdays. He was a black belt in both. At sixty years old and about 5'6," 145 lbs, he could have kicked just about anyone's hiney. But we all knew that he loved us. I really respected my Judo Sensei, or "Top," as we usually called him.

Being a Judo participant didn't change things at school. I was just a beginner at martial arts and was far from having the courage yet to stick up for myself. But it was a great class, and I'm really glad that I did it. That training certainly did come in handy years later. But that's a different story.

So strong was my shame at being a bullied wimp, that I lied to my parents about it. Being the son of a tough, muscular, hard-working former soldier of six foot four, I felt that I had a lot to live up to. I wanted my parents to be proud of me - especially my dad.

"You should've seen it!" I excitedly blurted with a smile. "This gang of guys was messin' with me but I took care of that!" *Time to spin a fat one! Will they believe me?*

"There was this big tough bully named Tim!" Of course, in my story, the bully was big. "He was really being mean to me. So, I pretended like I was running away a little so I could get his weight moving toward me, just like I learned at Judo. Then I spun around fast as lightning and, before he saw what was coming, I flipped him! Right over my hip!" I was really telling the story with gusto now!

"He hit the ground so hard that it knocked the wind out of him, and he couldn't breathe! Ha ha!... Then I demoralized him by faking that I was going to punch him in the face while he was helpless. He was terrified! But instead, I helped him up. His friends were all laughing at him. Yup! That kid won't mess with me again!"

It never happened. There was no big bully named Tim. I made it up. I wanted my mother to think that she had helped me by doing the research and phone calls to find Sergeant Daly and for enrolling me in Judo. I thought that she would feel proud if something that she had done had saved the day. I wanted my dad to think that I was strong, like he was. More importantly, I just didn't want him to be ashamed of me, which I was certain would happen if he knew what was really going on. It worked. They both bought it, and I got the approving looks and the warm atta-boys that I was seeking. Right when the bullying was at its worst, and my walks home from school at their scariest, I lied and created the impression that I had fixed my bully problems with Judo and that things were getting better at school.

It was a lie and I knew it, but the approval felt good. So I told the story again, and again. I told that lie for years. Mighty Mouse had pounded me so deep into my pit of self-doubt and insecurity that I almost managed to convince myself of the story's truth. My mother liked to hear the story. In fact, years later, when I was married with children, she asked me to tell that old seventh grade story again. So I did, just as if it had really happened. How do you stop it after so long? Now I had lied to my children. Some wounds bleed for decades.

I am sorry, Mom and Dad, for lying to you. I am sorry to everyone who has heard that story. It will never be told again.

After an eternity, seventh grade came to an end. For the first time, in all of my moves from city to city and school to school, I somehow had managed to go all the way through a school year without making any friends – without ever breaking free of being The New Kid.

The following September would find me starting the eighth grade at a new Junior High School. We had moved again. My parents had bought some property in the summer between my seventh and eighth grade school years, in the woods outside of Woodinville, Washington, and I had spent the summer watching the new house being built. Woodinville was about a half hour's drive South of Snohomish and was in a different school district. My parents were doing most of the work on the house, hiring contractors to do a few things. My uncle Don built the foundation. Dad did most of the plumbing and wiring. Grandpa, Mom, Shanon and I installed most of the siding. It was a tough summer break with lots of honest hard work.

Now I was The New Kid at Leota Junior High School. Every day, I would attend my classes, eat my lunch and walk the halls alone. I was getting pretty good at this by now. The familiar weight of being 'The New Kid,' of being alone, was there as expected. But, glory be! Mighty Mouse was not!

My grades were much better there than they had been at Snohomish. I was playing on a local Youth Football team. No friends just yet, but I was hopeful. Every afternoon, my brother and I would be dropped off by our busses. We would walk up the gravel road to our property and step into the tiny travel trailer that was our home. It was parked a few yards from the massive new partially-built house. We had no shower, so we did sponge baths. Well, we were supposed to do sponge baths, but those often went neglected. Outside the trailer, Dad had built a large teepee out of alder trees and canvas. There was a five gallon porta-potty inside, which require emptying daily into hand dug holes in the woods, and buried as quickly as any shovels had ever moved. Shanon and I had the honor of doing that chore. We called our unheated master bathroom 'The Peepee Teepee.'

For my electives, I had chosen Metal Shop and Cartooning, and I enjoyed both very much. I was settling into a routine at Leota. I had made a few acquaintances that had the possibility of becoming friends.

The new house would be done soon and I was looking forward to moving in. Leota was a very pretty school and I liked it there.

But, a few months into eighth grade, it happened again, and I had to leave Leota. For reasons that I still don't fully understand, the house "fell through." I remember that term being used. It was a very stressful time for my parents. I don't know why, but they lost the home and the new property. Something had gone wrong, financially. Soon, we were back in the Hillcrest house, and I was back at Snohomish Junior High.

Chris was a really funny guy. We sat near each other in two classes, Geography and English. It seemed to me that he and I had a lot in common. First off, I loved his name! We laughed at the same things and enjoyed cracking jokes in class. I decided that I wasn't going to have a repeat of seventh grade. I was going to have some friends, and I chose Chris. Wouldn't it be fun to have a best friend with the same first name as mine? One day, I plopped myself, uninvited, next to Chris in the school cafeteria and I ate my lunch with him. He seemed friendly enough while we ate, which I took as an encouraging sign.

Where did they go? I was alone in the hallway outside the cafeteria. Chris and his friends Kevin and Paul and the other couple of boys whose names I can't remember, had ditched me. I chased after them, and I eventually found them. I walked with them and tried to participate in the conversations. I felt so awkward. I laughed when they laughed and I walked where they walked. Then they were gone. I had been ditched again. I laughed out loud, "Ah, you got me again! Hah hah! But, I'll find you!" I made sure that I was loud enough that they could hear me if they were anywhere close. I wanted them to think that I was cool with what they were doing.

Trying not to cry, I would look and look and eventually I would find them. This went on for a few days. I would sit and eat with them in the lunchroom and, afterward, they would lose me in the halls. How were they able to lose me so easily, when I was probably a faster runner than any of them? It was because I didn't have the heart to chase. I would walk, talk, laugh, and will myself to believe that the initiation was over and I was one of the gang now. Then, as if on cue, they would scatter. Maybe they had a code word. Over and over, I felt the wind rush out of me, as an emotional fatigue would replace any previous whispers of hope, and I would stand still watching them go. Then after a short time of recovery, I would play their game and find them again. If this was all they were willing to give me, I would accept it without complaint. After all, who was I to complain? Just a worm. At least they didn't beat me. *Why doesn't anyone want me?*

It was a Friday, late in the lunch period. They had lost me again. This time, I didn't follow. I wandered into the huge lunch room and sat alone in the middle of a long straight table. I looked down at the tabletop in front of me, at the dark imitation wood grain. I don't know how long I'd been there, when I finally looked up. I ran my eyes around the lunch room, not really looking for anything in particular. There they were. Chris and his gang were over by the exit door, poking their heads around the corner by the dishwashing window. They were all looking at me. Paul, the biggest kid in the group, and kind of their leader, looked me right in the eye and smiled. He beckoned to me, as if he was saying, "Come here" with his hand.

Why? So you can ditch me again?

I didn't smile back. I shook my head and looked back down at the table in front of me. A long moment later, I heard the bell ring. I stood up from the table, noticed that Chris and Paul and the others were gone. I stepped out and just before I walked away, I reached down and I swept my hand across the table. My palm felt a cool moistness as a small mess of tears smeared across the imitation wood grain surface.

You'll make lots of new friends, Chris. It'll be great. You'll see.

8

Firewind

I love this smell, I thought with a smile, breathing deeply the warm perfumed air. It was a hot day in the Western foothills of the Sierra Nevada Mountains, and the heat always seemed to bring out the smells of the pine and the sage and the other plants that covered those hills. I never have understood why. Maybe those plants secrete more saps and resins when it's hot. Maybe it was my imagination.

There was an ugly bush that grew a lot in that area. I don't know its real name, but Dad told me that it was called "Mountain Misery." It was a good name. It sounded to me like a name that some grizzled miner forty-niner had given it a century earlier. I could almost picture him, with his wrinkled leather skin, his gnarled nine-fingered hands, and his penetrating knowledge-filled eyes. The word had a homespun pioneer sound to it, and I liked that kind of thing. Quite the romantic at ten years old, I often loved imagining that I was seeing and hearing and smelling the very same things that long-dead colorful characters of the past had seen, heard and smelled. Okay, I still like to do that.

Dad had spent some time working for a small civil engineering company when we first moved to Placerville. In that job, part of his time had involved sitting at a drafting board, creating and revising maps and property diagrams, but he had also spent a lot of time trudging over the hills and valleys, surveying topography and determining property boundaries. It might have been a good job if not for one thing. He learned, working as a surveyor, that he was particularly sensitive to the effects of poison oak. He learned it the hard way. I can still remember him, tough and uncomplaining, but with pain in his face, standing in front of our wood-burning stove, covered in pink lotion, trying to get it to dry; trying not to scratch the angry red welts and hives that covered him. No place on his body was safe from the blistering blight, and I mean *no place*! It's a sad yet somehow hilarious memory image to me now, thirty five years later.

Close your eyes, dear reader, and imagine the scene. You probably don't know my dad, so picture your own dad, standing in front of a roaring fireplace, face twisted with itchy irritation, trying not to cry, scream or laugh, standing on one leg, waving the other leg and both of his arms in giant circles to maximize the airflow over the lotion, in nothing but his Fruit-of-the-Looms, with giant patches of pink medicine covering him. Have the picture in your mind? I do too. Bwah, hah hah hah hah!! I mean, umm… poor guy.

Other than Poison Oak, Mountain Misery was the Northern California plant that Dad disliked the most. Those resins that I mentioned a moment ago would secrete in massive quantities on the hottest of days, and that plant smelled bad!

When you're climbing up and down the hills, carrying your heavy surveyor equipment, on an almost stifling windless hundred degree day; hot stinging sweat rolling into your eyes; pointy fox tail stickers in your socks, nagging you like a disappointed mother-in-law with every step you take; the air filled with the piercing never-ending high pitch screech of a thousand locusts hiding in the forest around you; your nearest water jug back down the hill in your truck, you wonder if it could ever get worse than this. Then you hike right into a grove of ripe Mountain Misery. Yup, it just got worse. It's a smell that just associates itself with hot dusty misery.

But, here I was, drinking in the pure mountain air today, and loving it; not a trace of Mountain Misery anywhere. Today, I was loving the smell of the California Sierra foothills. But it wasn't just the pine and the sage that I was loving. Today, there was an extra ingredient that added to my pleasure. It was the unmistakable smell of dirt bike exhaust! My helmet was cinched tight under my chin and Dad's Honda was running strong. At ten years old, it wasn't as easy to ride double with Dad as it had been when I was seven, but we were making it work. Mom and Shanon were going tandem on the other Honda and we were having a great time. That sweet smoky smell that I had enjoyed for so many years meant that we were all together, doing what we loved. Decades later, I still love that smell.

My parents had two matching 1972 Honda 125's. For years, we had ridden those bikes, doubled-up with our parents. When we were as young as two and four, my brother and I would ride, sitting between our parents' legs, hugging the metal gas tanks with our thighs. But today, at eight and ten, we rode behind Mom and Dad, with our arms wrapped around their waists.

Up a tiny winding one-lane gravel road, in the hills above our house, there was a huge expanse of land that we knew only as "Mr. Lange's property." None of us had ever met Mr. Lange. He was the faceless entity, the *King of the Hill*, who lived in that distant brown house on the upper reaches of that massive beautiful area of land. My brother and I used to hike and bike all over Mr. Lange's acreage. We loved to throw rocks into his two small lakes. We and our friends, the Harwell brothers, must have roamed many miles through the years, zig-zagging and exploring those hills with Buttons, the smartest dog that I have ever known. We loved that chunk of land.

Today, my brother and my parents and I were exploring Mr. Lange's property on our trusty Hondas. What a great time. This was the first time, though, that I had been a little bit nervous about trespassing there. This time, it wasn't just a handful of harmless kids with a dog. This time there were adults. This time there were motorcycles. That whole day, though I was loving the motorcycling and the time that I was spending with my family, I had a constant feeling in the back of my mind that we were doing something wrong.

I have to admit, we were an odd family. We had a thing that we liked to do; call it a hobby, or maybe a strange habit. We loved junk. Garbage! "One man's trash is another man's treasure," Dad used to announce proudly. We loved to look through trash and find those treasures.

We loved antique stores and thrift shops, and we loved garage sales. But it didn't stop there. It was not unusual for us to be driving down a street in town and have Dad pull off and silently drive behind a shopping center. We only did this when Mom wasn't in the car. Dad would pull to a stop and out of the car two boys would dart, right up over the sides of the dumpster and into the awaiting scavenger hunt. No words were needed. We knew our job.

Through the years, we'd found some amazing things! We were rewarded, many times, with something that had been some other man's trash but had become our treasure.

Once, when I was seven years old, while we still lived in Newbury Park, in Southern California, we were out on one of our family motorcycle adventures. We had stopped and were all off of the bikes for a few minutes, taking a break. Four-year-old Shanon had wandered out of sight, over a hill. He had discovered a place where people had been, perhaps for years, dumping things. There were mattresses and old bottles and car parts and piles of other rusty dusty artifacts. He thought he had discovered the motherlode!

"Gaaaarrrrbaaaaaage!!!" He was screaming like a crazy person as he ran back down the hill toward the motorcycles. "Gaaaarrrrbaaaaage!!!" We still laugh about this as a family all these years later. Screaming and waving his little arms over his head, that cute blonde preschooler was the happiest little *garbeologist* in town! That was what we called ourselves. We fancied ourselves much like treasure hunting archeologists, but we were garbeologists.

So, here we were, a few years later, deep in the heart of Mr. Lange's property, standing before an ancient wooden cabin under a grove of tall ponderosa. Who knows how long it had stood there? The motorcycles were turned off and Dad was trying to see through a small dirty window into the darkness. He came around to the door and he pushed it open a couple of feet. The rusty hinges complained as the door slid slowly.

I watched curiously as my father poked his head into the cabin. And I laughed as he pulled his head back out, turned toward us smiling and said, "Gaaaarrrrbaaaaaage!!!"

My whispering feeling of wrongdoing whispered no more. It shouted. That quiet dread about trespassing, that had gnawed at me throughout the ride, now spoke loudly to me, but I kept still as I watched my father sifting through, and choosing from, the garbage in that cabin on Mr.

Lange's property. The owner, it seemed, didn't care about the cabin or its contents. Everything was strewn all over and covered in dust. The door had obviously not been opened in years, maybe decades. This, I suppose, was why Dad felt that it was alright to take the stack of very old National Geographic magazines and the book or two that he had found inside. After all, who's going to miss them? But, it bothered me. To be fair, it's important to mention that, for decades, Dad has regretted the decision.

They were the tallest flames I had ever seen. Would they come this far? Was our home in danger? I stood in our backyard, watching, and I was struck by how different a forest fire looks than the fires that I had seen almost every night in our wood stove. Instead of the familiar yellow, these flames were dark orange, almost red.

For a few hours, emergency vehicles of every size and color had been speeding by our house, rumbling up that bumpy one-lane gravel road that I had bicycled so many times. Bright yellow airplanes were swooping down from above, dropping some kind of red mystery liquid into the flames. I could smell the smoke, but that wasn't what was making my eyes water. Mr. Lange's property was burning. Could this really be happening? As I tried not to cry, my beloved wandering grounds were being consumed before my eyes and there was nothing I could do about it. I was torn between sadness at the loss and a difficult to describe thrill of seeing destruction so powerful, so strangely entic-ing, even beautiful; like I had never seen before. That's a confusing twist of feelings for a ten year old boy to chew on silently, as I also chewed on a long dry piece of grass. I almost always had a piece of grass in my mouth; the longer the better. It's a country boy thing.

"Do you hear that?!" Dad yelled. His eyes went to the sky. He quickly spun around in little circles, as though trying to see every part of the sky at once. "Where is it?" He was rarely this excited. His hearing was better than mine, and I wondered what he could mean. Then I heard it too, though I didn't understand what it was.

"It's a radial, and a big one!" He pointed Southwest. "It's coming from over there! Watch, boys. You're about to see something!" He stared straight ahead, an expectant smile on his lips.

What's a radial? I wondered. *Isn't that a kind of car tire?*

"There it is! Oh my goodness!" his voice actually cracked.

Just then, a massive yellow airplane came over the hilltop. It must have been twice the size of the other fire bombers that we had been watching. It was loud and seemed to be moving so slowly that I thought it might drop straight down onto its belly. Past us it lumbered, almost directly overhead, so low that I could see every rivet. Straight for the flames it dove. I watched in awe as its belly opened and out came almost twice as much red fire chemical as the other planes had been dropping.

"Boys, that airplane helped us win World War Two. Honey! I have to get over there, I just have to!"

Dad loaded us two boys into the old light blue Volkswagen Bug and we zoomed toward that bumpy narrow dirt road. As we left our long gravel driveway, I looked back and saw my mother, standing on the roof of our house, a running garden hose in each hand, facing toward the flames, though they were still a few hundred yards away. *Fire, you will not touch this house, so help me God!* her posture and her expression seemed to say. It's one of my favorite memories of my mother.

I was very impressed by all of the bustle and busyness going on at the fire. There were so many people there. We could hear the airplanes overhead, somewhere on the other side of the brown-black smoke cloud. Men were shouting and moving around, but everything seemed very organized.

There was a big flat-nose bus there, painted an ugly shade of gray green. And there was a long line of men with shovels. They were all digging, looking like they were making a new dirt road. I wondered why they were doing that. I had never seen black people up close before. *They sure have big round hair!* I wondered why they were all dressed the same. Is that their uniform?

"Dad, who are those men? Why are they wearing chains?"

"Those are prisoners, son. That's a prison bus and those are prisoners. They're here to help fight the fire. See the two policemen with the rifles? It's their job to watch the prisoners."

Wow!

I stared at them. *Real prison men, like in the movies!* How many new things could a ten-year-old boy see in one day?

They were working where there was no shade and they sweated in the sun. It looked like such hard work. Not all of them were black, but it was the black men that I watched most closely. I had moved from home-to-home and state-to-state many times in my young life, but all of those places had been suburban or rural. I had never seen black people up close like this. How the sweat shined on their dark skin! I wanted to take them some cold water to drink.

I looked at the policemen. They paid no attention to the fire or the airplanes. They seemed not to notice me standing there staring at them. They looked only at the prisoners. They wore dark sunglasses and they held stonelike expressions on their faces. I felt like I had stepped right into *Cool Hand Luke* or *The Longest Yard*. My dad liked movies so I knew very well who Paul Newman and Burt Reynolds were. *Any moment now, one of the men is going to stage a daring escape attempt, and I am going to be right here to see it.* I knew that one of them had an intricate plan and allies on the outside. I looked around for Charles Bronson.

"That's obviously not water that they're dropping," I heard my dad shout. I turned away from my prison movie to see him talking with a fireman. "What's the red stuff? I've never seen that before."

I listened intently as the fireman explained that this was a new kind of firefighting weapon. He explained that it was a chemical solution that did far more than simply wet or smother the flames, like water could do. This red stuff was much heavier and colder than water and clung more to objects than water did, creating a better protective layer over things. But, best of all, it was an oxygen inhibitor. It pulled the oxygen out of the immediate area in an effort to starve the fire.

I knew from Science class that fire required oxygen a lot like we do. I thought about what it would be like to have the oxygen pulled from my own immediate area. In my imagination, I saw myself choking and suffocating, gasping for breath, as a bright red chemical coated me, tearing the air away. *Wow*, I thought. *That's some dangerous red stuff! What a terrible way to die!*

Up close, the flames were the mightiest, most awe inspiring thing I had ever seen. They must have been a hundred feet high and I felt their heat on my face. The immense power of it all was more than I could imagine. I heard the giant pine trees hissing and cracking as the glowing orange monster engulfed them. But I heard something else. Now that I wasn't thinking about suffocating in red goo or about prisoners making a break for it; I heard a sound that I hadn't noticed before. It was like a rushing river, roaring. Near the flames, trees and tall grass were leaning this way and that. They twisted and moved in a violent dance, as wind like I had never before seen tossed them like toys. It seemed that they should come up by their roots at any moment.

But, it's not a windy day today. I stared in confusion. *Where had that wind come from? Why don't I feel that wind over here where I'm standing?*

I asked my father about the wind. He smiled and answered, "That's firewind, son."

He explained how, during World War II, firebombs had been dropped on cities in Germany, England and Japan from airplanes a lot like the very one that we could hear at that moment circling above our heads, and how those fires had been so large and had created so much firewind, that there were firestorms with winds as strong as hurricanes.

Firestorms?

My imagination immediately did its thing again. I had a Mind Movie, right there on Mr. Lange's hillside, of hurricane winds lifting objects and sucking them into raging city-size infernos; of windows and doors being blown off of their frames, and trees ripped from their roots, in exotic faraway lands of Europe and Asia, while squadrons of giant radial-driven airplanes turned away in perfect triangular formations, like geese, and flew away, leaving the ferocious firestorms that they had created.

I turned back from my dad and looked at Mr. Lange's fire; at the wind-blown leaves and grass and tree branches, violently flying through the air close to the flames.

Never mind the big yellow airplanes, or the prison men, or the policemen or the red fire jelly! This new thing – this Firewind – was definitely the coolest thing I had ever seen! I stared and stared, my mouth hanging open, as a large brown bush of Mountain Misery blew almost over in the wind, straining to stay upright, and then, in the intensity of the heat, burst into flames like a bomb. *Firewind!* I stared and I stared, and I whispered, "wow."

"Oh… that's gonna stink." Dad laughed.

I stood there transfixed; my attention riveted to the scene being acted out in front of me. My mind paid no attention to the other sights and sounds around me. *Firewind… Wow.*

"Chris!!! Run!!!"

What? Did someone call my name?

"Run!!" It was Dad's voice. I came back from my trance and looked around me.

My seven-year-old brother was running away from me in one direction, toward a small open-front wooden shed, Dad in another toward a thick area of green leafy trees. "Hit the Deck!!" That was the voice of the fireman that Dad had just been talking with.

What's going on? What's that loud roaring noise?

The new sound was coming from above me. I looked up in time to see a fast moving object coming toward me from the East. A giant bright yellow B-17 Bomber was coming fast. It was opening its bomb doors and a huge mass of red was hurtling directly at me.

"Chriiiiiiiiiiiiis!!"

I had no time to run. I dropped onto my belly in the dirt and covered my head with my arms, and I waited. *It's an oxygen inhibitor...* the fireman's words repeated in my head... *It pulls the oxygen from the immediate area... it pulls the oxygen from the immediate area... It pulls the oxygen from the....*

So, this is how I die. I sucked in as much air as I could and held it.

Wham! I felt it hit my back. So cold. So wet. Like spring snow. Like frozen slush. I squeezed my eyes as tightly as I could and I held my breath for dear life. *It's an oxygen inhibitor... It pulls the oxygen...*

"Ahem..." There was a tapping on my shoulder. I turned my head upward, my eyes still squeezed shut, my bulging cheeks full of air. "Care to join us?" Dad said with a laugh. You're not getting into the car like that!" and he laughed again. The fireman and my brother looked on, both laughing.

I'm alive! I'm alive! And I'm really wet! Ick! This stuff is gross! I stood.

"Your back's all red!" my brother yelled and did his patented high-pitch Shanon-giggle.

Maybe that red stuff didn't inhibit the oxygen quite as badly as I'd figured.

Now all of us were laughing.

A little while later, there I was, standing on the back bumper of a light blue VW Bug, holding the roof-mounted luggage rack with both hands, dripping cold, feeling and looking like someone had poured an extra-large red cherry-flavored Slurpee down the back of my yellow t-shirt. Slowly we bounced our way back down the one-lane gravel road. *Mom's gonna love this.* And I laughed again.

"You meant evil, but the Lord meant it for good." That's a quote from the fiftieth chapter of Genesis, in the Bible. I sometimes chuckle now, when I look at the bookshelf in my living room and see the worn leather-bound 1867 Bible that sits there. It's the oldest book I have ever seen. The pages still turn and the spine still holds the book together nicely. Other than some color fade and some corner wear, the Bible is in pretty good shape, considering that it's a century and a half old.

That's what a dry environment will do for an old book; a dry environment like a wooden cabin on an arid pine hillside, under a pile of newspapers and old magazines.

Mr. Lange's forest fire had burnt and blackened many acres of land that hot Summer day in 1978. But his home and ours were saved by the hard work of those firefighters, bomber pilots and prison men. But, of the ancient wooden cabin that we had trespassed earlier on our motorcycle outing, there was nothing left but ash. The theft of that Bible had saved it.

Perhaps the reference to Genesis 50 is a little unfair. I don't mean to say that what my father did that day was truly "evil." But there is a delicious irony in the fact that a stolen bible sits atop my living room shelf. A rare 1867 Bible, containing an authentic signature from a long-dead 19th century previous owner, still exists today because it was stolen from a garbage strewn cabin on a dry California hillside a little more than thirty five years ago. A cabin that, just a short time later, would be a pile of ash.

Maybe we should look, instead, inside that same stolen Bible, to the book of Romans, in chapter eight where it says, "All things work to the good for those who love The Lord and are called according to his purpose."

When I see that old Bible sitting on my shelf these thirty five years later; I sometimes get visited by memories of tall trees in flame; of prison busses and rifles; of yellow t-shirts stained red; of garbeology; of loving family and motorcycle outings.

And I remember Firewind.

Insert a warm nostalgic smile here →

9

My Own War

My flight was running on time and I was happy about that. Though there is a certain amount of satisfaction sometimes when I climb into an airplane that I helped design, I never have enjoyed air travel very much. There's a lot of waiting around and, when I try to read a book, I often get so drowsy that my eyes want to close. I love books, so air travel should be a great thing; a time to do nothing but sit and read; a license to loaf. But, for cryin' out loud, I usually get sleepy and I wimp out.

I sat in the concourse area, people-watching. I had about an hour and a quarter until I would be boarding my flight from Louisville to Chicago. I was very tired from my three day business trip at the Mid America Trucking Show. The show is held in Louisville, Kentucky every year, and is the premier U.S. event in commercial trucking. Part of my job had been to go there and to visit as many exhibits as I could, and to learn as much as I could, including a couple of very specific exhibits where there were people that I needed to talk to.

The other part of my job was to take my shifts standing beside a big pretty new truck, looking like an enthusiastic representative of the Design Engineering Department, answering questions and shaking hands. That's what I do now, having left the aerospace industry in the early 2000s. I now design Cab components for big eighteen-wheelers.

As tired as I was, I knew that there was very little reason to pull a book out of my briefcase as I sat waiting for my flight. I doubted that I would get a page into it before Mister Sandman would come and do his thing and I would start falling asleep. Nope. Today, at Louisville International Airport, Gate B6, it would have to be people-watching or nothing.

I saw cowboys in full shiny-boot western-shirt San Antonio regalia. I saw vacationing families with bored cranky children. I saw one very tall black man in a bright red full body Chicago Bulls sweat suit and massive high top shoes.

I had to chuckle when I saw *Super Family.* They were sitting across from me on the other side of the busy concourse. A seven or eight year old boy, probably named something trendy like Colton, or Liam, with bright colored Nikes, and perfectly combed dark hair, very likely combed by his mother, sat there happily. His fingers flew with lightning precision on his handheld video game. A bored and unhappy-looking girl of about fifteen (I silently named her Mikayla) with perfect teeth, glistening blonde hair, tight black yoga pants and brand new Uggs (a soft suede shin-high flat bottomed boot that, though ugly, hot and clumsy, are, at the time of this writing, ridiculously popular with the American high school and college-aged white girl,) iPhone in one hand and Starbucks cup in the other. Mom, a lovely athletic-looking trophy wife if ever there was one, looking fetching her figure-flattering, shiny two-piece bright white sweat suit and big dangly earrings, shot a now-you-listen-to-me-young-lady look at Mikayla, who was obviously not impressed. Meanwhile, a tall handsome one-hundred-percent-oblivious Dad paces nearby talking out loud into the air, Bluetooth earpiece firmly in place, gesturing with his hands. I can't hear him where I'm sitting, so I imagine him enthusiastically using terms like "leveraging assets," and "cross-functional synergies," and "We-need-to-get-more-traction-on-that-initiative."

"But, MOM..."

"Not another word, Mikayla! Wait until we get to Costa Rica and get checked into our massive ocean-view, air-conditioned suite. Then you can have all of the lobster and caviar you want!"

I know! I overdid that part of the imaginary conversation. But, hey! I was people-watching. My game – my rules! *Grin*

Having beaten that horse to death, I looked around the airport some more, and I saw one of the top-ten cutest things I have ever seen. A daddy was pulling his big suitcase-on-wheels by the handle. Perfectly balanced on the suitcase, head back and mouth open, was a little boy of about two and a half, fast asleep. His arms and feet hung lifelessly to the sides; his toes about an inch off of the airport floor. So adorable, it made me laugh out loud with fondness. My teenagers would have called that, "Totes adorbs!"

Looking around some more, I saw soldiers in camouflage fatigues and tan combat boots, each with his identical GI carry-on bag. They didn't seem to know each other. They were coming into the seating area, one by one, each of them giving the others a nod of the head and then moving on to find a seat by themselves. They varied in height, weight, race and gender, but they all had identical uniforms. I admired the modern digital desert pattern camouflage that they all wore. Instead of stripes or colored blotches like military camouflage used to have; the new pattern is a blur of tiny, neutral-colored squares and rectangles - a lot like pixels on a computer monitor. On each soldier's shoulder there was a patch that designated his or her outfit. The soldier closest to me, a muscled redheaded youth of modest height, had a shoulder patch that read "Airborne." *Wow! Special Forces.* I couldn't help but be impressed a little. A lot, actually.

My head fell, and I caught myself, jerking my groggy head upright and hearing the last half of a loud unappetizing nasal snort noise blaring outward from my face. Yup, I was that guy! Luckily there was no drooling, this time. I got my bearings and looked around. A young couple with a baby was sitting directly in front of me in the not-so-comfy black vinyl seats, the pretty young mommy looking right at me. She giggled a little. I blushed a lot.

If I don't get some caffeine into me, I'm not going to make it.

I discreetly read the shoulder patch of every soldier as I walked by them on my way to the Starbucks counter. I saw infantry and medical and other insignia; even one engineering patch. That one made me smile a little.

Moments later, as I was walking back to my seat, a piping hot double grande vanilla breve latte in my left hand, I stopped in front of the young Airborne soldier and I held my right hand out to him. "Thank you for your service," I said to him with a smile. He almost leaped to a standing position. He crisply and purposefully thrust forward and grabbed my hand in a firm confident grip, "You're welcome, sir!" he said as he looked me directly in the eyes. I walked away, feeling a little bit safer, knowing that such a fine young man is defending me and my family; knowing that there are tens of thousands that are just like him.

Why can't I sleep tonight? I need to go to work in a few hours.
It had been nine days since I had come home from the Truck Show and I had been doing just fine. But, somehow, tonight was weird. It was wrong. I heard the rhythmic breathing of my wife sleeping beside me as I tossed back and forth, trying to find a more comfortable position.

My mind would not come to rest, but it raced – wound up like a two dollar watch. The young Airborne Ranger's face and shoulder patch kept coming into my mind. Why had he been there at that Louisville airport? Where had he been going? Was he safe tonight? Was he happily going through his work at some faraway duty station, or did he have a rifle pointed at him right now, crosshairs focusing on his chest?

Should I pray for him? I did. I prayed hard for him.

Does he have parents somewhere who love him; who fear for his safety every day?

Then something strange happened that has never happened before or since. I started thinking, almost hearing, verses in my mind. I'm not a poet and, other than a few naughty limericks, I had never written a poem of any kind. I'm certainly no songwriter. I can't even read music or play an instrument. But, as I lay there unable to sleep, a poem was taking shape in the air above my bed. I tapped into my memories of the soldiers at the airport. I imagined their parents; their dads. I thought of my own son, then sixteen, and my daughter, eighteen, students in high school and my eyes filled with tears.

Several minutes later, in the early morning hours of Monday, March 25th, while all of my neighborhood slept; I was in my living room, in the comfortable green chair that sits right in front of the big bookshelf that holds numerous true-life military biographies and memoirs that I love to read, and one slightly faded 1867 Bible. There was a college rule spiral notebook laid out on the matching green footrest in front of me.

My pen bled blue. Words spilled out onto the page as tears spilled onto my face. I can't explain what happened. It was a surreal experience that seemed almost dreamlike. A beautiful poem was writing itself and I just needed to get out of its way. Verses and rhymes squirted onto the page almost all at once and it was hard to keep up, yet somehow it took me hours; hours that seemed to fly by in minutes.

My rough draft on that spiral notebook is a mess. There are verses written out of order. The intro was written almost last, and the closing almost first. There are lines and fragments of lines written in the margins, arrows pointing to places where things should be inserted, sentences crossed out, words misspelled, punctuation and capitalization virtually ignored, blobs of ink to obliterate mistakes. It's a big blue farrago of jumbled letters and squiggles. But I like it! I'll keep that ugly mess because, whenever I look at, I remember that weird early Monday morning, and I smile.

And now, dear reader, you get to see what it was that so wonderfully wrecked my sleep on the morning of March 25th, 2013. If you will indulge me a little, I present to you the first-ever poem of a normally very unpoetic Chris Ford.

I have no doubt that, to a student of poetry, this is garbage, but I provide it without apology. After all, simply put, it is what it is, no more; no less.

My Own War -- Christopher S. Ford © 2013

I said a prayer over them before they left,
Though my mind could scarcely hear me.
Heads were bowed and eyes were closed,
Those I loved most gathered near me.
The men turned and walked toward uncertain futures,
My son among the three.
Young soldier, so handsome and strong, I wondered
Would he ever again need me?
Did he know of the pain I was feeling just then?
Does he know how much I care?
Of the memories that flooded me to almost overflowing,
Of training wheels, baseballs and bright blonde hair?

I knew that he might lose his life sometime soon
For such are the risks during war.
This could be the last time I look upon him breathing,
As the soldiers came nearer the door.
Behind my fake smile, my mind exploded
In a silent terrified scream.
This can't be real, it isn't true.
Please! Let this all be a dream.
But pride was there also for my boy now a man
Who would answer his nation's call,
Who would trade in his youth for a uniform and gun
That his homeland never should fall.
My own war between honor and selfishness raged,
My heart swollen with duty and fear.
With joy at the sight of my brave new hero,
Fearful sobs that no one could hear.
I gave him a wave, and encouraging wink.
His mother cried softly beside me.
Oh God! I thought, please help me.
I'm needing you now to guide me.
Just before they disappeared through that ominous door,
That point of no retrieval,
Beyond which my son would face both good and bad,
Triumph and pain, good and evil,
He looked back, caught my eyes, and for a long moment just stood.
We spoke with no words needed.
He thanked me and he loved me and we both understood,
And my pain and my fear both receded.
For I was sure at that moment, in that place in time,
That he knew how much I love him.
I surrendered his safety, his future, his soul
To our Loving Father above him.
And then he was gone, the doorway was empty.
The soldiers had passed from our sight.
And from that moment on, his mother and I
Would pray with all of our might.

"Train yourself to look for the comedy in your chaos."
Mike Moore

"Time spent laughing is time spent with the gods."
Japanese proverb

10

Guero Enchilado

To my wife, Cheryl, and our two friends, it was just a burrito house at the hungry end of a tiring day. For Dan, a well-earned Dos Equis; for Barb, a place to warm some cold toes. To me, though, this place had special meaning. Cold tired bodies slumped back into worn wooden restaurant chairs with audible groans and, for the sixtieth time that day, we all started laughing.

The place was called "Pancho's," but it had nothing to do with the large chain of Pancho's restaurants in the American Southwest. This Pancho's was a cute little hole-in-the-wall a few miles downslope from the Steven's Pass ski resort, on Washington State Route 2.

For years, I had passed Pancho's on the way up and on the way down that mountain. Going back a decade or more, I could remember watching the neon lights of the Pancho's sign, blurry through the snow or rain as I looked longingly and hungrily from the back seat, my dad driving us back from a day on the mountain. No matter how the ski day had gone, I was always hungry on that ride home. We never stopped at Pancho's, because we knew that Mom would have hot chocolate and a warm dinner waiting for us just a little farther down that winding highway. I knew that if I could just wait another hour it would all be okay, but oh how I wanted to stop at Pancho's - every single time.

In front of that little restaurant, the giant Pancho's sign was of a funny Mexican cartoon man, sombrero pulled down over his face, leaning against a wall. He was a cute little hombre, but we never did stop to see him up close.

It happened every Summer as well, as we travelled home from our favorite camping spots in central Washington. We always did our camping over on the east side of the Cascades - the dry side. Having lived through our share of rain all year long, every July would see the Ford family pack up in our various camping vehicles through the years, and head east to "dry out." That's what Dad called it. They were "dry out" trips. And, sure as the rain, Pancho was always there to greet us back to the wet side as we drove home from camping, tired and looking forward to sleeping in our own beds.

No, we never stopped to eat at Pancho's. Yes, I always wished we could; every single time.

Later on, it was from the high school ski bus that I would stare at the sign as we blew by it cold wet and tired. The bright pink and green neon that surrounded little Panchito always caused a smudgy blur on the wet bus window.

Years later, driving a car of my own, I had often driven by the sign of little Pancho, blinking green and pink, and I'd always wanted to stop, but something had always kept me from doing it. Sometimes it was because I'd had a car full of friends. Other times, I might have been in a hurry.

There was one particular ski day, when I was on my way home from a day of *shreddin' the gnar* on Big Chief Mountain, that I almost stopped to meet Pancho. I hadn't been able to find anyone to ski with me that morning, so I had gone by myself. That day I learned that skiing alone was not nearly as fun as skiing with a buddy, but more importantly, I learned that driving home alone after a full day of heavy skiing is just downright stupid.

It was dark and raining and I was so tired. I felt my eyes wanting to close, so I unrolled my driver side window a little to let some cold air in. Well that wasn't helping much, so I rolled the window the rest of the way down to let the rain in. *Maybe that'll help.*

The struggle continued. Eyebrow muscles purposefully strained upward, the drooping upper eyelids paying no mind, my eyes were slits. When you get to that point, fighting for consciousness, sometimes even the mind will turn against you. *I'm sure it'll be okay if I just close my eyes for a moment. Mmmm, that's nice, now open them. Doing alright. Let's try that again. Mmmmmm.*

Hooooooooooonnnnnnnnnnnnnkkkkk!!!!!

What was that?!

I had fallen asleep and drifted across the oncoming lane and into the shoulder on the other side. An Eastbound logging truck was screaming by me just a few feet from the handle of my passenger door. The thick brown trunks of fir trees were whizzing by on my left.

Whoa!! If I had crossed his lane just a second or two later…. I hated to think of what that would have looked like for the poor volunteer fireman that would have responded to that call, for that was all they had for fire departments in these little mountain communities.

One might think that such a close call should have jolted me fully awake, but it didn't. Moments later, I was unfocusing and starting to drift again. I cranked the radio as loud as I could stand it and I started screaming, "Stay awake!! Stay awake!! Wooooooooooooooooooo!!!! Stay awaaaaake!!! I'm an idiot!!! I'm an idiot!!!! Eeeeeeaaaaaaaaaaarrrrgh!"

Up ahead, I saw Pancho, leaning against his wall, resplendent in his pink and green as always. *Should I stop? Get some coffee? Do some jumping jacks? Should I stop?*

No! Yes! No! Just get home as soon as possible! There's no place like home… there's no place like home… there's no place…

A moment later, a dirty white 1976 Mercury Capri blew by young Panchito, skis safely mounted in the roof rack, rainy mist flying from the tires, windows open and a desperate, messy-haired, screaming, wet-faced idiot howling at the top of his lungs. "Aaaaaaaaaaaaaghhh!!"

Little Pancho never batted an eye. It seems he'd seen this kind of thing before. The customers out front, however…

Today though, it was going to be different! All of that was coming to an end. Today, I was finally taking my seat inside Pancho's. Notwithstanding anything that I had ever known to the contrary, there really was an interior to this building. It wasn't just a clever storefront with the likeness of a cute little ethnic fellow hanging by the door.

In a way, the place was part Mexican restaurant, part ski lodge. There was a lot of natural wood on the walls and plenty of neon beer signs. Dart boards, sombreros, old black-and-white photos of skiers from bygone decades, a jukebox, NFL Football posters, old snow shoes, a velvet bullfighter. The dining room was packed with tired laughing white people, all dressed the same. There were a lot of ski sweaters and colorful turtlenecks, and there was a lot of messy hair - the result of hours cramped up under a moist stocking hat; the standard skier look.

The four of us looked the part as we half-heartedly perused the menu. "What are free-joe-leez?" Barb asked.

"Heheh, those are frijoles. It means beans," I smiled.

"Then why don't they just say beans?" For some questions, a tired smile is all the answer required.

It had been quite a day for Dan and Barb. When you've grown up in a part of the country where the highest point of land is the hill built up around the freeway overpass; where, if you stand on your tiptoes and look far enough toward the horizon, you can see the back of your own head; where the topographical map of your hometown has no lines on it; then you're probably from the North American Heartland. To them, the mountains of Northwestern Washington were an amazing eye opener. They had "ooh'd" and "ah'd" all the way up to the summit that morning, enthusiastically pointing out the gaping canyons, the towering craggy rock pinnacles, the tall picturesque icy waterfalls and the lovely snowy fir meadows that the North Cascades are famous for. They couldn't get enough. Every direction that they looked, they felt like they were riding through a postcard or a scenic calendar. And they were right.

They were good folks, as people from Nebraska often are. Up on the slopes, they had listened intently to my tutelage about how to put ski boots on, how to stand back up after you've fallen, how to ski forward, how to slow down and how to turn. They had tenaciously tackled the "Daisy" run all day, until they had their snowplow turns pretty much figured out. The four of us - Dan, Barb, my wife Cheryl and I - had laughed and worked our way through the day. There was a lot of muscles that weren't accustomed to being used that way. There was a lot of falling down and a lot of laughter; and one pretty good snowball fight. Having been a snow skier for some time, I've got to believe that the other three were a lot more tired and sore than I was as we nestled into our warm Mexican dinners that evening at Pancho's.

"I think my rear end hurts the most," Barb groaned.

"Want your husband to massage it for you?" I asked with a laugh.

Dan let out a long exhale, with one eye closed, "Chris, you'd better do it."

"Oh no you don't!" my wife squeaked.

A sudden four-person, perfectly-timed explosion of laughter.

Every table had a small red glass jar with a candle burning in it. It was a popular thing to have at restaurants in the seventies and eighties. It helped to create a certain amount of quaintness, I guess. I miss those little red candle jars.

But, at Pancho's there was a second glass jar at every table, about two and a half inches tall and about the same diameter, with a little glass lid. There was a small horseshoe shaped hole on the edge of the lid from which protruded the handle of a tiny utensil. Tired or not, I had to know what this was all about! I held the container in front of me and I lifted the lid. My face sweated. I took a sniff. My whole head sweated. I set the jar down in front of me and I pondered. Peppers! Mexican restaurant peppers! Should I try one? Do I have the guts?

A bit later, our meals having just arrived, the conversation was no less silly than it had been all day. As we chatted, nibbled and laughed, my eyes kept going back to that little pepper jar. I just had to know!

So, I carefully pulled the tiny fork out of the jar and, as if by magic, a hush fell over the table. I looked around at three other faces, all with half-smiling looks of curiosity and excitement.

Schadenfreude. It's a rarely used word that I've always gotten a kick out of. It's in the English dictionary, but its origin is obviously German. Its pronunciation is like this: Shaw-den-froy-deh. Hard to spell, but fun to say! It refers to a feeling of pleasure at the misfortune of others. Two full decades after our visit to Pancho's, I watch with fascination every Spring as I see schadenfreude demonstrated for me in graphic proportions. I am a youth baseball umpire now as a hobby. At many of the ballparks at which I work, there are parking lots situated far too close to the playing area. Every time a high arcing foul ball gets hit out of play, the players all freeze and listen. It doesn't matter whether they're nine or sixteen; the boys all do the same thing. They become silent, filled with anticipation, and they wait. When they hear that hard ball hit the pavement, they exhale in disappointment and go right back to playing baseball. Oh, but when they hear that ball slam into the roof or hood or windshield of a car, cheers ring out from the ball field. Why? Why do they do that? Why are they happy that someone has just had their windshield broken or their hood damaged? It's schadenfreude. Literally defined, the word means harm-joy.

We humans don't understand why we do schadenfreude, we just do it. It's real and, simply put, it is what it is.

My three Pancho's companions silently watched me as I peered into the murky little pepper jar. Even though they were my friends, and my wife, they wanted to see me try it. Their little schadenfreude-filled minds wanted to see the stupid white guy's head explode from eating the mighty Mexican pepper. Unintentionally finding myself at center stage, I held up the tiny three-pronged fork and smilingly asked, "Should this be called a *threek*?"

I received a mild courtesy laugh for the joke; the comedic equivalent of the golf clap - and the intense stares continued. I guess I had no choice. I reached in and I forked a plump, medium-size pepper and I extracted it from the goo, placing it on my plate. With my left hand I held it firmly in place and with my right hand I knifed the pepper into a number of thin slices. Using my normal fork, I grabbed a generous portion of beef chimichanga and held it before me. Using my left hand, I laid a thin slice of the mystery pepper onto the bite-size pile. Into my mouth went the load.

As I chewed, I could see the disappointment on the faces of those around me. For some reason, they actually felt like they'd been gypped. I'd never promised anyone that I was going to stick that entire frightening monster into my mouth.

It's good. Tasty. Hmmm… it's getting pretty warm. Yikes, it's hot.

I wiped the sweat from my face as I chewed and I said, "Slap my hiney and call me Cindy!" And I went for my water glass. But a moment later all was fine. I grabbed another tiny pepper slice and combined it with another healthy dollop of chimichanga innards, and went through it all again. Then I did it again. And again. And again. Finally the pepper, the chimichanga and the entire glass of water were gone. Disaster was averted. My comrades' Schadenfreude would be denied. Or would it?

We moved on and the conversation wound around here and there, as only a tired, sore, margarita-laced conversation can, eventually coming, somehow, to the hair on Dan's back.

I rubbed a sleepy eye and said, "You should get it waxed."

Barb casually replied, "it would take more than wax. It would take a bulldozer." Group laughter again.

"Chris? What's wrong?" Cheryl asked me.

"I don't know… I don't… wow! My eye really hurts!... Oh, man."

Then I put it all together in my mind. It was my left hand, the left fingertips to be exact, that I had used to hold the pepper still while I had sliced it. And, hadn't I rubbed my eye a moment ago? With my left hand?

But I ate that pepper a half hour ago!

"Mmmmmmm… Oh… Oh, wow… this is really bad." My left eye felt like it was on fire. "This is really bad!"

Someone said, "Is this part where we call you Cindy?" All three laughed.

Schadenfreude!

By this time, with tears leaking down the left side of my face, I knew that I was in trouble. An uncontrollable keening sound issued from my mouth, as I stood and turned away from the table. Hand pressed firmly over my left eye, I ran.

Where!! Where do I go?!

It's funny how panic usually induces running. We start running sometimes, even before we know which way to run.

I ran to the bar. "Where's the restroom!" I screamed. I didn't care that I was interrupting. I didn't care that I was loud or that I looked like an idiot. The bartender pointed toward a hall at the back. Apparently I had the entire dining room's attention as I tripped over the leg of a barstool on my mad flight to the restroom.

"I remember my first beer!!" I heard a man yell behind me. Everyone laughed. I didn't care.

"Eh eh eh eh!" was the sound that I made as I ran for that restroom door. I knew that I would need to flush the eye with water. I ran to the sink, turned the water on and lunged forward. As soon as I let go of the faucet handle, it sprang back to the off position. No water.

The faucet was tiny and it barely cleared the edge of the sink. I tried several times, but I couldn't get my face close enough, and the water turned off every time I let it go?

"What?"

"No!"

What do I do?

Wet-haired and sobbing, I ran into the toilet stall, and I seriously considered shoving my face into the toilet water, but I didn't. Even in agony, I had my limits.

That would certainly be one way to flush an eye! In my pain, I allowed myself a quick laugh at that thought. I tend to do that; crack jokes when I'm dying. Once, when I was being rushed into the emergency room, writhing and sobbing on the stretcher, the nurse, who had been reading my chart, exclaimed, "Is this right? This is your ninth kidney stone?" Through clinched teeth, I whimpered, "Well, some people collect stamps." Yeah, I don't know why I do that.

Back to the Panchos' story…

I started grabbing toilet paper. I pulled and I pulled. It came out of the dispenser in tiny separate sheets. With a handful, I ran back to the sink. With one hand, I held the faucet handle open and with the other I held the wad of TP under the cold water.

With both hands, as I whimpered, I squeezed and molded the dripping wet toilet paper blob into a mush and I plopped it onto my eye. I leaned back so it would stay in place. It was helping a little but not enough! *I need more!* Back into the toilet stall I ran, dripping water on the floor, sobbing out loud as I went. I slipped and nearly went down.

A moment later, I was moaning in agony; writhing in pain as I stood shaking and clenching fists in the middle of the Pancho's men's room, with a dripping therapeutic toilet paper poultice covering a third of my face, cold water running down my neck into my clothing.

Suddenly the men's room door opened and in walked a man. He wasn't a guy, or a dude, or a fella. He was a man. He was about 6'3" with massive hairy forearms. He wore faded cracked black leather pants and big worn boots. He looked like he was about fifty years old, with a long black and gray speckled beard. His humorless gray wolflike eyes were surrounded by cracks and wrinkles that ran back into his dark graying temples. His shoulders were twice as wide as mine. His Harley Davidson t-shirt barely contained his massive chest, and a long salt-and-pepper colored ponytail cascaded from beneath a bandana head wrap. He was the kind of man who had seen a lot of tough road. I believe he could have pulled my arms right out of their sockets if he'd wanted to. This was very likely the toughest-looking man I had ever seen.

Deep in his own thoughts, he took a few steps into the room, then he froze in place. Before him stood the broken remains of a man. He saw me, in my colorful trendy ski clothes, wet and dripping, a glob of wet toilet paper mess on my face, leaning back awkwardly, pieces of toilet paper in my collar, agony in my expression, hair a wet crazy mess, standing in a paper-strewn puddle in the middle of the restroom, crying like an eight-year-old girl.

Embarrassed at my very unmanly condition, but unable to do anything about it, I looked up at this paragon of masculinity. He looked me squarely in my one good eye for a long moment. Then, in the deepest of voices that sounded like it was edged with gravel, he said, "Habanero?"

"Yeaaaaahhhh!!" I cried back to him.

He nodded solemnly, "I've been there, brother." And he walked by me toward the urinals.

Strangely, his emotionless words of encouragement helped me. In my pathetic weakness of the moment, if the manliest man I have ever seen won't belittle or shake his head at me, then neither will I!

It was a long time before I emerged from the restroom, but I did it with my head held high and my collar straight.

Yup. I've got this.

11

The Goodness

I didn't own a skateboard and neither did Scupper, but that other guy - the cool big kid with the curly hair - sure had a nice one. Scupper was a kid that I'd been playing with for a few weeks. I don't remember his real name because I never used it. For some reason, "Doug" is ringing a bell – I don't know. He was shorter than I was and I remember him having dark hair that hugged his head. It was Summer Vacation and I hadn't seen many of my normal school friends since early June. We had never been friends at school, Scupper and I. I suppose we ran in different circles. So, we found each other and we made do for the Summer. An eight-year-old boy needs someone to play with. Looking back, I'm pretty sure that, once third grade started up the following September, we went right back to ignoring each other. Kids are funny, that way.

That Summer, we played a lot of make believe war games, in Scupper's neighborhood, using L-shaped sticks for guns. "Pow" or "Bang" were the words that we shouted when we fired our imaginary pistols and rifles at each other, but we never used, "Boom" for that. "Boom" was a special sound effect reserved for bombs and hand grenades.

Neither of us really wanted to win these battles. No, it's a lot more fun to lose. We would often make sure that we shot each other simultaneously, so we could both go into our heart-wrenching death scenes. Sometimes, I would do a quick grab to my chest and, with a guttural cry, I would violently spin to the ground, lying still with my eyes open. Other times, when the actor's muse got a hold of me, I would draw it out in a long emotional pain-filled sequence, complete with an anguished gasp for air, an agonized attempt to rise, only to fall again, and eventually, an almost Shakespearian "Goodbye cruel world" lament followed by a dramatic collapse, tongue lolling out the corner of my mouth. All the while, in the grass just a few feet away, Scupper would be going through an academy-award-worthy demise of his own. Dying was great sport to an eight-year-old boy in the mid-1970s; at least it was where I lived.

Our elementary school was situated directly under a high altitude jet route. My dad explained it to me as an airplane freeway. Vietnam War era fighter jets flew over every day. Every once in a while, when there was sonic boom, which I guess was far more legal in the 1970s, every single boy on the playground would die. It didn't matter if we were playing kickball, freeze tag or chasing girls, the instant that massive boom hit our schoolyard, every one of us would belt out some kind of death scream and down we would go, leaving a hundred disgusted girls standing, shaking their heads at us in distaste. *Boys are morons!* Moments later, following a mass resurrection, we would all be right back to whatever we were doing before, healthy and alive - at least, until the next big boom.

That was the world that we lived in. Vietnam had just ended, World War II was still very real to us, and the Cold War was in full swing. John Wayne and Captain Kirk were everyone's heroes, and we all loved shooting the bad guys. Sometimes we called these playtime dramas, "Cops and Robbers." Other times, it was called "War," or "Army." Yes, there were times when the game took a diabolical and downright reprehensible direction as we played, (gasp!) "Cowboys and Indians." Oh the horror! Tongue-in-cheek enough for you? You know, we turned out alright.

Another of our heroes was the great Olympic Champion, Bruce Jenner. How stunned we all would have been if we could have known the direction that his very public life would take, about four decades later.

Best of all, for me, was Evel Knievel. Mr. Knievel had become a household name by jumping his Harley Davidson over larger and larger record breaking distances in exciting locations all over the country, breaking plenty of bones along the way. He was handsome, independent and crazy, and our country was diggin' that kind of rebellious character right around then. Scupper had an Evel Knievel bike! I had a scratched up old bike that my dad had scabbed together from used parts and then spray-painted black. Its brand new shiny blue banana seat looked out of place on that dull finish black bike frame. But it was a good strong bike, and I liked it. Scupper's bike, however, had a plastic gas tank and a number plate on the handlebars. It had fenders and other very cool plastic body pieces, all colored red, white and blue, with stars and stripes just like Evel Knievel's Harley. It was so cool.

We rode our bikes all over Scupper's neighborhood. We climbed trees, we played tag and we prank called strangers from his parents' master bedroom phone. Both of his parents worked all day, so we had the place to ourselves. When we got hungry, we ate sandwich cheese from the fridge or we picked little mandarin oranges from the trees in his backyard. Those things were tasty.

Scupper's house was in a typical suburban neighborhood, most of the homes having been built ten or fifteen years earlier. He lived in a cul-de-sac, at the top of a steep hill. At the bottom of the hill lived my little brother's friend, Reed. I don't think Reed and Scupper knew each other. Reed was at least two years younger, maybe three. Across the street from Reed's house, there stood the oldest house in the neighborhood. It didn't match the others, it was so much older. Its property was a little bit larger than the rest and it was badly over-grown. The house's ugly green paint was peeling.

Though I hadn't seen him yet, Scupper told me that there was a scary old man who lived there alone with two big ugly dogs that looked like they were as old as their owner. The old man's property seemed a little bit like a big weed in the middle of a flower garden, it so stood out. The sidewalks didn't even go onto his land; they stopped on both sides of his lot. Scupper's dad had told him that, back when the neighborhood was being built around him, the old man had refused to allow anyone to set foot on his land - even to build a sidewalk.

All Summer, Scupper and I had avoided that scary old house and its ugly property, as did all of the kids. We played and hid and chased and climbed everywhere else in the neighborhood, though, paying little attention to property lines.

We didn't ride skateboards. It wasn't because we didn't like them; we just didn't own one. That's why we were like loyal puppies following the big dog the day the tall curly-haired boy came into the cul-de-sac, shiny red board in hand.

He used big kid words like, "Cool," and "Whoa," and "Right on." I admired the way he ended almost all of his sentences with the word, "Man." He was really cool.

"I'll bet he's, like, ten, or something. Maybe even eleven. Wow. That's really old!"

"Whoa! This is a super cool skateboard hill, man," he told us, with a stylish sideways toss of his head to woosh his hair to the side. *Cool big kids do that with their heads.*

We played together all day. I was impressed and happy, because this was the first big kid that had ever treated me well, or wanted to play with me. It didn't take me very long to perfect the big kid's sideways head toss. *Far out.* After a few hours of doing anything that the larger boy wanted us to do, the whole while trying our best to make our voices a little lower, Mr. Big Kid decided that it was skateboard time. We stood together at the top of the hill, on the sidewalk across the street from Scupper's house, and looked down to the bottom. It was steep.

"See where the sidewalk ends, and the grass starts, by that ugly house?" Curly Hair asked with a cool head toss. "That's where the skateboard will stop, but my body will keep going." And, with that, he was gone. Down the hill he flew. So fast! So scary! So cool! I watched in awe as he stood sideways on that amazing red skateboard, and confidently speeded away from us. At the bottom of the hill, just after the slope started to lessen, the sidewalk ended. The big kid reached the grass. Just as he had predicted, the skateboard stopped abruptly at the sidewalk's end, and its rider kept going forward. He expertly ran across the old man's dandelion-strewn grass, slowing quickly to a stop just before reaching the rough cracked up driveway. He turned and walked back to where the skateboard sat waiting for him. He picked it up and walked back up the hill.

My assumption was that, when he'd returned to us, we would get to watch him do it again. That sounded good to me. I was shocked when he held his pretty red board toward us and asked, "Who's next?"

What? We get to do it? He's going to share his board with us? But, he's a big kid! Big kids aren't supposed to be nice to little kids. While I stood there trying to come to terms with this unexpected kindness and with the thrill of fear that shot through me - knowing now that the big scary hill would be part of my immediate future - Scupper filled the silence.

"I'll go," he said with a grin, as he took the board from His Tallness' hands.

"Right on," said the older boy.

Oh no! Scupper beat me to it. That "Right on" from the cool kid could have been for me.

Scupper carefully set the skateboard down on the sidewalk. Then he surprised me by sitting on it. He turned his head back toward us and, with a nervous smile, he said, "Umm, think I'll try this sitting down."

Off he zoomed. Down the hill he went, the hard red plastic wheels making "tick-tick-tick" sounds as he passed over the tiny sidewalk gaps. On he shot, like a missile. Just as he reached the grass, he rolled off of the skateboard onto his belly, then hopped up from the grass with a smile and a fist pump in the air.

"Yeah!!" crowed the big kid. "That was so cool!"

Scupper quickly scurried off of the forbidden grass, skateboard under his arm. This was probably the first time that he had touched that scary property. By now, I was halfway expecting to see the faded wooden screen door fly open, and a suspender-wearing bald man to shout, "Hey, you kids!" with two old sway-back dogs at his heels. But nothing happened.

Moments later, it was my turn. I stood at the top of the hill. Scupper and Skaterboy stood watching. Though I had never ridden a skateboard before, it never occurred to me to ride it sitting down. No way. Scupper had done the brave thing by going first. Well, I was going to do the even braver thing, by going upright. *Tall and strong! Like a big kid!*

Down the hill I shot, wind tugging at the legs of my shorts. I heard and felt the "tick-tick-tick" beneath me. The speed surprised me. It felt so much faster in person than it had watching from behind. This was fast! I could hear the rush of wind in my ears. *Okay, here comes the grass line. Run it out, like the big boy did.*

I hit the grass with a speed that I hadn't anticipated. Before I had time to run, I was soaring through the air. My eyes widened, and my arms shot out before me as I flew like Superman, dandelions passing beneath me. I would probably have screamed, had there been enough time to.

Over the grassy area I rocketed, and I knew, before I got there, that I was going to land in the driveway. It was over in an instant. My hands and knees took the punishment, instinctively sacrificing themselves that my face and head would be spared. The rough, worn asphalt of that old driveway shredded me. I was bleeding badly from all four limbs as I stood. The scream that had refused to come, while airborne, came now with strength behind it. I cried in pain and fear, like a hurt and panicked eight-year-old can.

I don't know how loudly I screamed or for how long, but, very quickly, help arrived. It was Reed's mom. "Chris? Is that you?" She knew who I was. She grabbed me around my arm and pulled me across the street to her front yard, where she turned on her front outdoor faucet and washed my wounds. The open gash on my right hand kept bleeding. Reed's mother held my hand under the water, allowing it to poor right into the wound. It hurt so badly. Where, moments earlier, I had been so concerned about being cool and acting tough, none of that mattered to me now. I cried and cried and cried.

A day later, I sat soaking in a bathtub of warm water. My injuries had scabbed and my gauze bandages were imbedded in my wounds. My mother said that it was time to change them, but they wouldn't come away from my skin. She ran me a bath and told me to undress and sit in the water. My job was to slowly, little by little, as the warm water softened the scabs, pull the gauze out of my sores. While I was doing that, she and my five-year-old brother would go to the store to buy some better bandages, and some other medical things for me.

Dad was at work, so I was alone in the house as I slowly tugged on the wet bandages. Each time I tugged, I cringed and gasped, but I made some small progress. It was a slow painful process. Finally, after a long time of tiny pulls, each causing little stinging tears in my scabs, the bandage of my left knee came free. I had never had such a bad sore before, and I didn't know what it would look like, but I was not expecting this! The injury was deep and the flesh around it was irritated and swollen. This, combined with the wrinkling that happens from being in a bath for too long, made it look rotten. I stared at it for a second, horrified by the terrible sight, and I screamed! No one came. No one was there. I screamed and I cried, certain, in my eight-year-old mind, that my knee was infected and ruined. My high-pitched eight-year-old voice echoed in the bathroom tile, making my screams sound nightmarish. I heard the echoes as I continued at the top of my lungs. It may have been the first time in my life, other than my 0.75 seconds of flight the day before, that had ever experienced true terror.

Eventually, the frightened screams devolved into mournful sobs, then, after a time, pathetic whimpers. Finally, there was silence. Mom was still gone, so, after a long time of trying to work my courage up, I resigned myself to seeing another ghastly sight, and I went to work on the bandage of my right hand, which was stuck in the scab as badly as my knee had been.

By the time my mother returned, I was dried and dressed. My private bathtub breakdown would forever (until now) remain a secret. Once dried, my wounds didn't look so awful. Though I didn't let it show, I was very discouraged and sad. Maybe it did show. It had certainly been the most stressful bath of my life. It hurt to walk, and I couldn't use my right hand at all. I watched as my mother pulled medical supplies from a brown paper bag.

"Look at this, Chris. It's a new kind of bandage. Better than gauze. These won't stick to your sores." I was very happy to hear that as she showed them to me. I sure didn't want to go through that scab thing again. She reached back into the bag and removed a brown plastic bottle. "Hydrogen Peroxide," she said. I had no idea what that meant.

Then she removed a tube of antibiotic ointment, which she always referred to as salve. "This will help you heal faster."

The last item to come from the bag was the best. It was the item with the greatest healing power of them all. With a small smile, she reached toward me and laid it on the table where I was sitting. I had never seen one before. It was a Mountain Bar. "You can have that after we get you bandaged."

She poured peroxide on my wounds and smothered them with salve. Bandaged and medicated, with my right arm in a sling made from a pillowcase, she handed me the Mountain Bar. It was crunchy and chocolaty, and it had cherry filling in the middle. It was so good! I savored it slowly and I didn't have to share any of it with my brother. It had been a rough two days, filled with pain and fear - but, at this moment, it had all turned into creamy, peanutty goodness. Thanks, Mom.

Decades have passed. I still have the scars. Sometimes I get a sharp pain under the scar on my hand, especially when it's cold. But, all in all, it worked out alright. It could have been so much worse. Instead of my hands and knees, it could have been my head. Our hospital pediatric wards across the country are full of children with traumatic brain injuries. That could have been me. I am thankful.

About thirty six years after the skateboard crash, having just driven me home from a hospital Emergency Room, where I had just endured my ninth kidney stone (I've had twelve at the time of this writing), my wife, Cheryl, knew just what to do for her drugged up, hurting husband. She set out my prescription pain medication, with strict orders not to take another until the appropriate time. She propped me up in our big living room easy chair with a pillow, and she wrapped a blanket around me. On the end table beside me, she set a tall glass of water with a small wedge of lime - the way I like it. Then she surprised me as she smiled and handed me a Mountain Bar. It may sound funny, coming from a man in his mid-forties, but, I almost cried. I must have told her the story. She had remembered! Chocolaty, peanutty get-well magic in a colorful wrapper, more healing than any prescription. The taste of love. The Goodness.

I almost look forward to the next time I have something go really wrong, just so I can relive the sweet, nutty, get well goodness of a love-filled, chocolate covered Mountain Bar. At the same time, if I never taste one again, that would be pretty good too.

"*There is no such thing as chance; and what seem to us merest accident springs from the deepest source of destiny.*

Friedrich Schiller

12

Always on Friday

"It's not here," she whispered sadly. She stood for a moment, eyes scanning the parking lot. "Nope." She stayed still for a while, checking her wrist watch a few times, hoping that it would come, but it didn't.

One last check of her watch, "Oh!" she exhaled with frustration as she turned toward the door. "Maybe next time." As she pulled open the door of the office building, she smiled to herself, "What a silly girl I am." She walked down the hallway toward her desk, where she would spend the rest of her day typing, filing and writing reports. "Maybe I'll try again at lunch."

She liked her job as an Executive Secretary. She worked in a large office building that housed hundreds of people in multiple departments, that included Administration, Finance, Marketing and Engineering. She enjoyed the professional atmosphere and was proud of the fact that she could type faster than anyone she knew, which was probably why she was one of the few in her department entrusted with the fancy new IBM Executive typewriters, making her the envy of her peers.

Seattle was a fun place to live in 1965. The jet age was ramping up and The Boeing Company was on the cutting edge of Aerospace technology. Jobs were plentiful, money was good and, despite some rumblings of something going on in Southeast Asia, the country was enjoying a peacetime economic optimism that carried over into everyday life. This was especially true in Seattle.

At twenty-four, Dixie was a fun-loving young lady who enjoyed staying busy. She was living with two young roommates who also worked at Boeing. She had done some dirt track auto racing, back when she'd still lived with her parents, and she had some nice trophies to show for it. Her father and older brother were very involved in the local dirt track racing scene and they had built her a nice car. They'd purposely made it a bit heavier than some of the other cars because they wanted their pretty young driver to be safe. She lost some of her competitive edge in the straightaways, where the lighter cars had the advantage, but it was in the corners where she would take them. Back then, the ladies raced in their own "Powder Puff" division at the local quarter mile dirt tracks, and Dixie had been good at it. But her racing days were over. She was an adult now with an adult job and adult responsibilities, and though she sometimes missed her parents and siblings, she enjoyed her adult life.

She liked to keep her dark hair shorter than most girls did; sort of an Audrey Hepburn / Leslie Caron kind of thing. She was taller than a lot of her friends and she was attractive. Along with her job as a Boeing secretary, she did some modeling; nothing real serious, but plenty of fun.

There it is! Oh, it's gorgeous. She'd had better luck on her lunch break today. There it was, right where she'd hoped it would be; big, bright and beautiful. It was the perfect blend of beauty and fierceness. Aggression and elegance. It was almost angry looking, silently screaming of power and ferocity. But, elegance and precision were there also. It was a lovely piece of master craftsmanship, with an extra energetic optimism in its bright yellow paint job. It sat alone on the pavement. She could almost hear it sparkle.

As a race driver and car enthusiast, Dixie's appreciation for the brand new Corvette Stingray was understandable. It was the model with the 427 cubic inch engine. This was a car! It was more than a car! Dixie smiled as she stared.

She stood a while, then she looked around. As enjoyable as it was to admire the wonderful machine, it wasn't the car that she had come to look for. The subject of her quest had yet to be found. Her target had not yet been acquired. She had heard that the driver of the bright yellow treasure was a single guy who worked in her building somewhere. More than the car, it was he who held her curiosity, and it was he that she was outside trying to catch a glimpse of on her lunch break today; as it had been the day before, and the day before that. She would probably wait a few minutes after her shift tonight, as she had the night before, and the night before that.

So it went for several more days; always looking, never finding. Sometimes the car was there and sometimes it wasn't, but she was never able to time her parking lot visits in such a way that she could see the Corvette's driver. The mystery grew in her mind. Was he short or tall, dark or fair, thin or stout, handsome or… well… not?

She knew that this was a little bit funny, even weird. But, what had started as curiosity had become something more. It was like an itch that she couldn't scratch. She just had to know!

Dixie had spent her later teen years living with her family in a big, white turn of the century two-story house in North Everett. Everett was a decent-sized town about an hour north of Seattle. They lived right across the street from the Everett General Hospital, so it had been a natural fit for Dixie to work there as a "candy striper" when she was young. She did well in school, and she was particularly good at art. She enjoyed many kinds of art but she was especially fond of painting.

She was the third of four children - five, really - but the first had died as a baby. The oldest living was her sister, Doris. Next in line was a brother, two years older than Dixie, named Don, and she had a younger brother named Del. Doris, Donald, Dixie and Delbert. Apparently her parents were fond of the letter "D," though they both had names that began with "O."

It was the kind of home where people felt welcome, and there was often more teenagers there than just the four who called it home. The house was big, the dinners were good, and all were welcome. Dixie's parents had, more than once, taken in a young person who had some tough things going on at home. There was always an extra bed available. It was a warm and fun place.

Along with racing dirt track, her family had another pastime that they enjoyed. They could dance. Dixie and her siblings loved to dance, and they could do it well. Throughout their teen years, they had practiced together in their big living room; laughing and learning as they boogied. They were great times.

So, it was an easy answer when, years later, Terry, Dixie's roommate and fellow Boeing secretary, asked her if she would like to go to a local dance at the Renton Inn. Dancing? Of course she would!

There was a very famous and exciting nightclub movement happening in some of the bigger cities around the country, in the mid-1960s. It was called, "Never On Friday." It had originated in Los Angeles and had quickly spread to New York, Chicago and other cities. "Never On Friday" was a series of dances, very much designed for the younger over-twenty-one crowd, and anyone who was anyone was at those dances. It was very fashionable.

Someone in the Renton-Seattle area decided that it would be fun to do something similar, so they held a dance at the Renton Inn. They wanted to take advantage of the fashion and mystique of the Los Angeles dances, but they couldn't call their dance, "Never On Friday," so they called it, "Always on Friday." Clever.

The small group of girls sat near the wall at a round table, watching the dancers and enjoying the band. There were two stages, one at each end of the large rectangular room, on which the bands would take turns playing. Terry and a couple of other friends were there with Dixie, as was Dixie's sister Doris. The girls sipped their beverages and tapped their toes to the beat. *Would anyone ask them to dance? Maybe? Maybe not. Either way is okay; this is still fun.*

"Excuse me." Every head at the table turned toward the voice. "Would you care to dance?"

They watched, not at all surprised that it was Dixie who had received the invitation. Smiling, she reached for his hand and stood. It was an unusually large hand that she held as they walked toward the dance floor. Even in her heels, she had to look up a good distance to see his eyes. *Hmm... Six foot four? Yeah. Something like that. Maybe six-three.*

He might have been the tallest person in the room. Song after song, they danced the night away. Through the fast dances and the slow, the two fell more and more into rhythm with each other. Soon, they'd both forgotten their respective groups of friends, and neither of them were interested in dancing with anyone else. At some point, during the long evening of dancing, Dixie learned that the tall dark haired stranger was named Troy. She thought that she may have heard a trace of an accent when he spoke, but she wasn't sure. It was hard to hear very well with the band playing so loudly. *Texas, maybe?*

"Looks like Dixie has made a new friend," said a voice from the round table. The girls looked on wistfully.

Her friends had wanted to leave for some time, but since Dixie had no other ride home, they had waited. They didn't want to interrupt what was happening on the dance floor; like the tiniest of buds just starting to open into what might become a flower. Who were they to interrupt? Eventually, though, the evening had grown late and the friends were long past ready to leave.

"Dixie," Terry whispered, after having tapped her dancing friend on the shoulder. "We would like to go now. We're tired and it's late."

For a moment, Dixie froze. *Of course you do. I'm sorry. You're right, it is late. We should go,* she thought silently. *But I want to stay! Oh, how I want to. What do I do?*

Troy watched the short interaction from about ten inches above, and he read Dixie's silent hesitation like a book. It made him happy, because he could see that she was feeling exactly the way that he was.

"Maybe I can help," he said, looking into Dixie's upturned eyes. "If you'll stay a little longer, I'll be happy to drive you home."

Dixie's eyes quickly shot back to Terry's, who gave Dixie a playful grin, and turned without speaking. Without saying a thing, she leaned back into the dance, picking up the rhythm perfectly, her left cheek against his chest, her right hand in his left.

The two glided as one through the remainder of the song, lost in worlds of their own, a smile on both of their faces. So it went for the rest of the evening.

"I'm glad you stayed," he told her later as he helped her into her light sweater.

"I am too," she replied with a smile as she took his arm. Together they walked out of the dance hall, which was really a large temporarily converted conference room. Down the hallway, around the corner and through the main lobby of the hotel they slowly walked, arm in arm, until they emerged into the hotel's covered entry area. It was late, so there was very little movement there. There was a bellboy helping a couple remove luggage from a car. A taxi sat with its engine running.

Troy stopped walking and reached into his pocket. As he stood facing her, fishing in his pockets, Dixie glanced past him to the parking lot behind. In the distance, a little beyond the taxi, sat a bright yellow 1966 Corvette Stingray.

Adrenaline shot through her, causing prickly tingles to race across her scalp like a hundred tiny needles. *Oh my goodness! It's here! That means… Oh my goodness! He's here! My mystery man is here! I was in the same room with him this whole evening! He's here right now! Which one?! Which guy in that room? Could it have been that short guy that danced with Terry? Or maybe the guy in the skinny tie. Which one?*

Troy did not notice the catch in Dixie's breath. He smiled and reached toward her. "Gum?" he asked, as he popped a piece of Wrigley's Doublemint into his mouth. Her mind racing, she declined with a slight movement of her head.

"You alright?"

She answered with a barely audible, "Mm-hmm…"

As he turned toward the parking lot with a smile, he asked, "You ready?"

She held his arm again as they walked. She could hear the "tap-tap-tap" of her high heel shoes on the pavement beneath her. *He's here… I can't believe he's here!... whoever* HE *is… The Corvette man is here… somewhere. Is he at the dance right now? Did I see him? I wonder where….. he….. um….*

Wait!… What are we… what are we doing? Is he? He can't be? We're walking toward the car. No! Yes? Is this really happening? OH MY GOODNESS!!!

Her brain cartwheeled and her knees went weak as his key slid easily into the bright yellow passenger door. She froze in place, staring at the door as he opened it. He stood smiling, holding the door for her. How long had it been since she had taken a breath?

Almost as if it was someone else who was doing it she felt herself nestle down into the smooth black leather seat, and she heard the solid thump as the door closed. Without thinking, she leaned to her left and unlocked the driver's door.

I'm going to have a heart attack!

A moment later, the massive engine roared to life, then gurgled like a happily purring dragon. She peeled her still-unbelieving eyes off of the Corvette emblem in front of her on the dash, and looked at Troy.

Still displaying the boyish smile that he had worn the whole evening, he asked, "So… where do you live?"

Three years later, I was born.

"Tomorrow is the most important thing in life. Comes into us at midnight very clean. It's perfect when it arrives and it puts itself in our hands. It hopes we've learned something from yesterday.

John Wayne

13

A Life Well Lived

Shanon and I sat together at a memorial service reception. We chatted as we enjoyed the excellent snacks. At forty-three and forty-six, respectively, it was still very obvious to any casual observer that he and I are brothers. I've always been a little bit jealous of how good my brother looks in a suit. Today he was in a very nice black pinstripe. I'm so proud that that sweet little boy turned into such a good man.

Shanon's father-in-law was being buried today. It was a bitter-sweet day with a fair share of both laughter and tears, as Bob's life had been remembered and recounted by various speakers at a nearby church a couple of hours earlier. Because I had lived for over a decade in a different state than my brother, I had hardly known Bob, but as I had listened to relatives, friends and colleagues share their stories, I'd found myself struggling not to tear up.

I wondered what kind of man could leave such a legacy of universal respect and gratitude. This was not the average memorial service where a perfunctory collection of nice things are said about the Dear Departed. These people spoke of genuine admiration and love; of lives that had been reached and futures that had been changed and hearts that had been inspired by a man who had seemingly loved everyone and had given of himself to make other lives better.

One of the speakers told a story that I think will stay with me for life. She spoke of a certain day, in a doctor's office. The doctor had just told

Bob that his cancer was terminal, and that the sixty-five year-old husband and father of three had about five more years, give or take.

Bob replied to his doctor, "It seems that we have a problem here, Doc. I have a lot left to do. You're giving me until seventy, but my plans go out to eighty. Looks like I need to find me a different doctor."

She finished her story by telling us that Bob had celebrated his eightieth birthday last April. We all cheered with triumph when she said that.

Even in death, his great work was continuing. Two wonderful ladies, sisters well into their seventies, were speaking today for the first time in over fifteen years. Maybe healing was starting today. Bob would have liked that.

It was clear that Bob had loved God, and he had taken his God-given mission seriously. His example was inspiring me to reaffirm mine.

"Wow, that was quite a service," I told Shanon as I dipped my prawn in cocktail sauce.

"Yeah." He replied, looking far away. There was a long pause. Still looking at some abstract point out in front of him, he continued, "I would be proud if I can live my life in a way that impacts half as many lives as Bob's did."

"Me too." And we shared a quiet moment of introspection. I think that we both were making some loose plans and maybe setting a few nebulous goals in those quiet seconds.

After a moment, Shanon turned to me with a smile and said, "Hey! Do you know where we are?"

"Sure! We're at the Red Lion Inn, in the banquet room." I wondered why he'd asked me that, and why he was smiling so brightly.

"This wasn't always the Red Lion," he said. "It's changed names many times through the years. Long ago, it was called, The Renton Inn. Our parents met in this room!"

"Whoa!" I shouted, not caring about my loudness. "Really? This is the place?" I looked around the room, trying to imagine what it might have looked like in 1965. I suddenly imagined a band playing on a small stage at the end of the room, and a circle of dancing young people. A sign across the wall said, "Always on Friday!" The story that I'd heard so many times, of how my parents had met, played again in my mind like a movie, only this time the movie's set was more accurate.

"Hmmm." I exhaled with a smile. "You know, I'm writing about that night. I'm just starting that chapter."

I looked to my right where Cheryl sat beside me. My dad had met my mom in this room. I now sat beside my own precious wife in this same room. My brother and his wonderful wife, Erinn, were here. Two excellent, loving marriages of twenty years plus. This room had seen the beginning of a family, and now it was seeing a sad goodbye for another. Families with a link. If walls could talk.

Things begin. Things end. Lives are lived. Some are lived well. Other lives are inspired. Paths cross and cross again. Some things are lost. Some are kept. Chance meetings. Exciting beginnings. Epic events set in motion. Fond farewells. Loss. Gain. Hope.

God Bless you Bob.

"*Making a living and having a life are not the same thing. Making a living and making a life that's worthwhile are not the same thing. Living* the *good life and living* a *good life are not the same thing. A job title doesn't even come close to answering the question, 'What do you do?"*

Robert Fulghum

14

A very good friend of mine has successfully talked me into writing this chapter and including it in this book. In fact, and you can thank her later (or not), she has talked me into two such chapters. Both are stories about stories. Here is the first.

A Rich Man

When I was fifteen, one of my high school teachers assigned us a writing task. It could be any length, as long or as short as we pleased. It was, if I remember correctly, meant to be an exercise in sentence structure and narrative description. She told us that it had to be about only one character, male or female - our choice, and that we must incorporate, in detail, a physical object that our character interacts with in some way. Additionally, we must include an animal and a building. They could be any object, any animal and any building, but all three must be present. Further, she told us that we would get extra credit points if we could effectively describe a setting, different from our own real lives, in such a way that the reader could see, feel and smell the scene around her. More extra points were promised to the young writer who would make his or her reader feel something emotionally. Surprise, Amazement, Horror, Disappointment, Concern, Pride, Shock, Patriotism, Compassion, Suspense, Justice, Outrage, Grief, Satisfaction. It would be our choice - our challenge.

She knew that this would be a difficult task for some, as she smiled over her captive audience. Silently, she hoped that this just might be that one special assignment that would catapult a dormant young mind into the creative light; that might help one special student to find his or her writing voice; awakening a young person to a love of words and story. It worked!

Well, it might have, for *someone* anyway. I wouldn't know. I didn't do the dumb thing.

I am sad to tell you, my friend, The Reader, that this one was a member of a very long list of incomplete assignments for The Chrisser. *Homework? Bleh! I hate homework.*

About two years later, though, something wonderful happened. I grew up, a little. It was my senior year of high school, and I found myself, without consciously meaning to, gravitating toward different friends and prioritizing my wants and my likes and my activities differently than I had before. My attitude changed toward homework. My attitude, in fact, changed toward nearly everything.

One afternoon, right in the heart of that personal renaissance, I picked up a pen, and I sat down to start writing, just because. But, what should I write about, I wondered. *How about a poem? Nah. An essay? How about a story? Hmmm. But what kind of story?* I suddenly remembered an old never-completed writing assignment from a previous tenth grade Humanities class, and I set to work. I stuck the butt end of the pen into my mouth, nestled down a little deeper into a not-so-comfy kitchen chair, and I thought.

Okay... What had she said? One character. An animal. An object. A building. Extra points for painting a vivid scene. Extra points for making the reader feel something. What would I want my reader to feel? Hmmm...

So it was, with a loose plotline in mind, that I laid ink to paper, just for fun.

The next thing that you will read will be a two-year-late writing assignment that was never turned in; an assignment that would ultimately do nothing for my two-year-dead tenth grade report card. Thirty-plus years later, should I now have the good fortune to make it into her book collection, I wonder if my 1984 tenth grade teacher will recognize herself in this story.

You will, most likely, notice a difference between the voice in the story, and the voice in the rest of this book. Of course, that would make sense, since it was written by a seventeen year old, and the rest of this book was written, little by little, over a four year span during my mid-forties. So, here we go. Bear with me, please, as it's a bit crude and the writer's inexperience shows, but, it was a start.

A Rich Man
Chris Ford, age 17
1986

This place was full of treasures. Here a twisted bicycle frame, there a rusty mailbox, and beyond, a pair of Volkswagen hubcaps. The old man walked here often. To others, it was a dump; a junkyard, a place they saw seldom and thought of almost never. On that rare occasion that they did visit the place, it was merely as a means to discard an item that they no longer desired; an item that had sat too long in their basement, backyard or closet, collecting dust or mold, while being replaced by some shiny new version.

They would spend only enough time to dump their rubbish, glance around the place with a disdainful eye, unaware of the scowls on their faces, and drive away, wiping their hands on their pant legs.

To the old man, this place was a wonderland. Every day he would come, and every day he would find peace and contentment. He would also, from time to time, find a few items that could turn a tidy profit at the thrift store or recycling company.

He always kept an eye out for unusual bottles or glassware items. He would take these items down to Ida's store. She sold a lot of antique knick-knacks and she was always happy to give the old man a few dollars for the things that he brought. Many of these she simply threw away after buying them from him. It made her happy to help him. She knew that most of his finds were unsellable, but she enjoyed his visits. Not many people came in these days. The truth was, he rather enjoyed the visits, himself.

Sometimes he would find copper or tin. These he would take to the recycler. These trips were less enjoyable than the trips down to Ida's, but they provided their own kind of satisfaction. Money in the pocket meant food on the table.

The old man took these items from the place with permission from the owner. Years before, when the old man was not so old, a freckle-faced red-headed boy, named Robby, would sometimes sit with the old man and drink Kool-Aid with him on the porch. Young Robby visited the old man two or three times a week while he was delivering newspapers. The old man treasured those times. Now the boy was man; a man with responsibilities, which included the running of this place. Robby had not lost his red hair or his freckles, but he no longer came to drink Kool-Aid. There were many things that the old man missed from his long years. Things change. He accepted that fact. It was a part of growing old.

Though sunny, today was cold. As he walked, he felt the wind biting at his face. He pulled his collar up. As always, the place made him smile. He had already found a small lightly dented toy dump truck, which he had placed in the deep pocket of his overcoat. He hoped that he could clean it up and, maybe, get a buck or two for it somewhere. It was a pretty good find. Not great, but pretty good. There were many days that he would find nothing at all, but he didn't mind those days, because he had gotten to see the place.

There were also days, rare though they were, that he would find something great. Once, he found a perfectly good silver whisky flask. He liked to imagine that its former owner, having finally made the difficult decision to stop drinking, had marched up to a garbage can somewhere and, with a stolid look of determination, dropped the flask, heard the profound life-changing thud as it struck the bottom, and with head held erect, turned and walked away toward a bright future of health and happiness. Deep inside, the old man new that the flask had probably been thrown away by accident. Either way, it was his now. He thought of the flask as he walked, and he felt the satisfying bulge on his hip.

"It truly is one of life's great pleasures, to feel the weight of a flask on your hip, and to know that it's full," he thought.

On his way home from the place he walked beside the long ditch as he always did. This was another of his special places. At high tide, water from the bay would slowly fill the ditch, and often, things would float in with the tide, to be left there when the water receded later. Usually, all he would find was leaves, twigs or an occasional tire. But he would always look anyway.

He was nearly home when, out of the corner of his eye, he saw sunlight glance off of something in the ditch. Upon closer examination, he saw that it was a bottle of some kind. The glass was brownish-green, and the bottle was of an unusual shape. It had a short neck and, rather than being a cylindrical shape, it was a tall thin rectangle. It was very dirty, and it looked like it had been there a long time. He scurried down the side of the ditch, displaying unusual spryness for one his age.

He pulled on the bottle, and it made a slurping sound as it slipped from the thick mud. His first thought was to wonder how long it had been there and why he had never seen it before.

"Hey! I'll bet Ida gives me three bucks for this beauty!" he shouted, though no one was there to hear. He was excited now as he walked the last leg of his journey. He couldn't wait to get home, for he had made quite a haul today. Yes, sir! Quite a haul, indeed! He could see his little brown house now, as he walked. Two large cats loitered lazily on the front porch. As he walked up the three wooden steps to his door, he said, "Hello, Guildenstern! And a fine good evening to you as well, Mr. Rosencrantz! I have done very well today, my friends. Come. Come along now. It's time for our supper."

At this, the larger of the two cats, a huge orange tabby, rubbed against his leg, purring happily.

"Yes. Yes, I love you too." He opened the door and the three friends walked straight to the kitchen.

After sharing dinner, he went to work on the dump truck. With soap, water and a little elbow grease, he soon had the little toy gleaming. He then turned his attention to the strange bottle.

"Ida's gonna like this one, boys." Guildenstern meowed in reply. It was the rough meow of a cat who had smoked ten packs of Camels a week. The old man dunked the bottle into the dirty dump truck water. He wanted to get most of the crud off of the outside before tackling that old cork.

He marveled at its shine as he held it to the light. There was something inside. It hadn't occurred to him to check the bottle for any contents. He shook the bottle. "What the slim pickins is in there, Rosencrantz?" For several minutes, he worked on the old cork, all the while maintaining a one-sided conversation with his companions. Finally, he was holding a rolled piece of parchment, tied in the middle with a faded string.

"Hmmf! A letter in a bottle, I guess! Probably some love letter. Okay, this should be good for a few laughs." He easily broke the brittle string and he unrolled the note. It had writing on it. He stared at it for a moment, not reading it, and he admired the ornately flowing script with which it was written.

"Well, now! Would you fellas get a load of this?" Then, he started to read.

"Millen and Millen. Attorneys at law. Boston, Massachusetts," he read aloud. His eyes panned down past the address on the letterhead. He stared, unblinking, at the date. "Whugh! Why, this was eighteen years ago! Holy Mackerel!" The cats just sat there, seemingly unaware that they were being spoken to. Out loud, he continued to read, "To the finder of this bottle, I bid you greetings. I hope that no water has damaged this letter.

"It is with great gladness that I inform you of your newly found wealth. To you, I bequeath my estate. And, for my rude presumption in completely changing your life, I owe you an explanation." The old man paused for a moment. "Hey, boys!" he yelled. "You believe this? Holy Mackerel! Let's see what else this ol' boy's got to say!"

He focused his attention back on the document and, with a smile on his weathered face, he continued aloud. "I have no living heirs to whom I can will my fortune. Of my friends and associates, I can think of none to whom I would like to give such a gift. It is with delight that I cater to my love of the dramatic, or eccentric, if you will, as I will undoubtedly befuddle those around me by leaving all of my wealth to you, my dear bottle finder. Please contact the firm shown above, and may God bless you. Millard James Thornton, the Last."

He stared at the note. He looked at the bottle, at the cats, at the toy truck, and back at the note. He couldn't believe what he had just read. He glanced around at the shabby furniture in his shabby little house, and he wondered how rich he was.

He picked up both the note and the bottle, and he carried them into his tiny bedroom. He changed into his long nightshirt, rolled up the note and inserted it halfway into the bottle, and placed them on his nightstand. As he lay awake, unable to sleep, he stared at the bottle. This was the biggest thing that had ever happened to him. Out loud, he said, over and over, "I'm a millionaire. I'm a millionaire."

"Guess what, boys!" he suddenly shouted. Both cats turned their faces toward him. "Liver! Eggs! Salmon! Anything you want, you got! Why, you want caviar, you got that too! Hah! Dad's a rich man now! You hear me? A millionaire! And you, my fine furry friends, are the richest kitties ever! What-cha' think of that? Huh?" The old man giggled for a while, and eventually fell silent.

For another hour, he lay awake. Images and ideas cartwheeled through his sleepy mind. He fell asleep, finally, with a mental picture of a smartly dressed butler serving him brandy. With sleep, the images increased into detailed dreams.

The next morning found the old man at the dump, as usual. It had always been a place where he could think. He walked home along his usual route beside the ditch. The icy wind tore at his collar. It was cloudy today. Near home, he stopped. He stood, motionless, staring out toward the bay. A rusted industrial barge was anchored motionless in the water. A Seagull screamed somewhere nearby. Quickly, as if the right moment had suddenly come, he scampered down into the ditch. He reached into the pocket of his overcoat and he removed the beautiful bottle. He bent down and inserted it into the mud, bottom first, then he turned away. Without looking at it again, he climbed back up to level ground and he walked away silently; back to his cats, his whisky flask and his little brown house by the bay.

15

Walk Tall

"Did you write me a story, like you said you would?" she asked excitedly.

"Yeah, I did," I replied with a smile. I was a little bit surprised at her enthusiasm. She had read my old story, *A Rich Man*, the day before, and immediately asked if I had any more. I had shaken my head and explained that I didn't usually hang onto my short stories for very long. Thinking of them a lot like a cartoonist might think of his doodles and sketches, I normally just let them lie around until they eventually disappeared into the trash can, with a coffee cup ring or two dried into the paper.

So I agreed, at her request, to write her a quick shorty that very evening, and to bring it back to her the next day. "It's nothing special," I said as I gave her the handwritten story. "I just ad-libbed a little and this came out."

She happily grabbed it from my hand. "I'm sure it will be wonderful." She spread the pages out before her as she sat at her kitchen table. Concentration creased her brow as silence filled the room.

Remembering how *A Rich Man* had moved her emotions the day before, I knew that she was hoping for something similar. She longed to, once again, have her heartstrings tugged and her romantic imagination caressed by another strong heroic character pressed into poignant circumstance.

Heh-heh… this is going to be fun to watch.

Walk Tall
Chris Ford, age 19
Spring, 1988

He walked tall. Each step had purpose. He could hear the light click of his boots as they came down with each sure-footed step to strike the sidewalk. The sound pleased him. He had never noticed it before today, but, of course, today was no ordinary day. He felt a little taller today. He wondered if anyone noticed.

"Of course they do," he thought with no air of sarcasm. "They just don't want to let on."

He had always believed what they had said about him. He had always been a follower. He had always thought of himself as just a little under average. Today, though, his mind was full of new ideas. He knew that no one would ever call him "Runt" or "Pencilneck" again. Those days were over. Today, he was a better man. He knew it; and he knew that they knew it.

His quick, powerful stride lead on, past the bakery, the barber shop, the card store. He suddenly realized that he was whistling, and he wondered how long he had been doing that. An involuntary smile played across his face.

He knew that everyone was looking at him. As he walked, a new thought gnawed at the base of his brain. He must be the reincarnation of some once-great warrior, Julius Caesar perhaps, or Alexander the Great.

They had all been there. They had all seen what he did. They had all been watching. There would be no more jokes made at his expense; no more snickering, he knew.

The entire town had seen. Even his old teacher was there. She would surely regret that day, long ago, when she humiliated him in front of the others.

He could see it all so clearly. He could see what a waste his life had been, until now. It would all change! He would take charge of his life. As he walked, he clinched his fists with a new vitality, and realized that he was no longer afraid. He had proven that he was, indeed, worthy of being called a man. He had proven it to all of them! He had proven it to himself. He now knew that he was important; that he mattered.

"Look at them," he thought. "They all admire me now. They look up to me!" It had been the greatest thing that he had ever done, and he knew that he would always be remembered for it.

He had swallowed thirty four goldfish. The former record had been twenty nine. Yes sir! It was a day that none would soon forget!

I knew that she had just read the last line when her head jerked up from the kitchen table and she pierced me with smoldering eyes.

"What?!" She yelled. "That's it?"

I giggled and ran, as she jumped up and threw her paper cup at me.

You'll be on your way up!
You'll be seeing great sights!
You'll join the high fliers who soar to high heights.
You won't lag behind, because you'll have the speed.
You'll pass the whole gang and you'll soon take the lead.
Wherever you fly, you'll be best of the best.
Wherever you go, you will top all the rest.

Except when you don't.
Because sometimes you won't…

Dr. Suess

16

West of Bliss

Pride and Joy. I had heard the words used together for years, but now I was looking right at it.

"That car is his pride and joy."

"Her dolly is her pride and joy."

"Playing tennis was my pride and joy."

There's nothing wrong with sayings like these. It's a well-known, and probably over-used, figure of speech – *pride and joy*. But not this day! This was no worn-out idiom. I was seeing pride - *real pride*; and joy - *true joy* - beautifully mixed together, and I stood watching with my head cocked a little to one side and my face, very likely, showing a mix of curiosity and confusion.

His name was unfamiliar to me, but, as I watched his face on our TV screen, and heard the respect with which the announcers referred to him, and the enthusiastic approval of the roaring crowd in the background, I knew that his was a name that I should learn.

I don't know if I've ever seen a man with so much dignity in his posture, in the set of his jaw, in the intensity of his eyes, in the confidence of his stride. As I was an unusually thin, awkward, unpopular sixteen-year-old boy, I figured that the man on the TV screen was everything that I was not.

The camera panned back so the TV viewers could see both the man and the cheering crowd behind him. The farther he ran, the louder the crowd. He was running at about half speed, and he glided like a well-oiled machine around the oval track of the Los Angeles Memorial Coliseum. High over his head, he held the Olympic torch, flaming in the wind. Watching live from twelve hundred miles away, I could feel a swell of patriotic emotion in my chest and an unexpected lump in my throat. I wished that I was there in that massive crowd, cheering for the man. I wanted to cheer in my living room. Had I been alone, I probably would have. I stayed quiet as my family and I watched.

Then the camera went back to his face. There it was again; pride and joy, both. Not once, during his entire run, did he ever smile or wave or even look around himself to take in the spectacle; but he maintained an admirable determined solemnity that captured me and drove home to me the importance of what was happening. This moment was a big deal!

There were a lot of things that I didn't know about Rafer Johnson, as I saw him running the flame up the steps toward the giant Torch of the 1984 Olympic Opening Ceremonies. But watching him, I knew that this was a man who had faced adversity and had survived; who had striven through pain and hardship, and had emerged; who had dealt with things that I couldn't possibly understand, and had risen to heights few would dare. His was the face of a champion, and I could see it in every camera angle.

There was one other thing that I did know about Rafer Johnson as I watched him on my TV screen – July, 1984. I knew that he was deeply honored to have been chosen to represent the athletes and the rest of the country as the man who would carry the flame and light the Olympic Fire. He didn't need to tell us about the honor. It was plain for us all to see.

Up he went, climbing the giant stairway. At the top, he turned toward the crowd of more than a hundred thousand, and to the cameras projecting his image all over the world, solemnly holding his torch out to them in salute, and there it was again; pride and joy. The massive crowd roared. It had been twenty four years since he had won his gold medal, but he wasn't breathing hard. For a long moment he stood, face made of oak; the sun shined on his sweating dark skin as a muscular arm held the fire high. Then he reached up and touched his torch to a spot directly above him.

As the flame raced from his hand, up to the giant five-ring Olympic symbol above him, which burst spectacularly into flames, and then farther up, burning its way to the massive coliseum torch high above him; Rafer Johnson stood still and statuesque, like a rock, with that same magnificent look of strength on his face. I was sixteen. I was mesmerized.

The camera zoomed around the stadium, taking in all of the roaring masses. The screen flashed to a panoramic blimp shot from outside. The giant Olympic flame danced happily, as though it somehow understood. Then, just before the TV went to a commercial, there was an image of the torch from inside the stadium, and there I saw, from a long distance, the tiny back-lit silhouette of Rafer Johnson. Still at his post. Still solemn and strong. Still standing sentinel.

It was the first Olympics event that I had ever really payed attention to, but this was not the first time that I had seen an Olympic torch.

Exactly four weeks earlier...

I was hot, I was bored and the rock I sat on was hard and uncomfortable. *What are we doing here again?*

We had been on the road for many days, so it was nice to be out of the truck for a while. I didn't mind the heat or the dust. I didn't even mind the boredom. It was a nice change. We had driven through the entire state of Utah that day, from South to North, and well into Idaho. We all had a serious case of car-seat-itis, or, as Mom liked to called it, "hot cross buns." Simply put, my hiney hurt. It had been good to stretch and walk around a bit.

"About another eight minutes," Dad said as he squinted at his watch.

We had seen a lot of exciting and impressive things on this trip; Arches National Monument, Bryce Canyon, Mesa Verde, White Sands and others. We had gone all the way to Juarez, Mexico, crossing over from El Paso. I had even experienced an unpleasant visit from Montezuma himself.

Best of all, we had visited my Grandma Ford, who lived alone in Eastern New Mexico. It would prove to be the last time I would see her.

We were on the tail end of a long scenic drive across the American West, as we rumbled through Southern Idaho, and we were looking forward to getting home. Tonight would be our last night sleeping in the trailer.

It was late afternoon, June 30th. My family and I were part of a small crowd of people patiently waiting at an unattractive roadside dirt patch. There were no cities nearby, only endless flat farmland, some dusty open prairie and an old road.

I thought a little about the dust-covered road that I sat beside, blazing hot in the relentless Summer sun; beaten and faded in the middle of nowhere, pocked with potholes, some filled with darker asphalt, some gaping open.

What if you could tell the age of a road by the colors of the repair patches, like counting rings on a tree stump? Like most young boys, I liked to ask a lot of worthless 'what if' questions. *What if I could see through walls? What if I had a money tree? What if I wasn't so repulsive to girls?* Normal boy stuff.

I chuckled at the thought of myself counting road blemishes and judging their colors. I was thinking that this old road probably hadn't been repaired in years, maybe decades. But this was where we were supposed to be, said Dad. He was pretty sure. We'd know in eight minutes.

Yaaaawn…

Wipe some sweat…

Spit onto the pavement to see how quickly it disappears. Wow, that was fast! Sweat ran down the side of my face. I wonder if I could fry an egg on the road. Or a cheeseburger! Yeah, that'd be pretty good. Hey, I am kinda hungry.

I didn't know what the road was called, so I privately named it Cheeseburger Road. It was a good flat place for rattlesnakes to stretch out and warm themselves, but probably good for little else. I wondered if anyone had even driven this road in the last year.

"Here they come!" someone yelled, and our small crowd of sweating strangers started to stir and move about. They were a little early, I guess. I saw a man go up onto his tiptoes to see over the others. I stood up from my rock, realizing that I was still holding Suzette's leash. She looked up at me panting; her little tongue sliding forward and back with each breath, and I laughed, like I always do when I see a dog doing that. A warm panting dog, to me, always looks like there's something hilarious going on. I know it's just the natural shape of a panting dog's mouth, but it looks like silent laughter. Suzette's cute panting face was especially funny. I just figured that she was laughing her head off, roasting there with me in Idaho.

I just laughed again, as I typed this, remembering that funny fuzzy face from so long ago.

Suzette was a "teacup" sized purebred French Poodle, but you wouldn't know it. Most of the time, instead of the traditional poodle trim, she was pretty overgrown and natural looking, like a tiny black Benji-dog, so she didn't look much like a poodle; not in the classic sense anyway. Like many other poodles, though, she didn't have a tail. It had been removed when she was a puppy because, well, she's a poodle, and that's what you do to poodles, or so I was told. She had been robbed of the most prized and valuable right and pleasure of all dogdom; the wagging of one's tail. All there was now was a dumb looking, thimble-sized appendage where a magnificent black tail should have been.

We had always had larger dogs throughout our family's times, and it had taken a while for us boys to warm up to the idea of having a squeaky little rodent dog. She would have big paw prints to fill, as we all still missed our brilliant and beautiful border collie, Buttons, who had been killed by a speeding delivery truck some time earlier.

"Okay." Shanon had told my parents. "A poodle it is."

"But no naming her Fifi!" I exclaimed.

"Absolutely not! No Fifi," he agreed.

Dad smiled at Mom and, with a little laugh in his voice, he said, "Well, sounds like we need to come up with a different name than we'd planned." All of us laughed.

Suzette was a good name. It was cute, it was French, and it wasn't Fifi!

As I looked down at her adorable laughing panting face that tired afternoon in Idaho, I remembered a time when that face wasn't so adorable. A Mind Movie from two weeks earlier spontaneously projected itself onto the mind screen.

We were sitting at our high Rocky Mountain campsite enjoying a little lawn chair time with some cold beverages. The campfire crackled contentedly and we all watched with amusement as the cute chipmunks cautiously came closer and closer. One of them was a little bit more bold than the others. He would nose his way up close to me, and then he'd run away. Every time he returned, he got a little bit closer. He wanted that cracker in my hand, but he was afraid. My family all watched with smiles on their faces. Chipmunks are so cute.

The late afternoon shadows lengthened. Soon we would be talking about dinner. I was hoping for sausage dogs hand-roasted over the fire. Mmmmmm… Others had different ideas, to which I would confidently reply, "Never argue with a bratwurst!"

"What beautiful scenery we saw today!" said Mom. "Did you boys get some good pictures with your new cameras?" We chatted a bit about the things that we had seen and how nice the day had been.

"Did either of you take pictures of that big Thor's Hammer rock? That thing was really neat."

Arguably the most photographed natural object in Bryce Canyon is Thor's Hammer. Tucked into the Rocky Mountains, Bryce Canyon is a giant crack in the Earth filled with wondrous, almost mystical-looking rock shapes that point up into the air like giant petrified flames. The rugged terrain is splashed with yellow and red and orange rock all mixed together with giant rough skinned western pine trees, with needles so long that they look like something out of an exaggerated painting. It's a breathtakingly beautiful place.

Tradition has it that this majestic canyon was discovered long ago by a cowboy who was looking for a stray that had wandered from the herd. Modern tourism literature loves to play up that no-nonsense cowboy's famous quote about the beautiful valley. Suffice to say that his colorful language indicates that this was not a fun place to lose a cow.

Right in the middle of it all stands a tall thin rocky spire that stretches skyward far taller than the rest. At the very top of the spire sits a giant almost-square block of stone. From certain angles, it looks a bit like a giant hammer. Thor's Hammer. Magazine photos and postcards of Bryce Canyon all have pictures from that angle; the hammer angle. From the backside of the stone tower, the less picturesque side, apparently the side from which we viewed it, the big rock that makes up the hammer's head looks a bit different; not so hammer-like. More like, well, a certain item of human anatomy.

"Thor's Hammer?" replied Shanon. "You mean, the butt?"

"The butt?" asked mom.

"Yeah!" I interjected as I held a piece of cracker toward the chipmunk and tried to make a chipmunk noise with my lips, which really tickled. I won't do that again. "It's not a hammer. It's a giant butt… a great big butt-on-a-stick."

"Yup, a butt-on-a-stick!" Shanon said laughing! "It's a buttsicle!"

"A buttsicle!" I agreed, as I watched the chipmunk sniffing the cracker. "It's the world's biggest buttsicle!"

Shanon and I laughed and laughed, while Mom just smiled and shook her head. "You guys are gross."

For the rest of our trip, we boys kept finding ways to bring up the word "buttsicle" in conversation. It never failed to get some sort of exasperation out of Mom, which somehow made everything better.

Finally, after a lot of patient coaxing, the chipmunk had taken the small cracker piece right out of my hand and had immediately run away. Then he was back again.

"You want more?" I asked with a gooey childish voice. "Yes you do! C'mon you little sweetie. Here's your cracker. You're sure cute… yes you are." It's funny how differently we talk to animals than we do to people. Then again, if I'd spoken to one of the guys at school that way, they probably would have punched me in the mouth.

Sometime later, after several comings and goings, each a little bit more daring than the last, there was a tiny chipmunk sitting on my left knee, trustingly eating a small cracker piece in apparent safety. He had finally surrendered his fear and decided that I was alright. His furry friends were watching and curiously creeping closer. Little Chipper was enjoying his modest helping of Nabisco's finest. Unbeknownst to both of us, it would be his last meal.

Suddenly, from my right came a streak of black. Like a speeding arrow, before I could react, Suzette was on my lap with a shattered chipmunk in her mouth. Ferociously she whipped her head from side to side, breaking bones and snuffing life. She dropped the dead chipmunk onto my lap and looked down at it growling - her teeth bared and her back hair standing straight up. With lightning quickness, the other chipmunks scurried into any hiding places they could find. The beautiful precious creature that I had been baby-talking to just seconds earlier, lay stone still on my thigh, eyes staring straight ahead, mouth slightly open. Inches from his face lay a partially eaten cracker corner.

"Oh no! Oh no! Suzette! Oh no! Gaaaaahhh!" I started to cry.

Immediately, Dad was on his feet. He rushed over and he knelt beside me and, with one hand he grabbed and held Suzette, while his other hand scooped the chipmunk off of my leg as I sat there wide-eyed, body rigid, unable to breathe.

The Bryce Canyon Chipmunk Mind Movie faded, and I was back in Idaho – panting poodle at my side on a dusty Idaho roadway. *"There are old chipmunks and there are bold chipmunks, but there are no old bold chipmunks,"* I thought, smiling in a sad, ironic way.

Suzette's thirsty tongue still slid in and out of her grinning panting upturned face. She looked deeply into my eyes as if to ask, "What're we doing next, Chris? Whatever it is, I bet it'll be great!... So long as I'm with you. We're best friends, aren't we, Chris?! Ha ha ha ha ha!!"

Laughing again, I bent down and I rubbed her behind her ear. Enthusiastically, she wagged her thimble.

"Here they come!"

The little crowd migrated to one side, the way a school of fish or a flock of birds will move like a single organism. Just beyond the small people-swarm, I saw him; the one we had come to see. He was approaching slowly, jogging toward us. He wore red running shorts and a white t-shirt displaying some kind of colorful logo. In one of his hands he held the flaming Torch of the 1984 Summer Olympics. A little behind, following him slowly on Cheeseburger Road, there was a number of identical vehicles and a surprisingly large entourage of support crew, all wearing matching t-shirts.

We were witnessing something new. This support crew had followed the torch across America, zig-zagging and wandering this way and that through city after city, state after state. Taking their time in a meandering route, they were carrying the Olympic Flame from New York City, where it had arrived by ship, having been lit in Athens, Greece, to the West Coast of America where the games would be held. Dozens of spare torches were stored in the vehicles along with extra torch fuel. Like a Pony Express relay, the torch had been handed from runner to runner and carried on foot, through thirty-four states, all the way to Idaho. Four weeks from now it would be in Los Angeles. It still had Washington, Oregon and California to go through. The runner group was comprised of a long diverse list of Americans. Some of the runners had been famous people, some had been average folks. In the end, it would take three thousand, six hundred thirty-six of them to cover the continent, but they would get the job done.

Our people-herd spread out, as if on cue, making a path for the man who slowly plodded through the gap, making eye contact with no one. Nor did he proudly hold the torch aloft, as one might have expected considering how many pictures were being taken of him. The torch was held low, almost at his side. His head was down, his mouth hung open, his stride was slow.

"He's dying!" I thought with a chuckle. I didn't know how far he had come or how long he had been running, but I did know how hot it was, and it was easy to see that he was suffering.

Shanon held his camera up and looked through it. It was the same camera with which he had captured the buttsickle two weeks earlier. He was so proud to have this new camera, purchased with his hard-earned paper route money. It was a new kind of camera that contained an internal rotating disc of film. As each picture was taken, the disc would automatically rotate, effortlessly lining up the next film frame for an almost instant exposure. No more hand advancing. It ran off of a battery. Cool new technology!

Shanon's first picture was taken from the torch runner's left as he jogged by. Then Shanon ran ahead and crossed in front of the runner to get a shot from the other side. It wasn't hard to outrun the tired man. The second picture was from the runner's right. For the only time in all the years that my brother owned that camera, the disc had failed to advance after the first shot. It had malfunctioned. As a result, Shanon accidentally ended up with the coolest double exposure I have ever seen. As if done purposely by a master photographer, my thirteen-year-old brother had a perfectly positioned shot of dual Olympic Torch Runner images crossing paths at an almost identical angle. Instead of being bleached and blurred, as double exposures often are, the image was excellent. The bright afternoon sky was somehow darkened as if it was evening, while the runner was bright and vivid, almost glowing. What a picture!

Shanon proudly held onto that picture for years, but, as I write this now, almost thirty-one years later, and though we've looked diligently for it, it seems that it was lost somewhere along the way. Pity.

The torch passed out of our sight on its slow course toward Olympic History. The 1984 Olympics, with such memorable images as Rafer Johnson's proud Torch lighting, Bart Conner's tears at the gold medal ceremony for Men's Team Gymnastics, Carl Lewis matching Jesse Owens' long-standing mark to win four golds, Gabbie Andersen-Schiess' inspiring anguished stumbling battle to finish the first-ever women's Olympic Marathon under the screaming encouragement of thousands, Mary Lou Retton's amazing dual perfect vaults to clinch the first-ever non-Eastern-European Women's All-Around Gold Medal in Gymnastics (sporting the world's cutest toothy smile), the almost liquid-smooth grace of Edwin Moses gliding over the 400 meter hurdles to his second Olympic gold, the amazing Greg Luganis sweeping the Diving events, and so many other memories, would prove to be a massive television success, and a huge patriotic tidal wave for me, personally.

That was definitely worth stopping for. That torch thing was pretty cool. These were my thoughts as we sat in our trailer, a couple of hours later, enjoying a very welcome dinner of canned chili. Not as satisfying as the cheeseburger that I had fantasized about earlier, but great nonetheless. We were parked in a rest area, just off of the West-bound lanes of Interstate 84, a few miles west of Bliss, Idaho. The plan was to continue west after dinner and go for another couple of hours before calling it a day. I was looking forward to seeing the beautiful Blue Mountains of Northeastern Oregon, and crossing the mighty Columbia River the next day, but I was looking forward even more to sleeping in my own wonderful waterbed. Just twenty four hours to go! I loved that bed!

We sat in our medium-sized fifth-wheel trailer behind my parents' great-looking two-tone brown 1978 Ford Pickup. I remember falling in love with that truck the first time I saw it.

It was a small rest area that we sat in, eating our chili dinner, with long diagonal truck-sized striped parking places painted in the middle. There was one other vehicle there. Two or three spaces to our left, sat a large c-class motorhome. A white-haired couple could be seen through the RV's dinette window doing the same thing that we were doing.

After today's long drive, that chili dinner was so good.

"Could you pass the buttsicle, please?"

"Hhhhhhhhhh!!" was Mom's expected and gratifying response. Two brother's silently grinned at each other.

Screeeeeeeeeeeeeeeech!

What is that?!

From outside came a terrible teeth-chattering sound. It was a thundering roar combined with a terrible high-pitched tearing, scraping, screeching noise. It was like fingernails on a chalkboard. We all looked outside the trailer's dinette window.

"What in the world…" was Dad's exclamation as a large dark green car speeded by the trailer, going way too fast for a rest area. I recognized it instantly as a Dodge. It was a lot like a green version of the General Lee car in the TV show, *The Dukes of Hazard*, but not quite the same. I would learn later that it was a 1969 Dodge Coronet, which is nearly identical to a Dodge Charger. Its front left tire was gone and the steel wheel was scraping the asphalt, throwing a fountain of bright tiny sparks and a mind numbing blast of noise in every direction.

The mysterious muscle-car was traveling toward the front of our rig and disappeared from the trailer window's view. We all looked at each other with a mix of expressions. Mom and Dad wore adult expressions of concern while Shanon and I, suffering from terminal boy-brain, simply grinned, saying things like, "whoa!" and "cool!"

After a pause of a second or two, we all stood simultaneously from the trailer's dinette table and headed toward the exit door on the trailer's right hand side. We had to see what was going on.

The screeching sound was gone by the time we spilled out into the rest area parking lot. There, in front of our pick-up, sat the dark green Dodge Coronet. The car's driver had pulled in front of the truck and had backed up until the two vehicles were just touching, his rear bumper to our front. The driver didn't seem to be in the car, and everything was quiet and calm. We stood still for a moment, not knowing what to do. Dad walked a few tentative steps toward the Dodge.

Suddenly all peace was shattered. Noise, action and confusion reigned as numerous police cars came swarming into the rest area. Engines roared as they shot toward us and tires squealed as they came to a stop. Policemen poured forth on foot, every one of them brandishing a weapon. "Get Back!" one of them yelled at us, and we obediently took several steps backward. The first two officers to reach us ran straight for our pick-up. The one with the pistol leaned over the truck's Hood and the other, pointing a shotgun, leaned over the bed. Both of them had their weapons trained on the elderly couple's motor home parked to our truck's left.

"Freeze! Police! Get your hands where I can see them!"

There were now policemen everywhere, all of them shouting, all of them pointing their weapons in the same direction.

"Get back in the trailer!" my mother screeched. Without thinking, we obeyed and piled in. I'm not sure how much protection a plywood and plastic RV wall would have provided in a firefight.

From a window on the trailer's left hand side, I saw a shadowy form underneath the neighboring Motorhome. Over their half-eaten dinners, the frightened white-hairs, their eyes as big as goose eggs, held their hands up as they looked out their dinette window, unaware of the skulking menace that lurked directly beneath them.

"Get on the floor!" yelled Dad.

We waited for the sounds of gunfire, but they never did come. As soon as the general noise had died down outside, we all came tumbling back out of the trailer. Crisis averted and peace restored, the officers were milling around talking to each other. One came to us and started asking questions, writing in a small notebook.

We had just witnessed the end of a long drawn-out high-speed police chase. The driver was a local man of twenty-five. The man, the officer told us, had driven away from police at a high rate of speed, through a nearby town, and eventually, onto Interstate 84.

In the 1980s, police cars were not what they had once been. It seemed that the push for economy and fuel efficiency had made its way into America's police departments. I can remember laughing at the ugly little Ford Fairmonts and Dodge Diplomat police cars of that era.

That evening, the police in Idaho had been badly outmatched by the young man in his massive V8 Hemi. The newspapers would later say that the police had been hitting speeds of 115 miles per hour during the chase; but the officer that spoke with us that evening told us that the old Dodge was easily pulling away. Without a helicopter, they had worried that they would lose him. Their ugly little Fairmonts were little more than toys compared to that V8 monster.

According to the officer, the big green Dodge, at one point during the chase, had pulled across the freeway's grass median and had driven against the grain; driving the wrong way, scattering surprised and terrified motorists. Thankfully, there were no collisions.

The driver of the Dodge had taken an off-ramp at one point, where he had come face-to-face with an officer on foot. The officer stepped into the road and bravely stood his ground, blocking the Coronet's way. As he raised his shotgun, pointing it at the oncoming Dodge, its driver mashed its throttle down. On it advanced, screaming toward the officer.

When Sergeant Eldon Sailer got up that morning and drank his coffee, he'd had no idea that this was the day that a man would try to kill him.

Blam! Officer Sailer was able to get a shot off, pointed at the speeding car's grill. Pumping another round into the chamber, he stepped to the side, avoiding the course of the big green would-be murder weapon and he deftly fired another shot as it flew by him. This second shot was expertly aimed at the car's left front tire. A split second decision had been made and the tire had been selected as the target, instead of the driver's window.

His shot was true. The tire was destroyed. But the chase went on. Though severely hobbled by the missing front tire, the young man's lead was great enough that he didn't give up on his crazy flight. On he went, back onto the freeway.

Eventually, though, the Coronet's driver knew that he couldn't keep this up. Soon his lead would disappear and his pursuers would be all over him. That's when he saw the rest area. If he could make it there and hide his car behind a camper, maybe, just maybe, the cops would drive right by. It wasn't much of a plan, but it was all he had.

"Where's the driver now?" Dad asked the officer who was interviewing us.

"He's in the back of that squad car," the officer replied, pointing to a white police car parked at the rest area's back edge. It sat alone. I could just make out a shadowy form in the back seat, sitting still.

"Mr. Ford, you and your family will need to stay here for a while, so I suggest you get comfortable. There will be another officer who will need to ask you more questions. Also, the reporters will be arriving soon. You don't have to answer their questions, but you're free to do so if you'd like to. Just don't leave."

Time passed. I strolled around the rest area, holding Suzette's leash. It was well after eight o'clock, so it wasn't as hot as it had been earlier at Cheeseburger Road.

Wow. A real police chase. And a bad guy, just like in the movies. A bad guy who tried to run a policeman down with his car. A bad guy who got my family involved.

What if...

What if he'd had a gun? What if my parents had gotten to him before the police did? What if one of us had gotten hurt today... or worse? What if...

We had driven by the town of Bliss, Idaho a little earlier that day. I had been staring out the window, reading license plates and road signs and daydreaming. Over the last two weeks, I had gotten quite good at that.

Bliss, Idaho; next exit.

Bliss.

What a name for a town!... I live in Bliss... Bliss is my home... Yep, Bliss... Welcome to Bliss. We hope you will enjoy your stay... Thanks for visiting! Come again!

You know, to be truthful... I kinda do live in Bliss. Well, I mean... I do have a pretty blissful life.

And I did. As we had driven by that green freeway sign in that cramped Ford, my sixteen year-old mind didn't lay it all before me in outline form, but yeah... pretty great; blissful even. At sixteen, I knew that I had it good. A lot of my schoolmates had divorced parents. Some had major issues to deal with. Some had trouble paying their bills. I had never faced any real tragedies or hardships. I was comfortable, well-fed and I was loved. I knew that there were people all over the world who dreamed of having what I had. The truth was that, at sixteen, I really had no idea just how sheltered my life had been and how good I really had it.

They say that *ignorance is bliss.* How true it is. I wonder how the people of Bliss, Idaho feel about that saying. Hmph.

As Suzette and I wandered the rest area parking lot, I pondered deeper thoughts than I had in a long time. *I could have lost someone I love today. There's a policeman's wife just a few miles from here who almost lost her husband today, and she probably doesn't even know about it yet. There's a man over there in the back of that squad car who made some decisions today that will change the rest of his life. He's going to prison. Wow. Prison.*
    Prison!

I was standing in front of his big green Dodge Coronet, still parked the way he had left it, backed up against the front bumper of our pick-up. The front of the car was riddled with deep marble-sized dents, like individual bullet holes that didn't quite go all the way through the metal. The grill and the windshield were destroyed. I walked around to the driver's side where the front tire was missing. The left front fender area also had bullet dents. There was almost no tire rubber left on the scarred mangled wheel. The officer had told us that Sergeant Sailer had fired two shotgun blasts, and that he had used something called "nine-pellet loads." He explained that, with that kind of shotgun shell, the pellets were so large that only nine could fit in a shell, as each pellet was about the size of a .22 caliber bullet. Unlike the birdshot that we had always used in our own shotguns, this kind of load had some serious knockdown power.

I placed my finger into one of the steel dents, and imagined what it would have done to a person.

Wow...

I felt something strange. Somehow I felt a small helping of innocence leaving me. I know that sounds funny, but there it was. The real world was invading my protected world. My previous absence of worry, of care, of tragedy; my unnoticed and unmentioned sense of bliss was still there, but, like the green Coronet in front of me, it had taken some dents.

I had to see him. I had to know. What does that look like? Was the young man evil? Did he care that his actions had endangered motorists and officers? My family? Is he sitting there reliving the moment that he decided to take a Policeman's life? Does he understand yet that he will be going to trial soon, and then prison? Was he scared, like a little boy in a man's body, terrified at what lay ahead? Was he defiant and proud? Regretful and vulnerable? Evil? Crazy? Remorseful?

I would never learn the answers to those questions. As I peered into the rear passenger window of the white squad car, expecting at any moment to hear an angry, "Hey kid, get away from that car," the detained man never looked up at me. His hands were cuffed behind him. He leaned forward, looking downward and to his left. A shaggy mop of blonde hair obscured most of his face.

Look at me.

Hey, look at me! I tried to will him to look.

Hey you. Hey, bad guy. Car chase guy. Do you know I'm here at your window? My name is Chris, and I was doing just fine before you came along. I saw an Olympic Torch today, did you see that? Look at me. I'm sixteen, and you scared me today. Do you care?

What do you want? What are you thinking about right now? What were you thinking when the policeman pointed his shotgun at you? You know, he could have shot you instead of your car. You almost died today.

Look at me. What would you tell me if you could say anything to me right now?

Hello?

The handcuffed man never moved. He never looked up. For a long time I stood there, in that Interstate 84 rest area, a little west of Bliss, staring at the back of his head, little more than two feet from him.

It was October of 2002 that I drove Mabel, my Chevy Malibu into that old Rest Area. Over eighteen years had gone by since the big 1984 Summer trip. I now had a family of my own and I was on the homeward leg of a long business trip in Fort Worth, so looking forward to seeing my beloved wife and children after two months apart.

No one was there at the rest area. I don't know what I expected to find there or why I had even pulled in, but there was no way that I could have just driven by. As I walked around, I found myself standing on the spot where the bullet-hole-covered Dodge had sat, or as near as I could remember, and I realized that I had never been back to Bliss.

A young man goes through a lot of change on his way to adulthood, and a lot of it happens at around sixteen.

I've been traveling *West of Bliss* ever since that hot afternoon; a little farther west with every challenge, every hurt, every loss. Every achievement, every victory, every joy. Bliss can be a very nice place to visit, but I wouldn't want to live there. It's in the tight moments, the frightening, the sad, the painful, that our greatest growth is experienced and our greatest victories are won. If you know God, it's during those times of challenge that we have the opportunity to trust Him and allow Him to stretch us; to surrender our desire for comfort; opting instead to rely on Him. That's when real growth occurs.

Oh yes, sometimes I do wish for blessed escape, for a trip to the isolated little town of Bliss, but it's not a place worth staying.

In my late twenties, when I was stressed about the responsibilities of running a young family, I heard a quote by a guy named William A. Shedd. I have no idea who he was or what he did, but his statement has stuck with me for decades. He said, "A ship in harbor is safe, but that is not what ships are built for."

You like that?

I do too.

Me? I'll go west.

"Whether he is shoveling snow or helping women and children into the last lifeboat on the Titanic, men stand tallest when they are protecting and defending."

Stu Weber

17

A Strange Critter

How well I remember the night that I died.

I was very accustomed to being young. Young was all that I had ever known. Officially, I was an adult and I had been for a few years, but I still felt very much like a kid. Maybe not truly a kid, but certainly not a "man." I remember feeling a little bit uncomfortable when someone would refer to me as a man. It didn't happen very often. I preferred being called a guy. Anyone can be a guy. Guy, Dude, Kid, Youngster, Buddy - those titles were fine. My coworkers at my previous job had all referred to me as "Junior." I had a British guy call me "Bloke," once. I was cool with that. I kinda liked it, actually. But "Man?" No, I hadn't grown into that title yet. "Man" requires a certain amount of confidence that I did not yet possess.

I observed my world through young eyes and ears. As I brushed my teeth every morning, it was a kid that looked back at me from the mirror. I'm not sure why I felt that way, after all, I was well into my twenties. I was a home owner, the husband of an attractive blonde, and I was living three thousand miles from my parents and brother. I was working in the Engineering Department at a well-known military helicopter company, creating complex mechanical designs on cutting edge three-dimensional solid-modeling computer systems, and making a very satisfying amount of money doing it. I had and did all of the things that should make a person feel like an adult, so why didn't I?

The Undisputed Heavyweight Champion of the World, at that time, Mike Tyson, was younger than I was. My two favorite NFL quarterbacks, Rick Mirer of the Seattle Seahawks and Drew Bledsoe of the New England Patriots, were both younger than I was. I considered all three of them to be 'Men,' but, well...

Maybe part of my problem was the fact that I looked so young. So did my wife, Cheryl. Neither of us could go into a bar with our friends without showing our driver's licenses. I got carded, once, just trying to buy a lottery ticket, which only required an age of eighteen. I got a lot of comments about how young I looked. Some of those comments were delivered as insults for how immature I looked, sometimes bringing back some of those Junior High feelings of inadequacy. "Did your mommy drop you off today?" Occasionally I would reply with something defensive like, "Just think how much better I'll look than you do someday, when I'm your age." Most times, I just stayed quiet, laughing it off like it was a great joke - a coping method that I had awkwardly employed in Junior High.

It all changed at twenty-six. I had been aiming at the wrong target all those years. Who knows the age at which a young person becomes an adult; when a boy becomes a man? Is it puberty? Whiskers on your chin? Hair on your chest? Graduation from High School, or College? Is it the moment that you lose your virginity? Is it marriage, owning a home, or your first real job? Who knows? Who cares?

At twenty six I became something I had never been before. Chris the Guy died, and from his ashes emerged Chris, Lydia's Dad. Young Chris - Kid Chris – Chris the Dude, Chris the Guy died at 10:31 PM, Eastern Standard Time, on October ninth of 1994, the moment that Lydia was born.

Those nebulous goals of "Man" and "Adult" were absorbed and fulfilled in the term "Dad." My focus had changed. My world now revolved around a new understanding. I had a wife and a daughter who needed me. I was Dad. I was Provider, Protector and Leader. I was trusted unconditionally, and I was depended upon absolutely.

As the nurse wheeled Cheryl out of that Connecticut hospital the next day, the pretty new mommy never took her eyes off of the tiny child that was wrapped in her arms. It was as though the rest of the world was a blur to her just then. Only this was real as a tear slipped out of her eye, and a mother's love was forever fastened to the tiny one sleeping peacefully in her arms. It was a quiet time of bonding that I treasured watching. I knew that this was a special moment, and I stayed quiet.

As my wife was having her thoughts of how precious and tiny Lydia was, and making her silent vows of eternal love and care; I was noticing how precious they both were, and my own silent vows were taking place.

When Lydia was a little less than a month old, we moved. As Dad, I had made a decision that I knew held some risk and probable hardship, but was right for my family. Pursuing a new job opportunity, we left Connecticut and drove our blue 1989 Chevy Blazer, Uhaul trailer in tow, all the way to Wichita, Kansas. A drive that would have taken us two days in normal circumstances took four.

In my care were Luke, an aging, overweight black lab who needed numerous potty stops, a three-week-old girl who frequently required diapering and feeding, and a tiny, petite wife who had recently given birth to a child that had weighed over nine pounds. I'll let you use your imagination regarding the kind of injury a child that size can do to a very small lady. Suffice to say, poor Cheryl was more than a little uncomfortable on that drive.

We stopped a lot.

A lot.

It was late on night number two of our trip. The darkness was made worse by a torrential rainstorm. It was the kind of rain that turns roads to rivers and parking lots to lakes. We were somewhere in Eastern Indiana, barreling down Interstate 70, windshield wipers frantically trying to keep up with the onslaught, and almost succeeding, when some very welcome motel lights came into blurry view.

I will never forget it. The trip from the motel lobby, up the elevator and to the room was a tough one for Cheryl. She was mind-numbingly exhausted from the long day. Her lower parts hurt and her upper parts were engorged. She needed rest, and had a newborn to feed. "Please, just get me to the room," she whispered. That wonderful strong little lady never complained, but I knew she was hurting. I walked slowly beside her, my arm around her as I helped her move along. Then the miracle happened. It's funny how such a small thing can mean so much, even miraculous in the right circumstances. There, right in the middle of our motel room, sat something that I've never seen in a motel. There was a big, old-fashioned, wooden rocking chair. The kind with the comfy rounded seat bottom.

She almost cried.

I helped her to the chair and I told her, "You just sit here. Don't worry about a thing. I will take care of everything." Without a word, she did as I said. I helped her into a sitting position and I laid the green diaper bag, which contained everything she would need to feed and care for her precious little bundle, beside her chair. And there it was again in my mind, almost audible. Dad! I'm the Dad!

You rest, my two precious ladies, I'll be back soon. I've got Dad Things to do.

Back into the cold November rain I went, with a smile on my face. My own comfort was not even a consideration, because my loved ones were warm and safe, and that's a good feeling. I still had a dog to care for, luggage to haul and dinner to provide.

About forty-five minutes later, dog walked and luggage hauled to the room, I was walking back from a nearby restaurant, carrying a stack of white Styrofoam to-go boxes, filled with yummy smelling fried chicken and mashed potatoes with gravy. Though I hadn't thought it possible, the rain had somehow increased and I was drenched. As I walked through the motel parking lot, I glanced over at the Blazer with its Uhaul trailer, and I smiled. *Hello, Miles. I'll see you in a few minutes. We have some unfinished business to attend to, you and I.*

As much as I loved my pretty blue Blazer, it had one major problem. It had spent its entire life in Connecticut. Those folks up in New England salt their roads in the winter. Cars don't last long there. As nice as the Blazer looked on the outside, its nether regions were filled with rust. Earlier that day, the tailpipe had broken free of the muffler. It was completely severed; rusted through. The pipe was still there, hanging from a single bracket. The pipe swung forward and back with the slightest movement, sometimes banging into the rear surface of the muffler.

There wasn't much that I could do that night, except try to stabilize the tailpipe enough to get us to Kansas. Dinner delivered and wife, daughter and dog resting comfortably in our room, I lay in the dark, a tiny flashlight in my mouth, beneath a rusted Chevrolet. The parking lot was sloped sharply, and the heavy rain was a river flowing from left to right. The frequent lightning flashes would momentarily light up what I was doing as I lay on that cold hard pavement. Rain water was rushing down the slope as it hit me broadside, piling up against my body, working its way around me, flowing under my neck and around my head as it rested on the ground. I elevated my knees so the river would find its way around me and flow beneath my legs. I was truly a rock in a stream. As I shivered and worked, I thought of my dad. He had always handled things like this. I remembered being small and knowing that if anything scary or painful or hard ever came up, dad would be there to take care of it - to take care of us. It was good to have such a dad.

"Now I'm the dad," I said aloud. *My family is fed and they're safe. My car is getting fixed and I've got this handled.*

Shouldn't this be awful? Shouldn't I be hating this weather, this mechanical problem, this whole situation… shouldn't I feel a heavy weight of stress, moving my young dependent family to a new state where I'll face a world of unknown responsibilities in just a few days? Why am I laughing? I'm freezing wet, my knuckles are bleeding, I'm hungry and tired. Could it be that I'm actually enjoying this? A new dad is a strange critter! Heh!

In I walked. A box of cold chicken waited for me at the table. From her rocking chair, my tired lovely wife, a well-fed newborn Lydia sleeping beautifully in her arms, greeted me with a warm smile full of gratitude as my sleepy dog lazily wagged his tail. Tired, achy and shivering wet, I walked in like a dad. I ate my cold chicken and mashed potatoes, a thin congealed layer of skin atop the gravy, and my mind was full of love.

Though I still looked like one for many years that followed, I have never felt like a kid again.

18

Sideways

Man, it was a gorgeous day! Like Uncle Remus sang in that old Disney movie, "It happened on one o' dem Zip-a-Dee-Doo-Dah days." The sun was so hot that it hurt the skin, but the water was cold. It doesn't matter how hot it is outside; when you're rafting this river you're wearing a wetsuit. Baby, that water is cold! The river runs fast, white and angry with some of the purest glacier-fed water that these mountains have to offer. And today it was running at record levels. It was white water paradise!

Marty had a way of putting a person at ease right when you meet him. He was about twenty-nine, with a big grin, a crazy explosion of red hair and a wide-brimmed Australian cowboy hat that was the envy of all aboard. He was to be our guide. With the help of some introductions, my three buddies and I had met the two brothers who were in our raft with us. They said they weren't twins, but I couldn't tell them apart. Their names were Mark and Mike. My three friends and I were a bit older than the brothers were. They looked like they might have still been in high school but it was hard to tell; maybe college. The rest of us were in our mid-twenties.

Since there were only three of us with any previous rafting experience, Marty put us through some fun rookie exercises; teaching us how to maneuver the big rubber beast. We learned how to work as a team; turning, slowing down, speeding up, back paddling and a few other moves. I was placed at the front left, since I had the most experience. The rest of the team was told to time their paddle strokes with mine.

"Here's how you hold the paddle," he smiled as he demonstrated, holding his hand over the top hilt of the paddle's long handle. "This gives you more power, but, more importantly, it protects the people around you from gettin' Summer Teeth." He laughed and said, "y'all know what Summer Teeth are, don't ya'? It's when some'r in your mouth, and some'r in the boat, and some'r in the river. We don't want any Summer Teeth today."

The day started with some medium-sized rapids that were cold, fast and fun. Marty shot us through them expertly, shouting commands from the back of the raft where he did the steering with his paddle, using it a lot like a rudder. He told us that the key to running big rapids like these is to power your way through them. He told us that most accidents happen when a raft gets sideways. "Bad things, Dude," he said with a laugh. "Bad things happen when your boat's sideways."

The river got faster and steeper as the morning moved on. The rapids got louder, whiter and angrier. And we owned the river. Marty was laughing and screaming as we shot through the bubbling storm. Old Man River was doing his best to stop us, but we wouldn't have it. Though some of us had just met that day, it was like the seven of us were born to raft together. What a team we were.

This was a popular river, and there were other rafts that day. But, it felt like we were the only ones there. It was us versus that river, and we were winning. Or was the old man only toying with us?

Marty would tell us the names of each rapid as we approached them. "This next rapid is called The Johnson. It's named after Roger Johnson... he died there." Yeah, he said that. After we'd recovered from the chill that had run down our spines, we shot that rapid, laughing, screaming and paddling in near-perfect seven-part harmony.

After "The Johnson," there was a nice long calm stretch of water. That was good. We needed a break. It was a nice opportunity to lean back and quietly enjoy the beautiful scenery of these rugged mountains. There was something soothing about the slow trickling sounds of the river at rest. The sun felt good on my face. "Dudes," Marty said to us with a thoughtful look. "I want to ask you something. Have you ever heard of the Meat Grinder?" When he said "Meat Grinder" his eyes flashed and his grin grew extra fierce. Have you ever seen that maniacal grin that Gomez Addams used to do on the TV show *The Addams Family*? It was a lot like that; eyes almost angry and fiendish, with a smile of pure delight. It was weird when Gomez did it on TV, and it was just as weird when Marty did it on the river.

"Have you ever heard of the Meat Grinder? It's a mean piece of river down the ways a bit." Marty told us all about it. It's a section of river with rapids so huge and nasty, so fast and dangerous that rafters usually stay away. Most professional river guides and local rafters pull their rafts out of the water and walk around the Meat Grinder, reentering the water below it. A lot of rafters stop there for lunch.

"People have died there, Maties. It's a big wicked pig." He paused for a moment. "Wanna do it?" We all looked at each other. There was fear. I saw it. I felt it.

After a moment, I heard someone in the boat laughing. It was a low, growly laugh that came deep from the guts, and it was coming from me. "Yeah," I heard myself say. And I realized that I was smiling the Gomez Addams smile. Oh yeah! I wanted this. I was scared, but I wanted it. I looked around the raft at six other Gomezes. We were ready.

We came around a slow calm corner. Up ahead, we could see a cloud of mist. I heard a roar like thunder. We drifted slowly toward it. Ahead of us, I saw people pulling their rafts out of the water, carrying them above their heads on the sandy beaches beside the river. One of the brothers - Mike or Mark, I don't know which - let out a deep bellowing noise that sounded almost like a bear. I joined in. I made a noise like I've never made before or since. The others joined us and all seven of us let it out. It was loud and it was gruesome and it felt so good.

It must have sounded impressive from the beach, because people came running. They stopped eating their lunches, others laid their rafts down and ran to shore.

They started pointing at us, shouting. Some were jumping up and down with excitement. They could see that someone was going to raft the Meat Grinder and they weren't going to miss it!

We're moving closer to it. Here it comes. Was this a mistake? It looks so much worse up close. It's getting closer... Oh my goodness, there's no turning back now! In a moment, the world changed. Old Man River let us have it! Now he had us! Now HE was in charge!

It started with a deep drop off, then a mountain of water, then a freezing cold wall hit me from the left. I held on, hugging the boat with my legs, pumping my paddle with all my strength. I remembered what Marty had said. "Power through it!" I was powering through it. Marty was yelling "Forward, Maties!! Forward!! You can do it!! Keep it up!! Forward!!" Somehow, over the sound of Marty's shouts, and over the roar of the rapids, I thought I could hear the people on the beach. I heard cheering. Like a crowd at a football game, they were cheering us on.

We rose on giant watery hills, then we plummeted almost straight down into canyons of foam, only to be thrust straight up again. Over and over we shot forward into nothingness as the river disappeared beneath us, slamming us down hard. Waves toppled over us from the sides, so cold as they poured down my back, that my breath would be taken from me.

Knocked into the floor of the raft by a freezing cold sucker punch to the face, I scrambled, as quickly as I could, back to my post at front left, thankful that I had somehow held on to my paddle.

I felt a strong blend of panic and joy. It was wild and wonderful and terrible. I didn't know if the moistness on my face was river water or tears. Did I just throw up? I didn't know. I didn't care.

Forward we shot. In stern jaw-clenched silence we toiled. It was violent. It was fast. It was terrible! It was amazing!

Then it happened. Marty yelled, "Right turn!! Right turn!!"
What?!

Had I really just heard that? Right turn? *But Marty, you can't mean it. Right turn? But that would turn us sideways, and sideways is bad! And this is the Meat Grinder - the "Big Wicked Pig." People have died here. Right turn?*

Marty?

"Right Turn! Go, go, go!"

There it was again. *That was Marty's voice, alright. But I'm front left. I'm the guy that'll be facing the monster if we turn right. Marty's trying to kill me. That's it. He's mad at me. He hates me. Maybe I'd made a comment earlier that upset him. Maybe he's just a bad man. Why would he do this to me?*

Well, I'm not going to do it! I can do it my own way. I know, I'll jump.

That's it! Or, maybe I'll just pretend I can't hear him. Yeah! That's what I'll do. I'm not listening, Marty.

All of these thoughts must have shot through my mind in a nano-second, just before I lead the team in a perfect right turn. Now we were sideways. Sideways in the Meat Grinder!

"Go, go, go!" He was yelling. We paddled with all our might. We were paddling toward the beach - toward the people lining the river's edge watching us, but shooting downstream sideways. For an instant, I caught the eye of a young boy. He looked like he was about eleven. There was terror on his face. I wondered what mine looked like to him. I wondered what his name was. I wondered if it would be hard on him, watching me die like this. After all, I was sideways. Bad things, Dude.

We rolled and heaved and dropped and rose and jerked and climbed and shook… and we paddled. A giant wave rolled right over the top of us, but we somehow emerged from it with all of us still in the boat, several gallons of water in the raft's floor. We paddled and paddled, as the raft went up onto its side, left side up, fully vertical, then slapped back down again with a massive splash. On we rolled, up – down – up. The beach was getting closer as we paddled more and more to the right. My teeth chattered from cold and fear.

Was that the river roaring, or did I really just hear an old man laughing? What are you doing Marty? Why am I sideways?

"Left Turn! Left Turn!" It was Marty! He wanted us to turn left. *Yes!* I turned us left! And I paddled. We were straight again! Things made sense again! On we paddled. Far beyond the churning maelstrom ahead of us, I could now see the end. It was like a distant finish line in a long boiling race course. We were going to make it. I was going to survive!

That's when I saw it.

It rose up out of the water to my left. It was big and it was black and the sun shined on it brightly. A massive piece of wet prehistoric granite stood in the middle of the river like a giant sea monster. We passed it by on the right side. The river was smashing into it with a force that I'd never dreamed was possible. The noise was almost unreal. Mouth hanging open in awe, I stared as we passed.

Had it been there the whole time? *Why didn't I see it earlier? It was as big as a house; how come I hadn't seen it from upriver? What if we had kept going straight? What if I had jumped out? I would have been killed!* These were the thoughts that flashed through my brain as we bounced our way out the back end of the Meat Grinder and shot into calmer water, spinning to a stop.

Then I knew it. It was Marty. Marty had known about the rock. Marty had had a plan. Marty knew when to turn and when to go straight. Marty knows this river! *Thank you, Marty. I'm so glad that I stayed in your boat. Thank you, Marty!!*

I've thought about that day a lot since then. It's helped me through some tough times. I became a Christian in my late twenties and I now understand that I have a guide who knows this river. He can see the boulders and the whirlpools and the submerged logs that I can't see. Sometimes, to get me where I need to be, He has to turn my boat sideways for a little while.

Sideways isn't fun. Sideways hurts. But, when I'm there; when I'm sideways in the big wicked pig, I can hug the boat with both legs and keep paddling, and I can know that He is going to see me through. I do that now, when struggles and hardships arise. I look back and I can see that, before I'd even met Him, He was already guiding me through the swirls and the rapids, decades earlier; knowing all along that He and I would one day be friends. I am thankful that, through all of those years, when I'd felt alone, I never gave up. I've always kept paddling. And, you can too, because He loves you, just as much as He loves me.

"If we couldn't laugh we would all go insane"

Jimmy Buffett

19

Atonement

It's always fun at Aunt Tootie's house. Tootie and Harry are Cheryl's great aunt and uncle. They're good folks with a big house; a house that they like to have full of visitors. They're very good at making people feel welcome and I like it there. I think we all do.

Tonight was one of those nights. The house was full of movement and sound, food and conversation. People were in every room. Warm smells emanated from the kitchen, as laughter spilled from the dining room where a big card game was in full frenzy. I was sitting in the family room chatting with Uncle Harry about something. Knowing him, it was probably either World War II airplanes or some John Wayne movie - maybe even a John Wayne movie about World War II airplanes. Suddenly, my three-year-old son, Mitch, came running in, "Dad! Dad! Hey Dad! Guess what! Hey Dad! Uncle Mike told me to pull his finger. And when I did… hee hee hee… he pootered! Hah hah hah hah hah hah!"

"Pooter" was a word that we used in our house when the kids were young. It was less clinical sounding than "pass gas" or "break wind" and a lot less vulgar than "fart." It was a good word.

What?! He did what?! But, that's just not right! That's supposed to be my line! I'm the dad! I've been waiting for Mitch to be old enough to get that joke and now that he is, Mike beats me to the punch! Now it's too late! That was supposed to be MY finger!

I had waited too long. I'd missed the proverbial boat; denied one of the sacred rights of fatherhood, the time-honored Pull-My-Finger ritual, one of the anchor pins of Western Civilization, passed down the masculine line from generation to generation. I had pulled my father's finger, as he had pulled his father's. Actually, he probably hadn't, but work with me a little here. I'm trying to use a literary device. (grin)

Some days or weeks later, who knows how long, I was at the office, sitting at my desk. My mind was deep in my work, when the phone rang.

"Hello?"

My wife's unmistakable voice came on. "Do you know what your son just did?!" Whenever she called him "my son," I knew that it was going to be an interesting story.

"You've got to be careful what you say around him!" she continued. "He's always watching you, soaking in everything, like a sponge!"

Now I was really intrigued. "What did he do?" I asked with a little laugh in my voice.

"I'll tell you what he did!" she replied with incredulity. "He stood there in the hallway and very casually pointed at the bathroom door with his thumb. Then he told me, 'Mom, I'm gonna go drop the kids off at the pool,' and he went in and closed the door! Then I heard the fan come on! I wonder where he learned *that* little pearl of wisdom!" she said sarcastically.

I tried to stifle my laughter. I didn't think that Cheryl was enjoying this story nearly as much as I was. Funny how differently a dad looks at some things than a mom does.

A moment later, just after I'd said goodbye and hung the phone up, I thought to myself, *Hah! This so atones for the finger-pull thing!*

I smiled and allowed myself a small office-appropriate chuckle. *That's my boy!*

With a chapter title like "Atonement," you thought this was going to be something important or profound, didn't ya? Gotcha! Heheh...

Sitting looking out the window
How lucky the birds
All the beauty they see

They travel so far
Wherever they please

As I watch them I know
Oh how I wish I could go

Betty Sampson, age 83

20

A Momentary Lapse of Raisin

"Daddy!" He shouted. "Daddy!" I could barely see him. His body was rigid. He stood still, holding his hands up in front of himself, as if to ward off a blow, and he didn't make another movement or sound. He was terrified.

"I'm here, buddy! I'm coming! Hold on!" I replied, just loudly enough to be heard, as I ran, hopped and balanced my way to where my seven year old stood shaking. He was halfway up a large boulder pile, about fifteen feet below the smooth surface that separated him from millions of tons of rock and earth. His entire world, at that moment, was a small bubble of lantern light, beyond which was a frightening black abyss.

We had never known him to have a fear of darkness or any kind of claustrophobia. If we had, we would not have taken him into that big hole in the ground.

"Hold on to your lantern," I told him as I picked him up.

"Get me out of here," he whispered back to me.

"No problem," I replied. "We'll be back up there in the sunlight in just a few minutes."

As we made our way back through the tunnel, he didn't speak. I'm not sure he could have. I could hear his labored breathing. As I carried him, his body was as rigid as a piece of wood. It wasn't until we came around a corner and saw sunlight streaming down through a big hole in the cave's ceiling that he started to ease. Once we got up into the warm mountain air, my son acted as though nothing had ever been wrong. He didn't make any mention of what had happened down in the cave, so I respected that, and I didn't either.

I took that opportunity to make a few wardrobe adjustments, and soon I no longer looked like the goofball that I had been when we had entered the cave. You see, when we had driven up to the cave entrance earlier, it had been a beautiful warm Summer day, on the southern slope of Mount Saint Helens, in the southwestern region of Washington State. I hadn't known, then, that the Ape Caves stay at a constant year-round temperature of 42 degrees Fahrenheit. I was in shorts and a t-shirt. The only extra clothing in our car was Cheryl's long-sleeved sweatshirt. I was six feet, two inches tall, and about 195 pounds. Cheryl was about five and a half feet tall and about !)% pounds. This shirt was tiny! I looked ridiculous in it, but I wore it. Way too tight and way too short, it did help some with the cold. Best of all, it generated a lot of laughter from my family, not to mention several other folks, including one chattering group of camera-happy Japanese tourists. I just stood there and grinned as they took my picture, a proud ambassador of my country.

On May 18th, 1980, Mount Saint Helens experienced a massive eruption, spewing ash and smoke and superheated steam into the ionosphere and a massive wall of mud and trees into the communities below. Now, almost three decades later, it was an awesome and beautiful destination spot for tourists, scientists and adventurers from all over the globe.

Some of the mountain's best features are the Ape Caves; hollow lava tubes with entrances and exits that pop up into the forest. The most visited of the Ape Caves is a large well-maintained cave with a convenient paved parking lot, picnic tables and a metal stairway that takes a visitor down about two stories into the black, where one has the option to follow the tunnel one way or the other. Both directions lead a mile or more before they eventually exit back into the world of light. There are no lamps or paved walkways. Without a lantern or flashlight, it's as dark down there as the inside of a tennis ball.

My family and I had made it only a few hundred feet. It was part-way up the first rock scramble, in an unusually large portion of the tunnel, that Mitch had reached his breaking point. That was the end of his spelunking adventures.

A few years later, Cousin Greg told me that he and his Boy Scout troop were going to be climbing Mount Saint Helens, and that, if I wanted to, I could come along. This trip was going to also include a long hike through the Ape Caves.

We call each other cousins, but we aren't really. He's my wife's mother's aunt's daughter's husband. Though technically inaccurate, the word "cousin" works pretty well. His kids, even one more level removed from me by relation, simply called me Uncle Chris; "Unkie," sometimes. I love those two kids!

A former Eagle Scout himself, Greg was part of the leadership of an older group of Boy Scouts. I don't know how the age groups work in Scouts or what they're called, but this was the oldest age group. They were all well up in their teens. They would be earning some kind of advancement badge for this trip. This is the kind of advanced Scout activity that you wouldn't take the younger boys to. Greg's son, Riker, was one of the Scouts that would be climbing. Since friends and relatives were permitted to come along, Riker's twin sister, Alexandra, would be climbing as well.

Climbing Mount Saint Helens had long been a blurry item on my personal Bucket List. Blurry because, though it was something that I had really wanted to do, I figured I would never do it.

So, when Greg invited me to come along, especially knowing that my beloved niece and nephew would be there, I jumped at the opportunity. The news that the trip would also involve the Ape Caves made it just that much sweeter. I raced out and bought a nice new pair of hiking boots and I wore them almost every day for the next several weeks, hoping to break them in before the big climb.

Now this was the way to see a mountain! On Saturday, we would be in the Ape Cave, the very bowels of the volcano. On Sunday, we would be at the summit.

After several weeks of excited anticipation and some treadmill training, I was deep inside the sleeping volcano. It was Saturday evening and I was back in that giant lava tube for the first time since the tiny-sweatshirt-day. We had separated into groups of ten or twelve and had taken off in different directions. I was the designated "adult" of the group that included Riker and Alexandra. Ten years older than I, Greg had decided to forgo the Ape Cave portion of the trip, saving his best effort for the next morning's climb.

Remembering my mistake of several years earlier, I was well dressed for the cave this time. I had my warm durable clothing, my now well-broken-in hiking boots and a very cool looking wool felt Australian cowboy hat. As we ventured deeper and deeper into the earth, I became more and more thankful for that hat, as large cold drops of water kept falling on me, making a very satisfying *thump* sound with each impact. That hat was the envy of all in my group, as their heads had grown more and more wet with each drop.

At first, the young people in my group were loud and boisterous as they'd joked with each other in the dark, yelling "echo!" and other silly things, or poking each other shouting "Boo! Did I scare ya?" But, as the tunnel descended downward, snaking this way and that, I noticed, after a while, that the group had become very quiet, each of us lost in worlds of imagination, as we allowed ourselves to be fascinated and humbled by the beauty and the strangeness of what was around us. This was not a normal cave, with stalagmites and stalactites and side caverns and interesting rock formations. This was a true tunnel; a snakelike tube that wound up and down and side-to-side, spiraling ever onward. At one point, we had to lay on our bellies and inch our way, one at a time, through a small opening, soft sand below us, tons of rock above. It's funny how everyone thinks of earthquakes at a time like that.

Back into the more tube-like portion of the cave now, we walked through the cold stillness. In the cone of my flashlight, I saw how smooth the walls and ceiling were in places, and I had the funny feeling that we were walking through the esophagus or the entrails of a giant sleeping beast; a dragon maybe. At other times, I felt transported into some epic adventure tale, searching for the lost city of gold or the land that time forgot.

Suddenly, behind me, someone gasped and said, "Look at that!" My attention had been on my feet. I looked forward to see what had startled the young Scout. When I saw it, I caught my breath, and I heard others gasping behind me. There before us, just as the tunnel took a sharp turn to the right, was a giant shadowy shape on the ceiling and wall. It was Indiana Jones! It was a massive perfect silhouette of Harrison Ford's character from the movie *Raiders of the Lost Ark*, twenty or thirty feet high, an image familiar enough that all of us were instantly thinking the same thing. It moved its arm, then it took a step.

The magic lasted for only a second, when reason took over and we all started laughing simultaneously as we realized that the giant shape was me. Someone behind me had his flashlight facing forward, casting a giant shadow of me onto the cave wall in front of us. With my new hat, my giant shadow was the perfect silhouette of Indiana Jones, right up until Boy Scouts started reaching into the light making rabbit ear shadows and other shapes with their fingers. Boys!

Our romantic spell broken, the silly noises and shouts of "echo!" picked right back up.

I didn't sleep well that night. I spent most of it laying on my back, listening to the sleeping sounds coming from my "cousins" along with the almost eerie silence of the snowy world outside our tent. I was too excited to sleep. What a fun day it had been! What a fun day it'll be tomorrow! *I hope I can make it! It's a big mountain! I wish Mitch and Lydia were here.*

Basecamp was at a lower elevation than usual, due to an unusually large snowfall that year. This meant that we would have farther to hike in than climbers normally would.

It took a long time, hiking beneath the early morning stars, steadily uphill along the snowy tree-lined trail to reach the bottom of the mountain's stratocone. This was where the cone-shaped sides of the volcano began, where the real climb would start, and I was already breathing hard and feeling tired. *Could this have been a mistake? I'm no mountain climber!*

Into my borrowed backpack went the perfect-for-caves-but-terrible-for-mountains Australian cowboy hat, and out came the lightweight baseball cap that I had packed as an afterthought. Though there was snow everywhere, it was way too warm for wool felt, and my badly sweating scalp was letting me know about it.

Several hours - and thousands of vertical feet later - far above the tree line, my bones ached, my muscles screamed, and my mouth hung open. It seemed that even my hair hurt as I slowly placed one foot in front of the other and somehow summoned the strength to take another step. Each time I placed my weight into one of the steps, my foot would slide back two-thirds of the way. As the day had warmed, the snow had become more and more soft and slushy, making it very slippery. Progress was slow. If not for the two adjustable ski poles at my sides, I would have fallen many times. *What am I doing here? I'm no mountain climber!*

I shoved my toe into the snow in front of me, just like the person immediately uphill of me had just done, just as the person immediately behind me would do a second or two later, and I took another anguished step. Our group, combined with several other climb teams, formed a long stairway to heaven, mashing steps into the steep snowy sides of the big volcano.

Eventually I clumsily stepped out from the long vertical line of climbers and sat down on a rock. I was done. I had nothing left. I sat there, staring straight ahead, ears ringing, head foggy, body wasted. I had to admit that I'm not twenty-five anymore.

It had been a long strenuous day of slippery-snowy torture. *Well, I did my best. No shame in stopping here. I'll just wait.*

"You okay?"

"Sir?"

"Hmm?" I looked groggily up at the voice. A young woman stood in front of me.

"Everything alright?"

"Yeah. I suppose so."

She had a large fancy backpack, expensive-looking sunglasses, a white ball cap turned backward and short safari green shorts. I noticed her tan face, muscular legs, short dark hair and well-worn boots. She was a veteran trekker. I'm sure that she saw exactly what I was as well: a weekend warrior, an armchair quarterback, a would-be bucket-list-checker-offer. A middle-aged wimp in a borrowed backpack, completely out of my element.

She smiled sympathetically and said, "You can do it, man!"

"I'm done," I replied shaking my head from side-to-side. I smiled up at her sadly, "Got nothin' left."

"Dude, you've come so far. You're almost there." She turned and pointed up the steep slope.

"What? Another false summit? I've seen enough of those today." It was true. So many times I had crested a peak or a rise, thinking I was done, only to be heartbroken to see that, just beyond it, there waited another steep slope to climb. Slope after slope, peak after disappointing peak, each more difficult than the last, led me to another false summit. I couldn't take one more of those.

"No, Dude. That's it. That's the summit... right there." I looked in the direction of her outstretched arm.

"That's another five hundred feet, at least." I complained.

"More than that," she replied. "Eight hundred. Maybe a thousand. But you can do it. Cowboy up, hombre. You got this!"

I watched her walk away toward the final slope, wishing I had her energy. *Maybe... Maybe I can.*

I don't know how much longer I sat there. The attractive young climber was long gone from my sight, but her words of encouragement still rang in my ears. "Cowboy up, hombre... You got this!"

Alone, I shouldered my pack and dug a toe into the snow. On I trudged, with every fiber of my middle-aged pencil-pusher body shouting "Stop the madness!"

No one behind me and no one ahead of me, I chose my own pace, as I somehow picked up a foot and slammed it forward into the snow, in a spot where a hundred others had slammed theirs. As a mechanical designer, I knew what forty-five degrees of angle looked like. This was not forty-five. This last long slope was steeper than that. *Fifty. Maybe fifty-five.* It was more like a snowy ladder than a stairway, and I weighed seven hundred pounds.

Oh, God! I have to stop. Why am I doing this? But I'm so close! Just a... a little longer! I can't quit! I can't quit! Ugh...! One more step! I can do that! Okay... Now one more! Gasp! Maybe I'll...

Down I went, face first into the snow. So steep was the slope that I only fell a couple of feet. My face felt like it was burning in the cold, and I didn't care. There I lay, face in the slush, arms out to my sides, each still clutching a ski pole.

On your feet! Get up! Don't give up!

I groaned aloud as I lifted myself back to a hunched-over

almost-standing position, and I took another step, jamming my foot into its place.

"Cowboy up, Hombre!" I shouted, one syllable at a time, and I took another step.

"You got this!" I dropped to one knee.

"Hombre!" I got back up.

"You can do it, Dude!" I stumbled out three or four quick steps. "Cowboy... up... hombre..."

I stood still, staring at something on the steep snowy slope right in front of my face. "What is that?" I asked out loud.

I reached out and grabbed it. *Looks like a raisin. Why in the world would there be a raisin...? Oh who cares,* and I popped it into my mouth. It was so sweet, and so good. I took about ten more slow climbing steps, willing my body to extract massive amounts of energy from the raisin. It wasn't working.

"What's that?" I reached forward into the steep sloping snow. "A peanut! Hah!" I slammed it into my mouth and savored the rich nutty flavor.

Several steps later, *Huh?* I physically gasped inward as I picked up a yellow M&M. "Thank you, God!" A tickertape parade of sweet buttery goodness happened inside my mouth.

A few minutes later, a chocolate chip.

Twenty steps after that, an almond.

Then another peanut.

Forty feet later, a raisin.

Then, a thin piece of something. I didn't know what it was, but I ate it. It was good.

Do these things always taste this good?

On it went. It was a modern-day Hansel and Gretel path of treats, a trail-mix-trail, baiting me onward, leading me. *Did my pretty young "you-can-do-it-man" lady trekker drop these just for me? Did God put these here? Or some sweet and wonderful volcano elf? Maybe it was a gift from Saint Schmatzcake - the patron saint of middle-aged knuckleheads. Hah! What a huge ministry THAT guy would have!!*

Almost half of the mysterious morsels were raisins. I imagined them filling me with life-giving raisin goodness, like spinach to Popeye. On I trudged, step after grueling step.

I didn't look out to enjoy the view, when I finally reached the summit. I didn't look down over the sharp icy cornice, into the crater at the steaming volcanic dome at its center. No, I dropped, like fifty pounds of potatoes in a forty-pound sack, and there I lay for a solid twenty minutes. I stared at the blue sky and tried to get my heavy breathing under control.

Eventually, when I had finally come back to life, I did have a chance to get up and look around me, to take some spectacular pictures and to gasp in awe at the massive destruction that fanned out to the north of the crater; to be reminded of just how small I am in this beautiful awe-inspiring world.

God, your creation is amazing. That He could make such a mountain, such a world, such a universe, and still care so much about a puny ant named Chris, was mind boggling.

Though coming down, a little while later, was easier than going up had been, the trip back to basecamp was not without its own miseries, including a several mile trek, in wet clothes, through forest trails on slippery slushy ground; once again relying heavily on ski poles to keep me upright, and another twenty-minute collapse at the end, this time on the tailgate of my truck, legs hanging limply toward the pavement, a mess of gear strewn around on the blacktop.

Physically, it was the toughest day of my life. Nothing else even came close. But I'm so glad I did it. "A ship is safest in harbor, but that's not what it's built for." Remember that quote, by Mr. Shedd, from a few chapters back? I think it applies here. Here's another quote for you, from a profoundly imperfect and intensely happy man: "A little suffering is worth it, if it'll make a good story."

21

What Happened Outside

She may have been the cutest kid I had ever seen. I don't know. That's a tough call, but I sure can't think of anyone cuter. Her name was Chelane, but everyone called her Lanie. She was our niece; the daughter of my wife's brother, John, and his wife, Lisa. She had an older sister named Krystal, who was also a very beautiful kid.

Lanie was very expressive when she spoke. Her already-large eyes would widen with amazement and her little arms motioned this way and that as she told us the most important things. We couldn't help but laugh; not with amusement, but with fondness. I'm not sure how old she was, but she was somewhere between diapers and preschool.

"And then... and then," she continued, "he did something that was very silly!'

"He did?" I asked her. "And what was that?"

"He licked my hand."

"He did?"

"Oh, yes!" she replied with a look of importance, like she was telling us the most amazing thing in the world. "And he wagged his tail!"

"He kissed you and he wagged? Well, that's what dogs do, when they like you."

"Yes," she agreed. "That's very good. 'Cause he likes me a lot. Rocky is my best friend."

"Then what did he do, Lanie? What was the silly thing?" I enjoy conversations with tiny people. I love to ask them questions and listen to their wonderful answers.

Her eyes got huge, and with a look of astonishment, she announced, "He farted!" Then she let forth a machine gun staccato high-pitched giggle, which was so adorable that I couldn't help but laugh along with her.

"He was very silly," she continued, still laughing as she spoke.

"Well, it's a good thing that you both were outside when that happened," I told her. "Rocky might have made the house smell funny, if he had done that inside."

"Yes," she agreed, with formal seriousness. "That would be very bad."

We paused for a moment. She looked like she was thinking about what she wanted to say next. I waited. When it came, I wasn't disappointed. What followed was the most quotable exchange in my entire lifelong relationship with my beloved niece.

"That's where dogs fart. They fart outside."

"They do?"

"Yes," she continued, "and people fart inside, especially my dad."

I tried not to laugh when she singled out my brother-in-law as the main indoor fart master. "So, is that the way it works?" I asked her. "People fart inside and dogs fart outside?"

"Mm-hmm!" She nodded her head, happily.

"Very interesting." I continued, "Does your dad ever fart outside?"

She thought for a moment and then, nodding, she said, "Yes, sometimes he farts outside."

This was fun. "So, Lanie, if people fart inside and dogs fart outside, but your dad sometimes farts outside, does that mean that he's a dog?"

Her little brow furled downward as she contemplated this new thought. Then, suddenly, her eyebrows shot all the way up, in the most adorable way, and with shocked realization, she gasped, putting her hand over her mouth. Then after a breath or two, with grave seriousness, she looked me in the eye and said, "Don't tell Mom. My dad's a dog!"

"What?! I don't remember that!" Lanie told me, almost twenty years later. Grown into a very fine young lady, with a university degree in "Human Development and Family Science," and a very respectable position with a Seattle area nonprofit agency, helping local families, she hadn't lost her expressive pretty eyes. We were all visiting at Grandma and Grandpa's house. "I said that?"

"You sure did! You were the cutest little toddler!" I replied laughing. "Your Aunt Cheryl and I used to have you and your sister come visit us a lot when you were little. It was always a good time. Remember the night, when you were about seven, and you threw up on the carpet?"

"I even had you, once, when you had Chickenpox," Cheryl added. "I felt so bad for you. You were a baby then. That was a long time ago. Uncle Chris and I were still dating."

It's a wonderful thing, watching tiny people change into grown-up people. What a privilege it is to be there to watch something like that slowly happen. What an honor it is to play a part, even a small one. I am so thankful for opportunities to observe, and sometimes participate, when growth and victory happen; for the tiny and the not-so-tiny. Bring me more, life!

*"Life is an adventure. If you treat is as such,
you'll enjoy its happiness."*

Manny Segarra

*"I don't care who you are.
That's funny, right there!"*

Larry the Cable Guy

22

Space Cowboy

"Shu Bahda Du MaMaMaMa! Shu Bahda Du MaMaMaMa!" I belted it out nice and loud. The windows were down and there was a ton of road noise. With all of that wind roaring through the car and the stereo cranked as loud as I dared, I just felt driven to sing all the louder. "Shu Bahda Du MaMaMaMa! Shu Bahda Du MaMaMaMa!"

My girlfriend sat beside me in the passenger seat, her face displaying a look that said it all. There's just something fun about finding that perfect balance between amusing and irritating your lady - or your mom, if you're a teenage boy. It's a guy thing! Can I get an amen?

The way that I was reading her signals, I was just about right on target, almost perfectly striking that balance. Mildly annoyed disbelief played across her eyes, while her mouth supported a small but extremely cute smile. She was having fun and wondering if she was going to allow herself to admit it, I was certain.

"Come on!" I shouted through the noise. "You know the words!... or, whatever they are! Ha ha ha!... Shu Bahda Du MaMaMa!"

I was in such a great mood, and I just let all of that happiness run away with me as I drove us through the beautiful arid lands of Central Washington State. Dry hills and dusty rock formations rolled by. The smell of desert sage was thick in the air.

Before Cheryl started dating me, I doubt that she had known who The Steve Miller Band was. Having spent plenty of the last few months in my car, driving from here to there with me, I'm pretty sure that she knew most of the words to most of their songs, but I still couldn't get her to sing along. "One day, she will," I kept telling myself. "I'll Miller-ize her yet."

Maybe today will be the day.

Today was special. Today we would do more than just play that old cassette tape. Today, we would see The Man, Stevie Gi'-tar, himself. We were on our way to George. That's right; George, Washington. Isn't that a great name for a town? Over on the other side of the mountains, there's a little town called Martha, Washington. We've got them both.

Just outside the tiny town of George, there's a real gem of a place. Right beside the Champs de Brionne Winery sat the beautiful Champs de Brionne Music Theater. Sometime later, it would come to be known as The Gorge Amphitheater. Out in the middle of nowhere, about halfway between Seattle and Spokane, lies one of the world's most scenic and majestic music venues. The winery sits just above the Columbia River Gorge, on the Eastern Rim, with a spacious view into the giant canyon, to the beautiful Columbia River below. A short trail walk from the winery takes concertgoers down over the edge into the Gorge, where they discover a huge amphitheater built into the cliff side. From terraced grassy "seats," one can look down onto a large stage and out into the Columbia Gorge beyond. It's a beautiful place to see a show.

That was where we were going today - to see the Steve Miller Band. It was the Summer of 1988, and neon t-shirts were in fashion, from brands like Gotcha and Pacific Coast Highway. I was in bright neon orange as I glided my old mercury over the rugged desert terrain, singing out loud with my Steve Miller Band cassette tape.

"I went from Phoenix, Arizona all the way to Tacoma... Philadelphia, Atlanta, L.A.!" On I crooned as the miles of sweet-smelling sage rolled by. I think she was happy that "Shu Ba Da Du Ma Ma" was over.

Sometime later, we were pulling into the massive dirt and grass parking lot. "I wonder where the best place to park is. We're going to want to be near an exit after the show," said the cute and ever practical Cheryl.

I turned my head to her and I loudly replied, "Noooooooooorthern California where the girls are warm, so I could be with my sweet baby. Yeah!" With that reply, I had officially shattered the precarious balance between amused and annoyed.

An hour and a half later, we sat together, on our grassy terrace, holding hands, bobbing our heads to the beat of - yet another - Steve Miller Band rendition of an old southern blues tune, wondering when ol' Steve was going to start playing his own hits. It was hot that day, and there were a lot of beer-drinking young people in bright colored skimpy clothes, baking on that hillside. So far, it had been an interesting and entertaining evening of things you don't see every day, including one not-so-funny comedian intro-act, two nearby fistfights, one tipsy young lady who thought this was the perfect place to pull her t-shirt up for people, and way too many old-time Delta Blues songs. It seemed that Stevie Gi'tar and his fellas were in a Muddy Waters mood today.

"I don't know any of these songs, so far," Cheryl yelled.

Over the pulsating amplifiers, I yelled back, "You're right! They're not playing any of their own songs." I wondered when they were going to play their hits. Where was "Swingtown?" Where was "The Joker?" "Abracadabra?" "Fly Like an Eagle?" "Wild Mountain Honey?" Or, my favorite, "Jet Airliner?"

I didn't want to admit it to Cheryl, or to myself, but I was getting sick. It had started small, a bit earlier, but had been rapidly progressing for some time. I kept hoping, silently, that it would go away. My head, by now, was pounding. My stomach was upset and nausea was almost all I could think about. The worst part of it was a strange disorienting dizziness.

The temperature had gone down considerably since the stars had come out, and I suppose that did help some, but I was really not doing well. I eventually told Cheryl about my problem.

Caring a lot more about me than she did about Steve Miller, she said, "We should go."

"No way," I moaned. "They're going to start playing their good stuff any minute. We can't miss that!"

Fifteen minutes later, I was ready to leave. Whatever was wrong with me was getting worse. This was a kind of sick that I had never experienced before. We stood up from our grassy seat, and I immediately fell back down. I tried to stand. Cheryl pulled me up. With one arm over her for support, we started to make our way across the bowl-shaped audience area toward the trail that would lead back to the parking lot. Slowly, we stumbled our way along.

"Dude, have another beer!" someone teased as we worked our way by.

"I'd say he's had enough," someone else yelled.

I didn't know if I was going to make it. It took all I had in me to just place one foot in front of the other. This was the sickest I had ever been, and I was getting worse. Without saying so, I wondered a little if I was going to die.

Finally, after a lot of struggle, we had made it up the steep path, out of The Gorge and onto the flat land above. Before us stood an infinite ocean of hoods and windshields. Parked cars stretched out away from us in a giant fan shaped mechanical dreamscape that we stared at in disbelief. In the artificial light of the parking lot lamps, all the cars seemed to be about the same color; a dull yellowish gray.

"Which way?" she quietly asked. Echoing music boomed out of the canyon behind us.

I looked to the right, then to the left. My aching head swam and my mind clumsily scratched for any memory of where we might have left the car. "I don't know," I weakly whispered, trying not to fall. Everything looked so different than it had before all of these cars had gotten here.

Straight ahead we limped, arms around each other's waists, making painfully slow progress, panning our heads left and right, trying to find that little white Mercury with the round Vuarnet Sunglasses sticker on the back.

I dropped to my knees in the grass and dust. It was over. There would be no more walking for me.

"You stay here. I'll go find the car," and she was gone.

I don't remember falling. I'm not sure that I was conscious when it happened. My head rested in a soft bed of fine dust as I lay on my back, looking up into the stars. I felt like I was slowly rotating, like I was laying on a giant phonograph album that slowly turned, taking me with it.

Nausea and pain filled my world. Delirium was working its way in, invading my mind, as bile worked its way up my throat. I lay there that way for a long while.

Suddenly, through the mist of a cluttered and confused mind, from somewhere far away, I heard a beautiful sound. High overhead it rang out, lovely and sorrowful. It echoed as it changed tones. It was a saxophone, I realized, but why? Where was it coming from? So beautiful, it played alone. Was I dying? *Go to the light!*

Wait! I know that tune.

It was coming from the canyon, from the Columbia River Gorge. It echoed as it richly sang to me. Then there was a voice. It was a man's voice. "I don't want to live in a world of darkness, I want to live in a world of light."

I know this song. It's Steve. That's Steve Miller!

They're finally playing one of their hits!

"I don't want to live in a world of darkness, I want to live in a world of sight, and you know...."

I latched onto the voice, fighting for consciousness.

Steve continued, mellow and smooth, beautifully echoing from just beyond my view, "I want to make the world turn around, make the world turn around, make the world turn around, around, around..."

"Yeah!" I shouted. "It is!" I laughed out loud as I lay there on my giant dusty turntable, slowly spinning, like the second hand on big clock. Loudly, I laughed again and again as I heard the strangely echoing lyrics filling the air around me. Madness was nearly there.

"...Make the world turn around, around, around..." what a nice voice Mr. Miller had.

"It is turning around, Steve!" I shouted. "Around and around, ha ha ha ha...!"

Suddenly, an electric guitar pierced the night, and I instantly became silent. It held a long mysterious note, high and unwavering. It bounced off of the canyon walls and made its way to me, enveloping me in its warmth. A tear curled back from my eye and ran into my ear, where it puddled and stayed. It was one of the most beautiful sounds I had ever heard, though my head hurt worse than I had known was possible. I yearned for sleep; for any kind of relief from the pain.

"I found the car." She was back. We were moving again.

Later, I don't know how long, we pulled up in front of her cousin's house in the nearby town of Ephrata. We had arranged to spend the night there. He had told Cheryl that he and his wife would be out with friends for the evening, but that they would leave the side door unlocked for us. Unfortunately, they had forgotten to. For over an hour, I lay in a reclined passenger seat, drowning in a pool of pain and sickness, waiting for Cheryl's cousins to come home.

"I'm so sorry about the door last night," she told me as she poured coffee into my cup the next morning. Warm pancakes sat before me, and, from the smell, I knew that bacon was on its way. That made me happy. I have great respect for the bacon industry.

Whatever had plagued me the night before was gone now. I had awakened that morning on the living room couch where I had collapsed the night before, fully clothed, dust in my hair, and, surprisingly, I felt fine. I attacked my breakfast with a vigor and vitality that would have seemed impossible the night before.

"He doesn't look sick!" Cheryl's cousin told her.

"I feel great!" I replied. "Flop another cake on here, will ya?" Man, I was hungry!

"What is that on your neck, Chris?"

"Hmmm?" I asked as I looked up smiling, mouth full of warm syrupy yumminess.

"Here… and here!" Cheryl reached and pulled the neck of my neon orange t-shirt down a few inches, and she sucked in her breath in a loud gasp. "Oh, my goodness! Honey, pull your shirt up."

Still chewing, I obeyed. As I lifted my shirt up, exposing my stomach and chest to my breakfast mates, I watched three sets of eyes bulge wide.

"What?" I looked down at myself.

"You've got Chickenpox, Christopher!" she said.

"Ha ha ha! You sure do!" agreed the other lady at the table. "No wonder you were so sick!"

"What? I What? Chickenpox?"

"Lanie!" My girlfriend shouted. "Remember?"

I groaned as I remembered Cheryl's sweet baby niece, Chelane, covered in spots, several days earlier. "Oh, no…"

All three of them burst into laughter at my sad expression.

She made me sit in a sleeping bag all the way home, saying something about needing to bring the spots out. Being the height of Summer, in a car with no air conditioning, it was a long sweaty drive back to Seattle.

I missed over two weeks of work. I can tell you that chickenpox, for an adult, is spectacular! There is no place that is spared. Every inch of my body was spotted with painful red bumps. I got them on the bottoms of my feet, between my toes, on my scalp, my tongue, my gums, the whites of my eyeballs, the inside of my throat. Get your kids exposed when they're young!

I love Classic Rock music. I can sing along with most of the favorites from the sixties through the nineties. But Steve Miller music will always be a little bit funny for me now. Wouldn't it be great if Steve, someday, reads this book, and thinks back to that night at George, Washington, Summer of 1988?

"You did it, Steve! You accomplished what your echoing sax-accompanied lyric wished for. That night, for a sick guy in a dusty parking lot, you made the world turn around!"

23

It's Like a Whole Other Country!

"Before we step outside, I need to warn you about something," I told them as I knelt down to their levels. They were seven and five years old, and absolutely unprepared for what awaited them beyond that clear glass door. Lydia and Mitch had spent all of their short lives in Western Washington State, in one of the most comfortable climates our country has to offer. I was there to pick them up after their airplane ride with Mommy from Seattle to Dallas. It was early August and I had already been there for a week.

Shortly after the 2001 terrorist attacks, the Aerospace industry experienced a serious downturn, and I had been having trouble finding work in the Seattle area. Western Washington had long been a hotbed of Aerospace design jobs, but in the Summer of 2002, work for a designer was hard to find, even in Seattle. I had already been laid off from two temporary contractor jobs at small aircraft design firms and I had been unemployed, now, for over a month. The only job I had been able to find was at a Helicopter company, in Hurst, Texas; right about midway between Dallas and Fort Worth. Would this be another temporary job, or was this going to be our new home? At this point, we had no idea. Congress hadn't signed on the new aircraft yet, so my official employee capacity there was that of a contractor; a "Job Shopper," as we like to call ourselves.

"Guys, it's going to be hot when you walk out that door. Really, really hot!" They both nodded their heads with expectant smiles, almost as if to say, *sounds like fun, bring it on!* "Do you understand me? I continued. "This is going to be hot, like you have never felt before. I'm talking about Africa hot!"

The looks on their faces were priceless when I finally got them outside those airport doors. The "Africa hot" warning hadn't been descriptive enough, I guess. It took about one full second for it to really hit them, then they did exactly what I had known they would do. They physically flinched, like they'd been slapped. Then their faces twisted into expressions of surprise and pain, and out of both of their mouths came odd painful sounds that were abundantly clear in their meanings. It was so hot, so humid and oppressive that it actually hurt.

I laughed a little and said, "Welcome to Texas."

I smiled, returning from my Mind Movie of my kids, that day at the Dallas airport three months earlier, as I cruised toward the Texas sunset; just me and my trusty steed, Mabel. Mabel was what I called my car. Her full name was Mabel Lou the Malibu, and I loved my comfortable brown four-door friend! What a great car.

I'd been on the road for several hours and my mind had wandered all over the place as I'd carefully trekked my way across the vast Texas Panhandle, traveling East to West. With my former three-month-long helicopter contractor job not even cold in its grave yet, a huge expectant smile stretched across the wide expanse of my mind as Mabel and I pointed ourselves toward Washington. It was late October and, after so many weeks separated from my three favorite people in the universe, I was going home.

"Flash! I'm getting hungry! Gonna stop at this next town for bite. You want anything?" I glanced over at the little black flashlight sitting in the passenger seat, who said nothing. "No? Well… suit yourself."

Boredom and loneliness can be a great enemy when you're away from the ones that you love. But, when one is armed with an imagination and an ironic sense of humor, one need never feel truly alone. To be truthful, when a guy knows God, there's always someone to talk to. But, when a guy, a lonely guy, is feeling the strange combination of lonesome, sarcastic and silly, the Heavenly Father is probably not the most appropriate or respectful choice for conversation partner, at least, not at that moment.

Yep, throughout this entire Texas odyssey, I had kept ol' Flash handy, and though he wasn't much of a conversationalist, I had found him to be an excellent listener as I had lived alone in Texas for those several weeks. I'm not sure that he really got all of my jokes, but he was always courteous and patient.

"How 'bout I get you a milkshake?... You're welcome."

I wondered if I would need to employ the stay-awake-and-don't-crash technique that I had used three months earlier when I had driven down there. Taking some advice from my brother, Shanon, who had assured me of its effectiveness, I had employed his unusual stay-awake method as I had driven across the flat almost featureless fields of Southeastern Colorado and Western Kansas. He was right! It had worked beautifully. Where I had been just moments earlier fading away and yawning, I was wide awake and laughing. For twenty or thirty minutes I had been, at the top of my lungs, singing various Jimmy Buffett songs in my best John Wayne accent. "He went to Paris... Pardner..." I was cracking myself up! "Wastin' away again... in Margaritaville.... little lady..." Hah!! What a riot!

When that method had run its course, I switched to a very convincing Pee Wee Herman voice. "HEH! Heh heh heh heh... He went to Paris... Aaaaaarrrgh!! Hee hee hee hee!" Once again, I was wide awake and laughing like a crazy person.

Today, as I was driving northwest, three months later, following my bumper toward home, I remembered those crazy Jimmy Buffett songs and I was starting to consider singing them again, when I called to mind what had happened a little while after my original John Wayne and Pee Wee Hermon party of the previous July, and a new Mind Movie began. Stopping at an old roadside Oklahoma convenience store that hot July day, I had been standing in front of the cold drinks, trying to decide between Mountain Dew and Gatorade, when I'd heard a voice from just beyond the refrigerator aisle.

"If I had just held my course and kept going straight, they'd probably be alive now." Then there was a pause. I grabbed the Mountain Dew and headed toward the cash register, taking me closer to the mysterious voice. "I know, I know," he said slowly. "I just wish...."

Now I could see him. He was young. Tall. Powerfully built. Leaning

187

against wood paneling, just beneath a dusty wall-mounted stuffed pheasant, he silently listened to the hand piece of the payphone that hung near the postcards display. He looked me in the eye as I passed by. He looked tired and sad. His curly brown hair was a mess and he looked like he might have been crying a little earlier.

Chin-deep in my own thoughts of loneliness mixed with adventure, I walked past him and continued on, toward Texas. Later that night, from a Texas Motel room television, the lady on the news spoke of a fatal crash that had occurred earlier that day in a tiny town a little north of the Texas/Oklahoma line, wherein an eighteen-wheel semi had hit a car containing a young woman and her mother. The story mentioned that the car had somehow driven into the path of the truck. The reporter praised the efforts of the truck's driver to avoid the small car, but the two women had been pronounced dead at the scene.

From my lonely motel room, I prayed for the young truck driver. Should I have been more observant? Could this have been one of those divine occasions; a meeting perfectly appointed by God? A meeting that I had missed? Had I been too self-absorbed, as I'd carried my soft drink through that Oklahoma mini-mart, to really see what I was looking at, to really hear what I was listening to, to notice the need that was right in front of me? Could I have been that one friendly face or sympathetic ear that he might be needing when he finished his phone call? Could I have been that one person who could have prayed with him?

Drifting back out of the Mind Movie, I smiled sadly to myself as I steered Mabel toward home these three months later. "Yep, I think I might have missed that one, Flash."

An hour or so later, a little south of Amarillo, I was driving through a small picturesque canyon. "Canyon, Texas? Really? That's the name of this town? That's funny! I wonder how they came up with that clever name." I asked my flashlight sardonically? The same question I had entertained a few moments earlier when I had driven through the even-smaller town of Happy.

Texas is an interesting place. They think a little bit differently there. For instance, in Texas I learned that I am, apparently, a "Yankee."

"Yankee? You do understand that the Civil War was more than a hundred thirty years ago, right? And that Seattle wasn't in the war?" I had asked him?

"It's north of Red River, ain't it?" my fellow helicopter designer had confidently twanged.

"Umm, yes. But, by that measure, even parts of Northern Texas would be Yankees," I said incredulously.

"Yup." he'd replied without hesitation.

They pride themselves, many of them, on being the only state in the union that flies its flag at equal height to the U.S. flag. "It's like a whole other country!" Some even brag that, if it ever becomes necessary, they could secede from America and reclaim their own sovereignty. *Well, that's rhat!*

But, though I chuckled about it as Mabel, Flash and I cruised through the town of Canyon, I was reminded of how their naming convention is one of the many things that I love about Texas. Texas has the best city names in the world! Whenever I learn of a new one, I get a mental picture of the tough no-nonsense hard-working pioneer folk that settled this part of our great nation. Many of their town names, Canyon included, have a picturesque simplicity that are just downright wonderful. Corn! Yes, there's a town in Texas called Corn. I love that!

A lot of their towns were, apparently, named for what the settlers and pioneers saw around them, including towns like Canyon, Cactus, and Notrees. Hah! Seriously! Notrees, Texas! One of my favorites is Levelland. *Yup, this is some purty level land we got here, Clem!* Some are a bit more thought provoking, like Buffalo Gap, Bee Cave, Broken Arrow and Big Cabin. I'll bet those towns have some great naming stories. Muleshoe, it seems, got its name exactly the way one might think it happened. Those straight thinking honest early Texans named the place for the mule shoe they found in the dirt there. I figure the towns of Turkey and Quail got their names in a similar way.

Another of my favorites is Wheelock, Texas. *Hey Ma, looks likes like we done broke the wagon. Got us a busted Wheelock. Hmmm... well, this place looks nice enough, I reckon.*

There's also a handful of towns that seem to have been named after some everyday things, like Corn, Elbow, Blanket, Noodle, and Oatmeal. Hmmph! Oatmeal, Texas.

As we meander down the list of quaint, interesting and sometimes downright confusing Texas town names, we come to a group that just makes a fella scratch a head and say, "Hmmmm;" names like Tarzan (really!), Hogeye, Bigfoot, and Ding Dong. There are people, in today's modern era, who get to write Ding Dong, Texas on their envelopes. How cool is that?

Among my favorites are the towns that clearly were named after specific objects and incidents that have been long forgotten; names like Weeping Mary, Old Dime Box, and some extremely funny names like Hoot And Holler and Jot 'Em Down.

As one might expect from a state settled in the 19th Century Wild West, gunplay and other cowboy intrigues seem to have made their way into the towns of Texas, in names like "Gun Barrel," "Point Blank," "Gun Sight" and evocative-as-all-getout, "Cut and Shoot." It also seems that there was, at times, a serious lack of imagination among our early Texas brethren, painfully illustrated in town names like Uncertain and Nameless. I have no idea what it meant but, believe it or not, there are four towns, in the great state of Texas, called Needmore. Exactly what it was that they need more of is a mystery - other than the obvious answer of *vocabulary*.

You can travel the world without ever leaving the state, because China, Italy, Sudan, Egypt, Ireland and Palestine are all towns in Texas. One group of Texas pioneers figured they would cover all the bases, and named their town Earth. Mildred, whoever she was, has a town named after her, as do Maud, Martha and Mabelle. Not to be outdone, Melissa, Christine, Edna and Alice all have towns named for them, as do the very lovely trio of Anna, Katie and Josephine. The fellas didn't do as well on the town name scoreboard, but they did turn in a respectable showing with the names Elmer, George and Fred. *I live in Fred, Texas! Welcome to Fred!* Almost as if they could see into the future of children's broadcasting, they've even got a pair of towns called Kermit and Elmo.

There were some optimists among the settlers of the Lone Star State, it seems. One such group of stalwart pioneers named their town Best, Texas. But they were out-down by the sweet folks of an even more optimistic stock who named their town Veribest, Texas. And let's not forget the very inviting Texas towns of Happy and Friendly, and the well-wishing town of Goodnight.

Not to belabor the point, I've saved my favorite category for last. *Well, ya see? We got this here town that we need to name and it's rhat in the middle of the panhandle. Hey, let's call it Panhandle.* Yup, it's the towns named by the geography experts that I somehow find the most interesting. Most of all there's the portmanteau names. Portmanteau, in case you're wondering, is a very cool term that describes what you get when you combine two words. Smog is a common portmanteau of Smoke and Fog. Motel is a portmanteau combining the words Motor and Hotel. Sitcom, brunch, spork - you get the idea.

On the border between Texas and Arkansas, there's the cool geographical portmanteau town, combining the two state names, resulting in Texarkana. Between Texas and Oklahoma, they've got, you guessed it, Texhoma! Clever! But it doesn't stop there, we still have two more states bordering Texas. Way over on the line between Texas and New Mexico, there's Texico, and, best portmanteau of them all; right there on the border between Texas and Louisiana we get to use our state abbreviations of Tex and LA. Yes! They made a town called Texla! It's a ghost town now.

I love these names! No-nonsense hard-working pioneer-prospector-rancher-cowboy-farmer vocabularies designed these wonderful historical names.

That first night, on my way home from Dallas, I would be running out of daylight right about the Texas / New Mexico state line, way up in the very northwest corner of Texas. I had chosen that less populous route because I wanted to see some country that I hadn't seen before. The northeast corner of New Mexico sounded like it would do nicely. When I saw, on my map, the name of a town that I would be driving through at about nightfall, I knew that I would need to stop there. It was, quite possibly, the best no-nonsense geography-loving cowboy Texas name ever! It was right on the Texas line. Its name? Texline. Yes, sir! What name could possibly be better for a Texas state line town name than Texline, Texas?

After checking in at the Texline Motel, I was eating my dinner alone in a worn vinyl booth at the Texline Café, the perfect aproned waitress,

Johnny Cash playing, bland coffee serving, cliché motor café. I sat there in my cliché restaurant booth, eating some cliché apple pie, in a cliché Texas town with a wonderful cliché Texas name, and thoroughly enjoying the whole cliché experience, thinking that this fun moment couldn't possibly get any more quaint and cliché, when it did. It absolutely did!

I almost laughed out loud when he walked in. If ever there was a cliché cowboy-prospector, this was the guy. His name was John and the ladies working at the café obviously knew him well. He delighted in teasing, tormenting and flirting with the waitresses and anyone else who would listen. His wrinkled skin had a yellowish hue and his brushy blond-gray beard hung below a smiling mouth and a bulbous pockmarked nose. His eyes twinkled with a mirth and zest for life that I envied. His perfect old-man-cowboy voice reminded me of Gabby Hayes or Walter Brennan as he laughed his old cowboy laugh, "Hee Hee!" He wore boots, overalls and yes, a droopy dusty worn-out hat. He was short and wiry, a little hunched over and a little bow-legged. If this guy had been in a movie, I would have probably laughed at the casting director for making him too perfect.

Calling me "stranger," he sat down at my booth uninvited. He laughed as he told me stories of prospecting in the hills. He spoke of mining for gold in California and for platinum in Oregon. He had mined and panned and prospected all over the West, hunted big game in Wyoming and Montana, wrangled livestock in Kansas and worked the oilfields of Texas and New Mexico. He'd even discovered the cure for cancer. "Magnets, son! It's all about the magnets! I can use magnets like this'n," he pulled a dirty black stereo speaker magnet from his overalls, "and I can extract ore from the earth or cancer from your bones." He pointed a crooked finger at my chest and cheerfully winked a wrinkled ice-blue eye.

I tried not to grin while he spoke. I sat there wishing I had a video camera. I was tired and I needed a bed, but I stayed there letting the old man pour out his mind about life and about love and about "the things that really matter, son!" I thought that, at any minute, he might break right into one of those wonderful old Country/Western ballads that tell the stories of young men hearing wisdom from an old stranger, and that just maybe he'd start extolling the merits of "old dogs, children and watermelon wine" or instruct me that I've "got to know when to hold'm, and know when to fold'm."

What started a bit comical gradually became more valuable. Once I got over the oddness and the humor of finding myself in the middle of a Tom T. Hall song, and I actually listened to the man, this quaint and curious situation took on a greater meaning. I didn't hear anything coming across that table that was overly profound or life-changing. I didn't find myself suddenly wanting to write down his sage proclamations or ask him about life's great mysteries, but I did hear him speaking directly to my situation – almost as if he'd been reading my mail. His words were an encouragement that I was doing okay – that, throughout the long and trying, confusing and frustrating situation that I was in right then, that I had been doing it right and that I should stay the course, painful or not. Though he knew nothing about my past three months or my looming uncertain and intimidating days to come, his words were almost a reward – praise from an elder for my recent toughness and hard work, like a compliment from a temporary Dad Figure. It felt good.

Two nights later, I pulled into my driveway. It was late. That day I had driven all the way from Little America, Wyoming to our home in Arlington, Washington, making a quick midday stop at an Idaho rest area a little West of Bliss. "Made it, Mabel. Thanks for getting me here."

My Texas adventure was over. My trusty Mabel had brought me home, into the loving arms of my young family. Soon, we would be selling our home and starting our next adventure, moving to Oregon where I would be leaving the less dependable world of Aerospace to design cab components for big trucks.

As I closed the car door and started my walk to the house, I remembered what ol' John had told me two nights earlier, in the Texline Café. "If you don't got family, son; you don't got nothin'. And you gotta do all you can for 'em! Even when it hurts – especially then. You gotta be willin' to die for 'em if that's what's needed."

Once more, I thought back to way I had spent my last three months and I allowed myself a small satisfied smile. "You're right, John," I whispered with a slight nod of my head. Before sliding my key into the door lock, I stood on my front porch and looked out over a sleeping neighborhood; at the street where I had walked my young trick-or-treaters door to door, where I had taught them to ride their bikes without training wheels, where we had built a snowman together the Winter before, where I had so many times walked the sidewalk hand-in-hand with my wife. So glad to be home.

"Good night Flash."

"The more they overthink the plumbing, the easier it is to stop up the drain."

Lt. Cmdr. Montgomery Scott
Star Trek

24

Dining with Greatness: A Study in Double Entendre

I looked at him with a stern stare and I angrily tossed my fork onto my half-eaten plate. The fork clanged loudly as it banged off of the plate and immediately smashed into my water glass, creating a second, higher pitched noise as loud as the first. My angry face darkened all the more as I bored into his eyes with my own.

The sounds of casual conversation diminished in our area of the restaurant as heads nervously turned toward our table. Sitting directly across from me, he stared back, just as intensely. Abruptly and purposefully, he leaned forward in his chair, managing to grow at least an inch taller, as his posture became rigid. His lips turned white and the muscles in his jaw worked as he shot darts back at me from eyes full of hate. He looked as though he could go off like a bomb at any moment.

For several seconds, we glared at each other. Eyebrows furled downward and fists clinched, neither of us willing to break the stare. Suddenly, with actions faster than I had anticipated, he made his move. I saw it coming, but too late. I couldn't stop him in time to save myself.

It came in with a blur of movement and hit me in the smooth skin between the eye and the eyebrow, on the left side of my face. Though I had raised my hands in defense, I had been as good as defenseless in the face of his lightning attack.

"What a shot!" I exclaimed, laughing loudly. "That was so fast!" I continued to laugh as I reached up and pulled it off of my face. The soaking wet, rolled up straw wrapper was still cold from where he had dipped it in his drinking water moments earlier.

"Dennis! You're like Jesse James with that thing, man!" I laughed.

Leaning back, hands behind his head, he grinned proudly and replied, "You mess with the best, you die like the rest, my friend."

"You guys are morons," said Dennis' wife, Kelli, as she shook her head, smiling.

Across from Kelli, to my right, sat Cheryl. She looked at me and said, "You're embarrassing sometimes, you know that?"

"Then our work is done here," I replied with mock formality as I reached across the table and high-fived my best friend.

The four of us laughed as people at tables around us, who moments earlier had been watching nervously, turned away, some looking irritated, others amused.

"I'll never get tired of that," Dennis smirked.

We went out to dinner with them a lot. We enjoyed their company and, frankly, there wasn't a whole lot else to do in Wichita. Tonight, we were, once again, at a nearby national chain lasagna joint. I wish I could remember the name of the place. For some reason, when I try to think of the name, I'm suddenly picturing a Garden... with Olives in it. Hmmm.

It was Saturday night and the place was packed. We had waited a long time for our table. The lobby had been so full that we had stood throughout our wait. There were not a lot of benches to sit on. The wait had been just fine with us, though. It comes with the territory. If you want to eat there on a Saturday night, you'll be waiting a while. No big deal.

Our dinner conversation moved from expert paper wad flicking to other things. Our infant daughters sat quietly in their high chairs as the restaurant atmosphere buzzed with the blended sounds of a hundred lasagna lovers, all using their respectful indoor voices.

Suddenly, Kelli looked over my shoulder at something behind me. She pointed subtly and asked, "Is that... is that... um... whatever his name is?"

I looked back in the direction of her eyes and I sucked in a lungful of garlicky air in surprise. I immediately spun back toward our table, trying hard to look casual.

"What's his name?" Kelli whispered.

"That's James Doohan," I replied quietly. "You know, Scotty. Scotty... from Star Trek. Mr. Scott."

"Oh, yeah! You're right!"

With not much more than a step and a lean, I probably could have reached over and touched him. The actor and his three companions were just being seated at the table next to ours. We all tried to act nonchalant, which, I think, we did a good job of. We continued with our meal, but I had a very hard time keeping my mind on anything that was happening at our table. That was Starfleet Commander Montgomery Scott sitting next to me! James Doohan, himself! Like every other American boy from the 1960s and '70s, I had grown up on a diet of Star Trek. Mr. Doohan and his co-stars had been with us in our living room countless times, for years and years. I couldn't help listening to their conversations a little. Okay, a lot.

He doesn't have an accent! He's not Scottish! What?

Of course, I knew that he was an actor, and actors often affect accents for their roles, but this was Scotty! Scotty has an accent! How many times had I heard his rich authentic sounding brogue belting out a plaintive "I'm givin' 'er all she's got, Sir! She cannit take it much longer!"

Nope. No accent. They spoke of business and other mundane things. I soon figured out that the man to his left was his agent.

"How is everything tonight?" asked the perky young waitress who suddenly appeared at my side. "Can I interest you in some dessert?"

We all gave her the usual, "No thanks, I'm way too full," reply. Then I quietly asked her, "So how long do movie stars have to be seated?" I meant it only as a conversational jest. Our earlier wait hadn't been that big of a strain, and, to be truthful, I would have been perfectly fine if Mr. Doohan had been seated immediately.

"What?" the young waitress asked, "movie stars?"

"Well," I continued at a low voice, smiling, "I was just curious, since, you know... we have a movie star here in the room with us... I was just wondering..."

Suddenly, way too loudly, figuring, I guess, that I was joking, she planted her hands on her hips and blurted with a smile, "There's no movie stars in here!"

Embarrassed, I sank down a little into my chair and buried my face in my hands.

"Is there?" she continued, a little less sure.

Dennis pointed over, in a very subtle way, toward James Doohan's table.

The exuberant youngster spun on her heal and then let out an excited high pitched squeak when she saw him. Mr. Doohan had, apparently, heard the entire conversation, and was looking right at us. She took two or three happy skipping steps straight at him and came to a bouncy stop at his side.

"You're a movie star!" she said happily. He looked up at her from his seat with an amused grin. You know, I think that there is a direct correlation between how cute a person is and how much they can get away with. I probably would have been ushered out of the place if I had done that.

"Aye, yer a lovely lass, ye are."

The accent's back!!!

"I'm thinkin that I'd like a virgin Bloody Mary. Can ye git me one of those, dear?"

After a while, we got over the mystique of the greatness in our midst, and we moved on, our conversations eventually trailing away to other things.

A few minutes after Scotty's virgin Bloody Mary had been delivered by a proud restaurant manager, I started to notice that I was sweating. In fact, I was a little faint and my head was hurting.

What had started out as a pleasant evening was rapidly turning into something very much the opposite. I smiled weakly and I tried to participate in the conversation, but things were taking a bad turn.

"You don't look well," said Cheryl, as she placed a hand on my forehead. "Oh, you're all clammy. Chris, what's wrong?"

By this time, my lower stomach had my undivided attention. "Cramps," I grimaced, hugging my stomach with my arms.

I tried to stay still at my seat. My bowels were making strange noises and felt like they were twisting and wrestling inside my belly. I took some shallow breaths and, with pained face, I said, "I don't know what's wrong. It really hurts."

My three companions looked on with expressions of concern as I sat several minutes taking short, uneven breaths. It wasn't getting any better.

"Excuse me." I whispered as I stepped away from the table. I tried to look and act normal as I walked through the dining room and the tables of happily dining families. I needed to get to a restroom.

I passed from one room to another, and down a walkway. It was getting worse. My head pounded, my belly screamed, and I wondered if I was going to make it. By the time I reached the crowded lobby, dizzy and cramping, I was a man on a mission. With no concern for casual appearances, I made a bee-line for the restroom door.

The door blasted open as I burst through it into the empty restroom. I ran into a stall, slammed the door closed and, as quickly as I could, became intimately familiar with one of the restaurant's least comfortable chairs, just in time. Barely.

I will let you use your imagination regarding what went on in that private torture chamber. We've all been there a time or two, right?

My time in that cramped stall did have the desired effect. Relief was immediate. But there was an unpleasant added consequence of my actions, for anyone else who might venture into the room while breathing. In fact, and I'm sorry to take you there, dear reader, but what I did to the air in that restroom was absolutely unreasonable and unacceptable, but impressive nonetheless.

I sat alone in my tiny stall, the scene of the crime, my aching sweaty head held in my hands. The courtesy-flush that I had done moments earlier seemed to provide no improvement on the atmospheric destruction that I had wrought, when I heard the restroom door open, and the sounds of many feet on the tile floor. I heard voices as well. They were female.

Adrenaline shot through me, making me feel faint. Silent panic pushed through my veins. I heard the voices and the footsteps abruptly stop; then there was a thin whisper, "Oh, my." I could picture three or four ladies standing there holding their noses, wondering if this restroom visit was something that they might put off until later.

I'm in the ladies' room! What do I do?

I didn't move. Rational thought is, it seems, inhibited, when one's pants are around his ankles. Maybe there's a pressure point on top of the foot. I waited until I heard several stall doors open and close, praying that none of them would sit down next door and notice my size twelves on the floor beside her. I got lucky.

As soon as I'd heard everyone settle into their stalls, I silently blurted a very quick prayer, slammed my clothing into proper position, and I bolted from my tiny cubicle of shame. There at the sink, just starting to wash her hands, stood a young girl of about nine years old. She looked up at me and her eyes suddenly bulged in surprise.

I'm caught! Oh no!

Out the restroom door I exploded, into the packed waiting room. Straight across the crowded lobby I hurried. Just before I reached the men's room, I accidentally made eye contact with an elderly woman sitting on a padded bench, who, judging by the shock on her face, had seen the door from which I had come.

Caught again! Game over! I'm going to be arrested. I just know it!

On the wall, immediately beside the men's room door, there hung an oval picture, an elegant profile likeness of an ancient first century Roman man on the wall. He looked at me accusingly with his one eye that faced me. *Oh, shut up!* I silently yelled at him.

Into the men's room I hurried, wishing I could have James Doohan transport me to Planet Exo III, or to the Motara Nebula, - anywhere but here! I run-walked straight into the nearest toilet stall, where I sat fully clothed, hiding. I waited, knowing that one, or both, of those two who had seen me would be talking to the restaurant manager about me and making the appropriate complaints. I was in big trouble.

I waited a long while and nothing happened. Finally, I worked up the courage to venture out of my hiding place. I stood for a long time at the sink, splashing and rubbing cool water on my pale sweating face. My headache pounded as I looked at myself in the mirror.

You're an idiot. You know that?

I eventually washed my hands and returned, timidly, to my place at the table, fearing with every step that I would be recognized.

"That took a while," Cheryl said with a smile. "Everything go okay?"

"Um, sure. Everything's good. Hey, can we go now?"

I've heard that most drownings happen when the victim is just a few feet from the surface; most car accidents within a few miles of the home. I just knew, as I speed-walked across that restaurant parking lot, a full baby hauler seat in my arms, that I was going to get stopped by someone, just a few yards from my car.

Come on, come on, come on, come on!

Why were my friends all taking so long to get into the car?

Gotta get away! Gotta get away! Come on, come on, come on.

Panicked chills raced down my spine as I drove us out of the parking lot. "You in a hurry?" one of them asked me.

"Noop."

Since that night, way back in 1995, every time I walk through the lobby of one of those very familiar lasagna joints that, oddly, still make me think of a Garden full of Olives, I remember that night in vivid detail.

In fact, next time you're standing in the waiting area of one of those famous restaurants, and you notice the ladies' room on one side and the men's room on the other, round male and female Roman profiles on the wall beside each door, I'm betting that you'll remember this story too. And no one will know why you're smiling.

You're welcome.

25

Because I Can

Sometimes I write a new chapter that has absolutely nothing in it, just for the fun of it.

This has been one of those times.

"Sextus, you asked how to fight an idea.
Well, I'll tell you how. With another idea."
                              The Tribune, Messala, *Ben Hur*

26

Perspectives from Behind Bars: A Lesson Painfully Learned

I could avert my eyes, but I couldn't close my ears. I stepped into place, in my normal wide stance, precisely positioned just behind the slot that separated the catcher from the batter, where I had an excellent view of both the pitcher and home plate, and I tried to ignore the vitriol that was being spewed from the bleachers on the first base side. It was starting to get to me. They had been at it for a while.

"Why do we always get the bad umpires?"

"This guy is awful!"

"He must have a kid on the other team."

"Call it fair, Blue!"

I don't mind a little chipping at my strike zone, or even insults to my eyesight. That stuff is rude, but it comes with the game, sometimes. But when they start to question my integrity or my honesty, that really hurts. In fact, it was making me mad. Just a few generations ago, a guy could find himself with a bullet in him for calling another man a cheater. Now, he yells it out in a crowd, in front of his kids.

It was Little League Baseball District All-Stars. There was a lot of formality and ceremony with this game - a lot of importance. The crowd was big, the field was in beautiful condition, and the two teams were in top form. Decorations were hung, the weather was magnificent, and music played on the loudspeakers between innings. These tournament games are my favorite umpire venues. Although I was the former Umpire In Chief of two combined nearby Little Leagues, an umpire clinic instructor and a veteran of over ten years, I was the junior umpire on the field that day - a position I rarely find myself in. My partner umpires that evening, Frank and Rob, were savvy officials with resumes that would impress almost anyone.

Both of them had umpired in various Little League Regional events. Both did high school ball as well. One of these guys had worked in two Little League World Series. If that wasn't enough, our two tournament officials, the Tournament Director and the Tournament Umpire In Chief were both umpires of the highest caliber, with more experience than I had. We five were what you'd call a true All-Star officiating crew.

But, today, it wasn't going well. If one could believe the fans and spectators on my right hand side, I hadn't done anything right all day.

The visiting team was up to bat. They were called the Rangers, and they were the team in the first base dugout; the side with the dissatisfied mommies and daddies, grandmas and grandpas. It was a very close, hard-fought game - so far. The pitcher started his wind-up motion, I relaxed my knees until my head came down to exactly the right height from the ground, and I locked in. Through the bars of my mask, I watched a beautiful fastball slip in, right on the outside corner, a little above the batter's knee. The batter didn't swing. Through my mind flashed the thought, "What a great pitch! Way to paint the corner, kid!"

I stood up without moving my feet, raised my right fist and, with a motion similar to knocking once on a door, I shouted, "Strike!" The shrieks and moans that came from the Rangers' grandstand were almost comical. Almost.

"What?!"

"Did he call that a strike?"

"What is wrong with this guy!"

I ignored them. Deep inside, I wanted to lash back. I might have, early in my umpire career, but that never works out. By this age, I knew better.

There were two outs. The Rangers were behind by one run, and really needed to get someone on base. The next pitch was inside. Smart pitcher.

An Ocelot in an Underwear Drawer

The batter swung a tight inside-out swing and hit the ball, sort of. The ball rolled into the infield grass a short distance and died there. It was the kind of poorly batted ball that I sometimes call a "wimpydinkle." The Mariners' pitcher was going to get to the ball easily. The only way batters ever make it to first base on a hit like that is when there's a terrible fielding error.

I rotated around the catcher - on his left side - and I scurried up the first base line several quick steps as the batter went full sprint mode up the line. I stopped, stood still and I locked in. Frank, the first base umpire, moved into position to watch what looked like it would be a routine put-out at first. The pitcher had picked up the ball and decided not to throw to first base. Instead, he was going to tag the batter/runner himself. He stepped confidently into the running lane, blocking the runner's path, and reached toward him with the ball in his glove for what was going to be an easy tag out. Suddenly, the runner made a move to his right, so quick that any football running back would have been proud, and he slipped right around the pitcher. The pitcher, caught off guard, suddenly reached as far as he could but, from where I was locked in, I could see daylight between his glove tip and the runner's left sleeve. He had missed the tag. The runner zigged back into the running lane and ran the short distance from there to first base. He ran through the bag pumping triumphant fists in the air.

"Yaaaaaay!"

"What a move!"

"Great job!"

The Rangers' grandstand erupted with applause and cheers for the clever batter.

Though Frank had rotated into position to make a call at first, I knew that, since the tag attempt had been made prior to the base, the call would be mine. I made eye contact with Frank and I paused for about a second, just to be sure that he was not going to make a call. This is a practice that I like to do to avoid two umpires calling a play at the same time. That can be very embarrassing, especially if they don't call the same thing.

Frank, looking into my eyes, did a very smart-looking one-handed point at me, and then I immediately burst into my call. "He's Out!"

209

Fist in the air. "Out of the base path!" I made an emphatic two-handed gesture in front of me, a lot like I was pushing something big to the right.

You would think that I had just robbed someone's home, the way that crowd came unglued on me. I was, at that moment, public enemy number one, and they were certain that I was a terrible, mean man who hated their sweet little boys. The vocal gymnastics went on for a long time. The Rangers' third base coach, as he walked across the infield, on his way to his dugout, angrily looked at me like I had a horn coming out of my forehead, but he wisely stayed quiet.

It had been a close call, but I was certain that, from my angle, I had the runner more than three feet outside of his originally established running path, as he had made his maneuver to avoid the tag. That's an easy out call, according to the rules. It was because he was attempting to avoid the tag that the three foot rule came into play. Had the runner swayed out of his base path at any other time, it would have been just fine to do so. But, according to the rules, if the maneuver happens when trying to avoid a tag, he gets three feet. No more than that. Besides, it wasn't as though they had been robbed of something wonderful - something that they had earned. The hit was a wimpy-dinkle; a poorly batted ball.

The game went on. The verbal abuse went on. It hurt. I've got to admit it. I didn't like it one bit. So many people were absolutely sure that I had blown that call, and they weren't afraid to say so, that I started to doubt myself.

Maybe they're right. Did I kick that call? Could I have been wrong? Maybe it wasn't quite three feet.

I would call a strike or a ball, and then wonder if I had gotten it right.

Is my strike zone junk tonight? They all sure think so! Maybe they're right.

More batters. More plays. Frank and Rob were doing a beautiful job out on the bases, and I stunk the place up.

I'll bet my two partners are really embarrassed at my lousy performance tonight. Oh please, just let this night be over soon!

"Strike three!" I called, just after a fastball had zinged in near the top of the strike zone. It had been a couple of innings since the base path violation call.

Angry voices from the Rangers' spectators area pelted me like rocks. There was one extra emphatic male voice that could be heard over the others. "Strike three? You've gotta be kidding me!"

In my mind I thought, "No, I'm not kidding you. In fact, I'm not doing anything for you. This isn't about you." But, I stayed quiet, as I bent down to sweep the plate clean with my small plate brush.

I've often daydreamed about walking out of the fenced area, between innings, climbing up into the bleachers and sitting down silently beside the loudest spectators, where I would watch quietly as the pitcher warms up. Then, just as warm-ups were ending, and just before the next inning began, I would stand up, in my daydream, and say to the spectator, "Wow, you're right. You really can see the strike zone better from way over here."

Ah, but it's only a daydream; a fantasy to delight the imagination. In real life, I silently stayed in, and I took it on the chin.

Finally, through a very close and exciting back-and-forth game, we had reached the bottom half of the sixth inning; the last inning of regulation play at this age level. The Rangers - the team with the angry fans - were now winning by a run. If they could just keep those Mariners from scoring, they would win the game and survive to play another day, ending the season for the other team. The elimination games are very often the most exciting because the players of those games have the most at stake.

The Mariners had a runner on second base. They all knew that, if they could figure out a way to get that runner in, they could tie the game and, at the very least, send it into an extra inning. The runner at second was one of their little fast guys, but they had two outs against them. Could they score that fast runner, or would the visiting team hold onto their tiny lead and take the narrow win?

It was close. It was intense. It could go either way. These are the types of All-Star games that I normally love to umpire. But I was not enjoying this one at all. My confidence was dented, my desire to be there was gone. My angry crowd had made me realize what a lousy umpire I am.

Just get through it. I can do this. It'll be over soon.

The pitcher for the Rangers was playing a great game. Secretly, I hoped that he would just slide three straight no-brainers across the plate, win the game, and we could all get out of here.

"Ping!" was the sound I heard as the Mariner player's aluminum bat launched the ball into Centerfield. It was a good hit. I cleared my mask - umpire lingo for "removed" - and I watched the ball sail. I could see that it was not going to be caught. Would that quick Mariners' runner be able to make it all the way home to tie the game? Maybe.

The Centerfielder picked the ball up from the grass and, fast as lightning, threw a laser shot to the shortstop. The runner, who had been on second base at the time of the pitch, was running like the wind. He had already rounded third and was speeding home to score the tying run. The shortstop, knowing full well how important that runner was, made an expert crow hop about-face and fired a beauty at the catcher, who was ready for it, standing helmetless in front of the plate.

With my mask in my left hand, I read the runner's angle, saw the throw coming in and adjusted my position to get the best view. Oh, what a throw! It's not often that boys of this age have an arm like that. It was wise of the Rangers' coach to put his best arm at shortstop. The throw was in time and on the money!

The Mariners' runner looked up in horror as the ball got there quicker than he'd thought possible, and planted itself securely in the catcher's mitt. On went the brakes. His plastic cleats dug in and he turned, like only a young boy can, and was immediately on his way back to third base, while the catcher gave chase.

Vocal bedlam issued from both sets of the bleachers as the Rangers' catcher threw the ball, just above the retreating runner's head to the waiting third baseman.

Brakes on again! Cleats dug in. The speedy Mariner was back on his way home, chased by the third baseman. The runner was in big trouble and he knew it. If the Rangers got him, it would mean the end of the game. His season would come crashing to a close.

The runner was stuck between third base and home, scurrying back and forth as multiple defenders got in on the action. Catch, chase, throw. Catch, chase, throw. We call this a "pickle," or a "hot box." Often, it's called a "rundown." No matter what you call it, it's the most exciting play in baseball.

Umpire Rob had rotated in to cover third base and I had the plate.

We watched as the runner was chased back and forth by the Rangers defenders, who were running him ragged.

The crowd, the coaches, the other players; all screamed things like, "Go, go, go!" or, "Get him! Tag him!" or, "Ruuuuun, Johnny ruuuun!"

The Rangers' first baseman had come down to the plate, to get into the play. A tall left-handed kid; he was a very good ball player. In came the throw. The lanky lefty caught it and took two or three hard running steps at the advancing Mariners' runner, who, yet again, was forced to turn and retreat toward third. Nearly exhausted, from the many short sprints he had run, he lost his balance as he started his run back toward third base. His stumbling momentum carried him badly to his left - into foul territory, as the Rangers' player chased him with the ball. The tired runner staggered, looking a little like a drunk man, and then regained his balance. Off he tore to third base, just as the throw was coming in from the tall defender that had been chasing him. The runner dove at the bag, the defender caught the ball, and laid the tag down in an instant. A cloud of dust rose around them.

"Safe!" shouted Rob with an emphatic two-arm safe mechanic. Somehow, the fatigued runner had slid into third, just under the tag. The game would continue. The runner was safe at third base. The crowd went nuts.

"Hey! He was out of the base path!"

"Didn't you see that, Blue?"

"He was out of the base path! What's wrong with you? Call him out!"

The Rangers' fans were at it again. No one had any argument with Rob's call at third. Everyone in the park knew that the runner had made it back safely. It wasn't Rob that they were mad at. It was the lousy good-for-nothing home plate umpire that they were livid with.

"He went way over to the side! How could you not see that?"

"You called it against us earlier! But you won't call it against them? This is unfair!"

"You've robbed us again, Blue! This game should be over!"

"He's been doing this to us all night!"

Male voices. Female voices. All angry.

I wanted to turn to them and defend myself - to explain the rule to them. I wanted to read to them, from the Little League Rule Book, that the three-foot base path rule doesn't apply in this play; that a runner can choose his own running lane and travel in as wide or as straight a line as he chooses, except when he's making a maneuver to avoid a tag. Only at that moment, while the tag is being applied, does the three-foot rule exist. When that off-balance stagger to the left had happened, there hadn't been a tag attempt. The ball had been eight or nine feet behind him, at that moment, in the hands of a running defensive player.

There was no call to make. I knew the rule and they didn't. There was nothing to do but continue the game. With splenetic shouts raining down on me from the angry mob, I moved back into my umpire's position.

"Hey! I asked you a question you stupid umpire! Answer me!"

I bent down and swept the plate, just as though I was totally deaf. "Batter, please," I said to the on-deck Mariners' batter at a conversational volume as I motioned toward the batter's box.

With all of the attention having been on the runner in the hot box, the batter had easily made it to second base. The Mariners now had two runners in scoring position with a new batter in the box. The exhausted runner at third base represented the tying run. The Mariner at second, if he could get in, would bring home the win.

Momentum had swung. The Mariners team and spectators, who had, only moments earlier, feared that defeat was looming, were now on their feet, excited and expectant. Eager shouts of encouragement poured in from my left as the new batter took his position.

As I nestled into my place, I glanced at the young batter. He twitched and bristled with excitement. His fingers gripped the bat, then relaxed, then gripped again. The tip of the bat, way above his head, rotated in tiny circles. Every muscle was coiled up, ready to strike. He had a look on his face that I could only describe as fierce.

This guy was ready, and the pitcher knew it.

You'd better walk this guy, I silently thought. *If you give him any kind of pitch that's close, he's going to take it deep.*

In came the first pitch. Low.

Smart pitcher.

Next pitch. Low. Again, the batter didn't swing.

If the Mariners end up winning this game, these Rangers spectators are going to kill me.

"Two balls, no strikes," I called out, displaying the count with my hands.

Here comes pitch number three. Low, but not terribly. It might even be at the bottom end of the strike zone.

"Ping!" Off it flew, through the gap in left center.

You guessed it! A bases-clearing double. Both runners came in and the game was over. The Mariners had come from behind, and they had won. They all spilled out of their dugout and happily mauled their three helmeted teammates. Aqua-blue uniformed players ran around in a frenzy, happily hopping up and down. Coaches hugged players. They hugged each other. Joyful shouts of triumph thundered from the Mariners' bleachers.

The sounds were very different, coming from the other side of the spectator area.

"Worst officiating I've ever seen, Blue!"

"That guy was out of the base path! Are you blind?"

"We should protest this game!"

One curly-haired pear-shaped baseball mom screeched, "You were robbed, Rangers! Hold your heads high! You're the rightful winners!"

Normally, umpires wait for each other and walk off of a field together after a game, and usually out the side of the winning team. This time, though, I wasn't waiting for my umpire brothers. I made a beeline for the gate and made good a hasty escape. I wanted out of there, away from the abuse, away from the hate. I needed to remove myself from the area, before someone said or did something that was over the line. Most of all, I wanted to hide my shame.

Man, I stunk tonight.

Into the small umpire's room I dashed. It was the little wooden scorekeeper box of the nearby softball field that we were using as an umpire's quarters during this tournament. It was hot in there and cramped, with all of our equipment bags and other gear, but I was happy for a place of refuge.

I grabbed a water bottle from the cooler and attacked it, almost as if I believed it had some magical calming properties, then I immediately started getting out of my sweat-soaked umpire gear. As I slid the big hard shell chest protector over my head, I thought about the umpire evaluation that I would be receiving in a few minutes from my Umpire In Chief. Greg was a great UIC, and I respected him. In many ways, he had been my umpire mentor for several years, and I knew that he wouldn't hold back. He was an honest man and he would tell me like it is. There would be no sugarcoating. This had not been a good performance for me. I was in for a solid chewin'-out, I knew.

I heard the sound of feet coming up the wooden steps outside, and I braced myself. In walked Rob, my third base umpire partner. I slid a sweaty shin guard off of my leg and I tossed him a water bottle.

"Okay, Rob. What've you got for me?" I asked him. I wanted to just get it all over with quick; like a fast yank of a painful loose tooth.

"You might have moved your head a little much on a few pitches. See if you can lock-in a little more." He turned toward his equipment bag, hanging on a nail behind him, and he started to whistle.

That's it? Isn't he going to scold me for being such a bad umpire? For my terrible strike zone? My incorrect calls?

Whistling was all I got.

Then came Frank. What a great umpire. He was a serious umpire dude who found a way to look better in his uniform than everyone else did; more umpirish, somehow.

"Your thoughts, Frank?" I asked him. "Let me have it."

He twisted the lid off of a plastic water bottle and smiled. "Maybe you could speed up the transitions a little between innings." Then he went right into changing out of his damp blue umpire shirt.

Puzzled, I removed the ball bag from my belt and I folded it. *They're just being kind. Leaving the shouting for the boss.* I placed the folded ball bag into its compartment in my big black equipment bag and I wondered why it was taking Greg so long to get here. I didn't want to endure what I knew was coming, but I didn't like this waiting either. It was a lot like waiting for Dad to come home from work, knowing that I was going to be in big trouble when he did.

After all, my strike zone had been a dumpster fire tonight. My calls were iffy, my quality was poor. I suddenly realized that Greg was late getting to the shack because he and Cory, the Tournament Director, were probably having to listen to a bunch of complaints.

Oh no. He's really going to be in a bad mood when he gets in here! I'm done. He'll never trust me to do an important game like this again.

Umpire gear stashed and sweaty shirts changed, we all sat down on our folding chairs and we waited.

Finally, after several minutes, the door swung open. In walked my umpire hero; the boss, Greg Handley.

Here we go! Let's get this over with. Has he always been this tall? Should I wait for him to speak, or should I just start things with a big 'I'm Sorry?'

"Evening, gentlemen," he said. "Quite a game."

He started with Frank. No matter how good an umpire does in a game, a good Tournament UIC almost always has something to say to you in your evaluation. His comments to Frank were brief and, truthfully, I didn't listen to them.

Then it was Rob's turn. Once again, Greg's evaluation comments were short. Well, of course they were. These guys were Frank and Rob. Great umpires who had just called a great game.

"Chris!" He almost shouted it as he swiveled toward me on his tiny black stool. He stared at me for a moment with no expression. I held my breath.

"You get better and better every time I see you work! That was one of the best umpired games I have seen in a long time! Great work, my friend!"

What? Did he just… what?

Frank and Rob, both standing now, smiled down on me like proud uncles as I sat before them, stunned.

"Your strike zone tonight was consistent and accurate, and I know that those two pitchers were challenging you on the corners all night," said Greg. "Those boys were good!"

I didn't know what to say. Had I been wrong about my epic amounts of stinkitude? Had the Rangers' spectators all been wrong as well?

"Great job on the two base path plays. You nailed them both - your call in the third and then your no-call in the sixth. I know that the spectators wanted a call on that last one, but you did it right. There was no tag.

"Guys, we have a big championship game on Tuesday, and I need an umpire team that I can trust. Are you three available? I want a solid crew working that game. Chris, will you be here?"

"Uh… sure. Yeah, I… um… Yes! Yes, I will be here!"

"Good," he replied in a very businesslike manner, writing names on his clipboard. "By the way, that was a tough crowd tonight. You did a good job not letting them get into your head."

"Thanks."

No, I didn't.

Ten months later, I was working the plate of a Little League Juniors division midseason tournament game. Juniors is Little League's fourteen-year-old division. It's one of my favorite age groups to umpire, because they play on full ninety-foot baselines and they have open stealing and pick-offs. Many of the players are as large as I am.

I had worked a lot of baseball since that crazy and memorable Mariners/Rangers All-Star game of the previous June. Today, I was at my favorite midseason tournament. Teams came from far and near to play at this prestigious event. So did umpires. There were seasoned experienced umpires from all over Western Oregon and Washington. I was, once again, working with great names. There was a lot of atmosphere. It was exciting.

My first three games of the day had gone well. Good competition. Good sportsmanship. Good baseball. But, this fourth one, not so much. So angry and argumentative were the fans of one of the teams that I had asked a passerby to go get a member of the tournament staff to be present. I didn't know what these spectators were capable of, and I wanted someone there with some authority, standing back watching things progress.

I didn't know it, but Fred was also there. Fred was, at that time, the Umpire In Chief of the state. On top of that, he was the Assistant UIC of the entire Western Region. He was standing back where I hadn't noticed him, I would later learn, watching the game.

"You were safe, Matthew!" an elderly woman shouted at a young player whom I had just called out on a tag at the plate; a play that I hadn't even thought of as very close. "This umpire is out to get us!"

A man yelled, "Are you kidding me, Blue?" Ahh, the old *are-you-kidding-me*. I wish I had a dollar for every…

"That was a terrible call!"

This crowd was every bit as bad as that Rangers All-Star crowd had been last June. Though they were a different set of people in a different age group, I couldn't help but notice that they were from the same part of Portland. Hmmm, tough neighborhood, I guess.

A little later, I was standing to the side, watching a relief pitcher take some warm-up pitches. A wild pitch made it by the catcher, who got up to fetch it. I was prepared for this occurrence and I said, "Let it go, Catch. I've got'cha' covered," I tossed him a new ball, and then I walked over to pick up the stray one. This is one of the things that I like to do, to keep things moving along. I also do it as a courtesy to the catcher; the hardest-working guy out there.

"It's nice to know that you can do one thing right, Blue," came a man's voice from the angry side of the spectator area. I paused a moment as I bent down to pick the ball up. *Did I really just hear that?*

"Come on," the same voice continued. "You know you stink today."

I allowed myself a little crooked smile, as I thought, *Hmm, I've never heard that one before. Kudos, my frustrated friend.*

"Hey, Chris." This voice came from Big Dave. He was sitting in the bleachers on the friendlier side of the diamond. Having umpired around the area for so many years, there were a lot names and faces that I had picked up on. I didn't know him well, but I did know his name, and I knew which kid was his. I moved over toward him, and he continued.

"What ever happened to baseball being fun?" he asked, as he shot an irritated look toward the parents on the other side.

"I'm having fun, Dave! Aren't you?" I asked him with a big smile.

He paused a moment and then he too smiled. "Yeah!" His smile grew as he nodded his head several times. "Yeah, I am." He continued to nod and smile. "Thanks for the reminder."

I looked out at the relief pitcher, still throwing his warm-ups, and I pointed at him firmly. All umpire gestures are done decisively and crisply. It kind of goes with the uniform. "One more, if you want it, Pitch!" I looked back at Big Dave, smiling, and I gave him a wink, just before I slipped my shiny black mask down over my face.

"Batter, please."

"*Cultivate the habit of being grateful for every good thing that comes to you, and give thanks continuously. And because all things have contributed to your advancement, you should include all things in your gratitude.*

Ralph Waldo Emerson

27

The Thread from Which We Hang

I didn't even know what he was talking about. I just knew that he was pulling the car into the wrong parking lot. *What's a microwave?*

Often, when we went out to eat as a family, my parents chose pizza. Our town had a Shakey's. It was one of those great old-fashioned pizza parlor chains with heavily-lacquered wooden bench tables, red stained windows and a small stage where they sometimes had a fat man in a striped shirt, a bow tie, and a flat-topped straw hat, playing Joplin on a piano. For the kids, there was a small raised platform from which they could watch through windows, into the kitchen, where the cooks were making the pizzas. I could remember loving that when I was little, but now, as a big mature eleven-year-old, I was a little beyond that. At least, that was what I told myself when I jealously watched my younger brother up at the pizza window.

When it wasn't pizza, it was Mexican. We did a lot of Mexican food outings. When it came to dinners out, our family was a two-trick pony.

Jimboy's Tacos was a favorite for my brother and me, and that was where we were going tonight. Admittedly, Jimboy's probably wasn't what you should truly call authentic Mexican, but it was sure tasty; and it was affordable. On the east end of the tiny California town of Placerville, there were several small shopping strips along Broadway. Jimboy's was tucked into one of those, but not the one that we were pulling into now.

This other small line of shops - the one that, to my chagrin, we were driving into instead of Jimboy's - contained an appliance store that was doing a Summer Sidewalk Sale. They had banners and balloons and other decorations, and a lot of merchandise and people out in the parking lot.

A little while later, we were in the middle a roped-off area of the parking lot, enjoying a microwave oven demonstration. The polyester-clad salesman had just tried explaining to us about how this revolutionary new appliance would bombard foods and liquids with microwave radiation, which would excite the molecules of the item, causing it to heat.

"But, it's perfectly safe, Mr. Ford. It's not the same kind of radiation that you hear about in those Martian invasion movies. It won't make your food radioactive, ha ha." Yeah, he may have laughed at that preposterous idea, but I wonder how many of us had that exact fear - at least for a few minutes, when we first heard about heating food with microwave radiation. I know that it more than crossed my mind.

"There we go," said the man. "See how quickly it got that water boiling?"

No Way, I thought, silently. *Boiling already? But it's only been a couple of minutes. There is no way..."* I leaned into the conversation, just enough to better see the mysterious machine. I looked into the see-through plastic door at a small clear coffee cup. The water inside was at a mad boil. There was no mistaking it. I had just witnessed a miracle.

The salesman opened the oven door, and its electrical running sounds stopped automatically. I stepped back to give all of the radiation plenty of room to escape into the air.

"Reach in there and grab that handle, Mister Ford."

No! You'll burn yourself! Don't do it Dad! These were my thoughts as Dad reached in. Of course he'll burn himself! We always have to use pan holders when we heat something to a boil. It doesn't matter whether it's on the stovetop or in the oven. I almost peed myself when Dad, big smile on his face, held the mug for all of us to see. A few small bubbles still rose in that steaming water, but the glass cup handle was, apparently, just fine to touch.

Amazed doesn't come close to describing how I felt. Now we can boil water in two minutes, and it doesn't even make the cup handle hot. Now we can cook entire meals in just moments. This was like putting men on the moon. This was a game changer.

I don't care how much it costs. We have got to get one of these things, I silently screamed. Outwardly, all I did was smile. We kids didn't tell - or even suggest - to an adult what they should or should not do. It just wasn't done in 1979. Not in our home, anyway.

Happily, my parents felt the same way that I did, and we left that little strip mall, the proud owners of a brand new microwave oven. I couldn't wait to see what it would do to a banana… or a lollipop, a golf ball… or a grasshopper… heh.

Just a moment later, we were cheerfully settling down into an extra-large booth in the middle of Jimboy's Mexican Restaurant. Jimboy's was very different then than it is now. At the time of this writing, Jimboy's has grown into a chain of very nice, stand-alone restaurants in multiple cities across California and Nevada. Back then, it was a little shop in a strip mall; in a tiny California mountain town.

I understand that Jimboy's has made another significant adjustment since last I ate there. To this day, over thirty-five years later, I place my cheese into the shell first when I make a taco. Before the meat, before the lettuce, tomato or anything else is permitted to desecrate my carefully chosen shell of deliciousness, the cheese must go first. It is a moral imperative.

And I'm not the only one! Last time our two families ate together, which happened to be on a taco night, I watched, approvingly, as my brother inserted a generous handful of shredded cheddar into an empty taco shell. He raised his eyebrows at me, and he asked, "Know why I do it this way?"

"Of course I do," I confidently replied. "'Cause you're a Ford! And that's what Ford's do, at least the smart ones." I tossed a crooked grin at my wife. "And… because you remember the excellent training that we received at Jimboy's!"

"Him too?" Shanon's wife Erinn exclaimed in surprise.

"Him too," my wife replied, nodding, not without a touch of sarcasm. "Cheese first."

We held our cheesy creations aloft, my brother and I, and we proudly saluted each other with the only two properly constructed tacos in the room.

I have not been to a Jimboy's in over thirty-five years, but, while I was researching this writing project, as authors often do, I learned, from pictures on their website, that they no longer practice the cheese-first principle, though I do understand that their tacos are still excellent.

So, it is we - my brother and I - who must take this knowledge into the wilderness of error, lest it be forever lost, and enlighten as many as we can. Cheese first, my friends!

Comfortable in our booth that night, and looking forward to some good warm eatin's, I was thinking about our new microwave oven, and wondering if we could reheat Jimboy's in it. The appetizing smells coming from the restaurant kitchen were making me realize how hungry I was. *Maybe we should buy a bunch of extra food tonight. We can have Jimboy's again tomorrow! At Home! It's like we've entered a whole new world of possibilities, with our very own microwave oven!* I was grinning about that wonderful thought when I heard a loud slapping sound immediately to my left.

Between our booth and the one beside us there was only a short wall, a little less than shoulder high. There were people in that booth. I had subconsciously registered their presence when we had taken our seats, but I hadn't given them any thought.

More loud slapping.

We all turned our heads in the direction of the sound. There was a boy of about my age sitting a little less than arm's length from the short wall that separated us. He had glasses on and a buzz cut hairdo. He had some kind of small metal device taped to the front of his throat, just above his collar. Now that he had my attention, he stopped slapping the top of the wall and gave me an intense look as he reached up and touched his throat device with one hand.

He twisted his face a little, like it might hurt, and he made a strange growl sound. I glanced past him at his family. There was an older man sitting beside him, probably his grandfather. Beyond Grandpa, in the restaurant aisle, there was an empty wheelchair. I had not been around handicapped people much at that age, and I wasn't sure how to act.

He shook his head. He seemed a little frustrated. He reached for his throat device again and tried once more to speak.

"You… you, ehmemma… meee…" I could see that it took some work for him to communicate. His words weren't spoken so much as growled.

I looked at him for a moment. Seeing what must have looked like confusion on my face, he started again. "You… lehma… rrrr." He paused, and looked down. Then he looked back at me and was opening his mouth to try again.

"Remember?" I asked him.

He smiled and nodded his head.

How do I tell him no? He wants so badly for me to know who he is, but I don't. What do I do?

We stared at each other for several seconds, when his mother intervened. She was across the table from the boy.

"Hi," she said with a friendly smile, looking at everyone at our table. "I'm so sorry to disturb you folks." Then she looked right at me. "Do you remember a boy named Johnny Bell?"

It took me a moment, then my eyes bulged to twice their normal size. Reading my expression, his grandfather spoke up, "John had an accident."

I looked back into the smiling eyes of my schoolmate and recess football comrade, John Bell. He was happy to have been recognized.

John and I had never been great friends at school, but we did play together sometimes. A grade younger than I was, he used to join us, sometimes, in our big two-hand-touch football games on the playground. He was a good athlete and a fast runner - tough to catch when he had the ball.

Now, he was living in a wheelchair and he had a strange hole in the front of his throat. I would learn, later that night, from Dad, about tracheostomies. I had never heard of such a thing, at eleven.

One of my favorite things about Jimboy's was the duck-hunting game they had on the front wall. A customer could walk up to the front of the store and drop a quarter into a metal receptacle, and carry the game's control box back to a table. It wasn't a very fancy or technical game, but I sure enjoyed it. From one's table, by pressing the single red button on the box, a player could control when one of the three men on the screen, hanging above the restaurant front windows, would fire his rifle. A white target blob that sort of looked a little bit like a duck would fly over the top of the three stationary riflemen, and then you would press the button to make the highlighted guy shoot his own white dot. If you timed it correctly and led the target just right, your dot would hit the other dot and make it go away. Sorry, duck! The game kept track of the score on a running total. I was pretty good at it.

John and I sat side by side, and we played that game over and over, separated by that little stub wall. After a while, Shanon and I had moved to John's booth and his mother had moved to ours. The parents all chatted as Shanon, John, Grandpa and I laughed and shot white dots. We had a great time.

It was during their chat that my parents learned some details of John's accident. He had been racing bicycles with friends on a quiet neighborhood street, when a dog, excited by all the action and wanting to play, ran in front of John. He hit the dog, broadside, and flew over his handlebars. Hitting head-first on the street, he suffered a traumatic brain injury. He was in a coma for more than a month.

If this bike crash had happened during a time when kids rode bikes with helmets, it might have turned out differently. Probably so. But, we didn't wear them back then. It wasn't even something that we thought about.

"You have no idea how much Johnny's been needing this," his mother told my parents as she wiped tears from her eyes. "I haven't seen him laugh in a long time. It's been so hard."

Normally, we were only allowed to play that duck hunting game a couple of times each. After all, "Quarters don't grow on trees." That evening, thanks - I think - to my dad and John's grandpa, the quarters just kept magically appearing.

Later that night, as I lay awake in my bed, I thought about John. I was glad that we had bumped into him and his family at Jimboy's. I was happy that he had laughed and played. It felt good to have been a part of that. But I had to wonder, would he ever walk again? Would he ever again attend a regular school, like I do? It occurred to me that he had been, just a few months ago, no different than the rest of us. Could it have been me in that wheelchair? Could it have been my brother? Of course it could have.

All of our work and play, all of our goals and plans and hopes, could just go away in a moment, or change to something that we'd never dreamed of. It was a lot to think about.

At eleven, I hadn't been in many situations, so far, to call up thoughts like those. It was sobering. I cried for John that night.

As much as it bothered me - this new understanding of how easy it is to lose everything - I told myself, as I lay in bed, that I would not let it scare me. I was certain that, if John could, he would love to run and play and take risks again. Yes, I thought, he would probably even get back onto that bike.

Life is fragile. It's a huge, loud, funny-smelling, heartbreaking mess of laughter, pain, joy and sorrow; beach towels, raincoats and barbecue sauce. And it can all be wrecked in an instant. But, I think, as I lay there that night realizing all of this, that I also, in my eleven-year-old mind, was able to see how important it all is. Instead of scaring me into timidity, hiding in a shell of protection, my chance meeting with John had made me realize how good I have it. And I was going to appreciate it and enjoy it as long as I could, because, who knows? I might be the next John Bell.

Though I've never spoken of it, that I can remember, with anyone in my family, that night with John Bell at Jimboy's Tacos has stayed with me as a memory that I will always cherish.

How I wish that I could talk with John now, these thirty-six years later. Is he alive? Did he ever walk again? Does he remember me, and that night of tacos and duck hunting? What lessons did he learn from those months and years that followed his accident? Would it interest him to learn that, long ago, when he was at his weakest, he helped someone to better appreciate life? I'll bet it would.

28

Forty Feet Down, Fifty Years to Go

With Toes buried in warm beach sand, the rest of me covered in sunscreen, I looked out over the crashing waves and the glistening tropical blue. On a towel beside me lay my sniffling, mentholatum-smelling new bride; achy head wrapped in a moist towel, Kleenex box at the ready. What a terrible time to be sick. Sinus pressure had nearly driven her crazy during our long trans-pacific flight a few days earlier, as her congested ears had refused to pop.

Today was about three days into our Maui Honeymoon. She lay beside me, in her green bikini, trying hard not to be miserable. Even sick, she was beautiful to me, and, as I had so many times these last few days, I wanted to pinch myself to know that I wasn't dreaming. *Is she really mine? Did she really marry me?*

Unaware of the love-struck dummy admiring her every inch, she sneezed hard, then moaned in pain. I smiled sadly. *So cute, even sick! What is this beautiful creature doing with a lummox like me?* That this tiny, sweet, lovely blonde would marry this beaknose pencilneck was a mystery to me and all who knew me. The moment she did, though, she made me "an inspiration to ugly men everywhere," a title with which I have proudly referred to myself ever since.

On the southern coast of the Hawaiian island of Maui, there lies a beautiful hidden beach that we had accidentally discovered by following the bumper of our rented, bright red Geo Metro. "Following the bumper" is a lifelong Chris-ism for driving without a specific goal or destination. Sometimes I just go, and follow my bumper, taking me wherever it leads - which it always does. Down a random dirt road, a little south of the resort town of Kihei, our trusty Metro's bumper had led us. There we found a long picturesque beach; Makena Beach it was called, we would later learn. Since then, this is where we had come almost every afternoon.

Sitting beside her in the sand, I smiled as I recalled the incident of a few minutes before. Trying hard to put on a happy face for her new husband, she had jogged down to the water and joined me to play in the surf. Up and down we bobbed as the waves rolled beneath us. The warm water felt wonderful as we laughed and played together in the tropical blue, holding hands, kissing and pulling each other close between waves. Looking back toward the beach, I saw four or five young guys sitting on a log, just beyond our towels. *Hmm, those boys weren't there a few minutes ago,* I thought. I noticed that they were all watching us intently and I wondered why. *Self-appointed lifeguards?* I thought with a grin. *Probably not.*

Within five minutes of their arrival, it happened. I learned why they had come. A big wave hit us hard; a wave that, I would later learn, Makena Beach is known for. My feet spun up over my head as salt-water flooded my sinuses. Eyes burning, I saw the wave's tube as it rolled violently over us. Spinning, flipping, I smashed, face first, into the gritty sand. Pain shot through me. Dazed and disoriented, I stood and looked for Cheryl. I didn't see her. Then, out of the foam she arose in knee-high water, sand pebbles stuck to her face, soaked blonde hair hugging her head.

Holding her head in her hands, she moaned, "Ohhh... *cough! cough!* ...that was awful!" Her eyes met mine. "That hurt so bad. Are you okay?"

Yeah... I'm fine," I replied. "Umm, Honey?" I continued. "I think that's yours."

She paused for a moment and saw that I was pointing. She turned to face the beach, looking in the direction of my outstretched arm, toward the little bright green object that was working its way up the sand on a small wave. It took her ocean-thrashed mind a moment to register what the item was, then, recognizing it to be her bathing suit top, she looked down at herself, screamed a short, cute yelp sound and covered herself up with her arms as she ran toward the wayward garment.

I glanced up at the young men on the beach log. They turned to each other with triumphant smiles as high-fives were offered all around. *Clever*, I thought, and I stifled a laugh as I watched them get up and walk down the beach, no doubt looking for another bikini-wearing tourist to appreciate.

As she lay now, recovering from her embarrassing body slam, congested and sick, I told her, "I'm going to take a little walk."

"Mmmmm…" I heard from somewhere beneath the towels.

At the west end of the beach - the right-hand end, as you face the sea - there rose a huge rock. It was about two stories tall and wide enough to span the entire depth of the beach and extend well out into the crashing surf. I walked to the vertical face of the rock and I saw what looked like a good handhold. I climbed and found another. Then another. This was too perfect. On I climbed, up the rock's face, finding hand and foot holds in exactly the right places. Curiosity led me onward. Now atop the giant rock, I walked its flat upper surface. In a sandy place, I found a footprint. It was pointing west - the direction that I was walking. Where were these clues leading me?

At the rock's far edge, I looked down into a beautiful secluded cove. Trees leaned out over emerald water. It looked like a scene from a beautiful tropical calendar. Fifty or sixty people were there. Some sun-bathed on towels, others chatted and laughed as they waded in the shallow blue, while still others bodysurfed the waves. None of them wore a stitch of clothing. *Ha-hah! I've got to tell Cheryl about this… someday.*

A few days later, Cheryl was feeling a lot better. Today we were going to enjoy our honeymoon's one big excursion. Today I would SCUBA dive for the first time. Today Cheryl would choose more sensible swimwear. It would take our tour boat over an hour to reach Molokini. The whole way there, I kept thinking of how much our boat resembled "The Minnow," and I couldn't get rid of the tune in my head. "Just sit right back and you'll hear a tale, a tale of a fateful trip…" You know the song. And you'll probably be singing it to yourself the rest of the day. You're welcome.

Cheryl brought a roll of toilet paper today to blow her nose on if the need should arise. The entire roll took off on a strong breeze shortly after our departure. Off it flew on the wind, unraveling like a large party favor as it flew higher and higher, into the vastness of the Pacific. *Litterbug!*

On the way to Molokini, I would attend a deckside SCUBA lesson. As I understood it (or misunderstood it, which is more likely), in 1990, a certified Dive-master could take up to four uncertified dive students down at a time, provided they all attended a class. My small group and I congregated on the boat's aft deck for our SCUBA lesson while Cheryl and her less adventuresome classmates attended their own snorkel class up front.

I learned a lot in that class. For instance, I learned that it is possible for a handsome, French-accent-wielding Dive-master to deliver a non-stop full-hour flirt attack on his attractive young female newlywed SCUBA students, right in front of their new husbands, while providing a surprisingly informative dive lesson. Well done, Pierre!

I had heard of "the bends" before, but, Monsieur Lady-Slayer helped me to understand it better. He explained that, because SCUBA air is compressed, it is very important that we allow ourselves to "equalize," or acclimate to the pressures, as we descend into the depths and arise again later. To ascend too quickly from deep water after breathing compressed air would cause a horrible, painful condition called "the bends;" something akin to bubbles in the blood - a condition that can even be fatal.

I also learned, that day, that SCUBA is an acronym for Self Contained Underwater Breathing Apparatus. There's your cool word for today.

Have you heard of Molokini, my Reader-Friend? Picture a round volcano crater, like a big salad bowl, whose rim is just high enough on one side to peek above the ocean's surface, but not quite tall enough on the other side. Better yet, Google it. It's cool!

The result is a protected, round area that is teeming with life. Inside there are no dangerous currents and no fishing or hunting. It is a rich, abundant, bowl-shaped wildlife preserve. Boats could, in 1990, cruise into the crater, provided they had the right permits, attach to special anchor points, and stay there to play and explore. It was an under-water paradise; a must-see for divers and snorkelers.

After the long trip out, and a full hour of learning, it was finally go-time. I was pumped! I sat on the swim step at the back of the boat, mask on my face, flippers on my feet. We slipped beneath the surface, my instructor and I, and we slowly descended down the anchor chain. My first thought was of how loud my breathing was and how quiet everything else was. We stopped partway down, and he pointed at my face; a signal that we had discussed earlier in class. This meant that my eyeballs were nearly being sucked out of my head. I blew out through my nose as I had been taught, decreasing the amount of vacuum in my mask, and I received a thumbs-up.

After an appropriate amount of time at that depth, eyeballs where they belonged and bodies equalized to my instructor's satisfaction, we continued downward to deeper water. Finally, we reached the ground level, forty feet below the boat. I had never seen a boat from below. What an odd perspective. From there, Flippered Felipe and I Peter-Panned our way across the colorful crater, over an intricate floor of coral and anemones and myriad tropical plants, to a small sandy place where we stopped.

He held up an index finger as if to say, "I will be back in one minute," and I watched him swim away to fetch SCUBA rookie number two. As he swam, I smiled at how much he looked like a giant frog from this angle.

Soon, I was alone. I had never been underwater. I had never breathed compressed air. I had never felt so completely alone, so incredibly out of place, so dangerously unqualified. *What am I doing here?*

Millions of gallons of water pressed down on me. Fear! It was sudden and powerful. Pressure! Drowning! Crushing! My breathing became erratic; short, shallow. Scared. Alone. Underwater. Death! Panic! I was hyperventilating, I knew.

I wanted to quit - to just give up and get out of there; back to the surface where I could see the sky and breathe my own air; back to where things made sense, and it would have been so easy to do it. I could just swim straight up. *But, "the bends!" I can't forget about that!*

Through my panic, I hurriedly reasoned that I had only three choices. I could swim straight to the surface and escape the crush, taking the consequences, bends and all. Or, I could stay where I was, be a wimp, lose my self-control and probably drown. My third choice was to quickly grow up, take control, and conquer this thing. Even a goofed-up knucklehead in the middle of a submarine freak-out could see that there was only one choice.

I can do this… slow it down… slow it down… one long breath… good, now another… slowly… slowly… breathe… in… out… in… out… focus on the next breath… in… out… good…

Little by little, I calmed myself. I listened to the bubbles that came from my regulator with every breath. I looked around me as I slowed my breathing… *kinda pretty here…*

I looked into the distance, through remarkably clear water, at the strange shape that was the boat's bottom, and I saw four giant frog legs hanging from its rear swim step. A moment later, two bubbling flipper-wearing humans were working their way down the anchor chain. Relief washed over me. *I'm not alone.* My thumping pulse, no longer audible in my ears, slowed to a more normal rate.

Soon they were with me at the one sandy spot in this corner of the crater; the scene of my private meltdown - my secret forty foot freak-out. You've heard of a bloomin' idiot? I had bloomed in a spectacular way.

Our guide gave us his I'll-be-right-back gesture and then he was gone; back to the boat for the next SCUBA noob. My new companion, a young muscly long-haired blonde guy, looked at me through his mask and, with a delighted smile in his eyes, gave me a two-handed thumbs-up. I returned his happy salute - because I could! Unlike Chris-of-three-minutes-ago, Chris-of-right-now was truly happy. We learned that it's not so easy to do a high-five underwater, but we got it done.

Soon, five bubble-spewing, flipper-flopping humans glided through the clear warm waters, over colorful flowers, waving grasses, and clams the size of car tires; one dive-master and his four astounded mesmerized pupils. It felt like flying. It was wonderful.

Fish of every size and shape. Colorful giant anemones. Purples. Pinks. Bright yellows. Blazing reds. I was surrounded by an explosion of beauty, soaring through a world so alien to me, though I knew that it was we who were the aliens. *I didn't know that it could be like this. Lord, your work is great. What a masterpiece You have painted.*

Out of a hole in the coral protruded the large and frightening, yet beautiful, purple polka-dotted head of a moray eel. Unblinking, it stood still with its bright white mouth open, displaying sharp teeth and powerful jaws. I knew that it could have bitten my finger off like a pretzel. Then I noticed that there were many of them, stone-still in the flow, like a forest of fanged statues. A shadow suddenly covered me for a second, and I looked up to see a large manta ray gracefully gliding over me.

The two pretty young ladies with whom our SCUBA instructor had flirted throughout his class swam on either side of him. They had no choice, since he was holding tightly to their hands. What a lady's man.

He eventually led us to a wide open area filled with every kind of fish. This seemed to be a popular fish hangout. I felt a tap-tap on my arm. It was my teacher. He reached into his backpack and produced a loaf of bread. I remember, for some reason, that it was Roman Meal wheat bread. Using his fingernails, he tore into the brown plastic wrap of my loaf, creating a large hole midway down its length. He pointed at the hole as he handed the loaf to me. Then he pointed all around us at the swirling throng of fish.

I nodded to him as I took the loaf, and I watched him swim away to take bread to my classmates. I tore at the plastic to make the hole larger. As sea water soaked into the bread, I held the loaf at each end and I squeezed my hands together, crushing the loaf lengthwise, then I pulled them apart, over and over, as if I was playing a small plastic-wrapped accordion. With every push and pull, more soggy bread drifted out of the hole, muddying the water around me with hundreds of gooey crumbs and chunks. Soon I was surrounded by fish greedily inhaling bread pieces. I was at the center of a full blown feeding frenzy. Tall skinny blue fish, bright orange fat fish. Fish of every color. They ranged from no larger than my pinky, to the size of my head. All over me they twirled and darted; under my arms, through my legs, so many of them! My high-fivin' dive-friend would later tell me that I'd had so many fish swarming me that he could barely see me. I tore more bread loose from the wrapper and I waved a large squishy bread mass around in front of me, clenched in my fist. A dirty trail of bread-strewn water followed my hand as I drew giant swirls and arcs in front of me. Beautiful fish of every kind chased my hand as I painted a living fish mural.

"Ouch!" A sharp stinging pain hit the end of my other index finger. So enthralled had I been with what my left hand was doing, I hadn't noticed the big ugly fish that had been moving in on my right hand.

With a bulging round eye, a massive dark colored, torpedo shaped fish, two feet long or more, regarded me as he fearlessly glided slowly by, triangular teeth bulging. I looked at my bleeding fingertip and I laughed, or as close to laughing as one can with canned air being forced between one's teeth. When you're expecting wheat bread, I'll bet human finger tastes pretty bad.

It was a great trip, filled with these and many other adventures, including awkward luau hula dancing; making Cheryl carsick on the winding Hana Highway; getting our Metro stuck in Maalaea Bay beach sand from following its bumper too well; and doing the all-time greatest icky-icky dance after walking through the thickest spider web I've ever felt. It was a wonderful honeymoon, Cheryl's illness notwithstanding.

The island of Maui is a beautiful place, filled with friendly people and spectacular scenery. Though it has been over twenty-six years, at the time of this writing, I understand that it has changed very little. The water is still warm. The food is still good. And teenage boys still hang out at Makena Beach to watch the predictable rogue waves tear bathing suits off.

These were our first days together as husband and wife; the start of a union so blessed and beautiful; a family so committed and love-filled. I don't believe that there has ever been a young man more happy and thankful than that goofy, skinny, sunburnt kid - Maui, Hawaii, 1990. Though I don't look so much like a kid as I did then, nor am I as skinny; my happiness and thankfulness have only grown. Thank You, God, for my wonderful lady, who still looks as good to me as she did on that island beach. With Your help, may I always strive to be worthy of her.

May you have Enough…
Enough happiness to keep you sweet,
Enough trials to keep you strong,
Enough sorrow to keep you human,
Enough hope to keep you happy,
Enough failure to keep you humble,
Enough success to keep you eager,
Enough wealth to meet your needs,
Enough enthusiasm to look forward,
Enough friends to give you comfort,
Enough faith to banish depression,
Enough determination to make each day better
than yesterday.
May you have enough

Poet Unknown

29

When it's Ten

Pain.

Pain almost unspeakable.

As if they had wills of their own, my hands writhed and twisted before me like grotesque claws. My shallow breathing was not getting me enough oxygen, so my vision was starting to fade at the edges. I knew that I would soon faint if I didn't get my breathing under control. I welcomed the thought.

In spite of the nausea, the dizziness and the strange peripheral blindness that was coming on, almost all I knew was pain. I was only dimly aware of my surroundings. Only the pain was real. All else was a blur. Bright lights. Concerned faces. A beeping sound. A nurse pressing a needle into my arm. *Was that a needle or a pencil?* Even that hurt more than it should; so much more. I looked down, expecting to see a horrible wound, but saw only a standard IV protruding from my vein. I watched as he taped it to my arm.

Immediately, my body reminded me that my arm was the least of my concerns. Deep inside my torso, just below the ribs, lived a raging monster. Pain pierced me; it increased its attack and it tortured me. In my weak and despairing condition, I tried not to cry. *Men don't cry! Men don't cry!* Tears came. I cried.

For what may have been the tenth time that afternoon, a violent heave came from deep in my belly. Nothing came up with it. A long shouting retch sound came out of me. It held for several seconds, while all my muscles seemed to tighten and flex, feeling like they would tear, and my upper body lifted off of the hospital bed. After a long while, the heave subsided, and I collapsed, breathing hard.

I knew that, if I moved or twisted too much, I might damage the wires and tubes that protruded from me. I tried to calm my kicking legs and twisting torso.

"I'm at ten," I croaked, barely able to make a sound. Then, with more focus, more effort this time, "I'm at Ten! I'm at Ten!" I labored to pull an audible wheezing gasp. "This is Ten!" My body twisted on the bedsheet, as I spoke. I tried to be calm as I sobbed this time, "It's... Ten!"

When the nurse had asked me, several minutes earlier, what my pain level had been, on a scale of one to ten, I had wanted to scream, "Ten!" but I had known better. Despite the pain, my mind had quickly calculated and I had said, "Eight!" *Heavy breath... heavy breath*, "Nine, maybe!" I hoped that it would not be so, but I suspected that the worst had not yet come, and I should save some pain scale for its frightening arrival. I had been right. Now it had come. It was here, the worst was here, and it was Ten.

Immediately, as if those had been the magic words, my Emergency Room care team shifted, noticeably, into an intensity that I hadn't yet seen. I heard commands being shouted, and I saw people acting more quickly than before. There were now more bodies in my curtain-walled room, moving about it purposefully; a nonstop chorus of urgently spoken medical lingo came from all around me. Whole people; healthy people, working together to fix the broken person. I wanted to thank them; to thank all of them. All I could do was cry, try to breathe, and focus on hope for a tomorrow that seemed impossible.

Was I truly helpless? No, I knew that there was still one thing that I could do; one thing over which I still had control. At the end of my fraying, burning rope, I did the one thing that I could. I let go. Like a child in his parents' hands, I surrendered. "God, I'm yours." I silently prayed. "I can't do this. I lay this in your hands. Please, heal me. Please, make it all go away. Or, give me the strength to face it. And, if it's your will that I die today, so be it. It's your decision, not mine. You alone are God."

"Alright! What've we got?" rang a voice that was new to the room; a commanding voice. My eyes remained focused on the ceiling, as the last syllables of my prayer were silently moving my dry lips.

"Forty-four-year-old male. Right flank pain. History of kidney stones," replied another. "He is at Ten."

At that, the newer voice started barking instructions and commands; big words; scientific-sounding words. There was urgency in his voice, but calmness as well. Confidence. I knew that he was there for me; that I had his undivided attention. He would help me. Behind clenched teeth and an iron hammer of agony, I silently thanked God for the owner of the new voice, and my eyes watered with gratitude. At that moment, though I hadn't even laid eyes on my doctor, I loved him; in a strange disembodied way. And, as that love was on my mind, pain rolled over me, like a hot slimy wave on a mission to crush me. This was pain. This was real. This was Ten.

Two hours or so before that pencil-size IV invaded my arm, before that blessed Emergency Room Doctor and his wonderful staff rescued me, I paced the hall, quickly, angrily, back and forth; banging the heels of my recently shined shoes into the carpet in frustration.

"Not today! Why does it have to be today?" I knew, very well, what was happening inside my body. I had been down Kidney Stone Lane many times before. In fact, this was my tenth. But why today, of all days? A kidney stone is never good news, but I would gladly have traded for almost any other day, had the choice been mine.

Today, I would see my oldest child, Lydia, graduate from high school. She would be graduating at the top of her class, having never received a grade lower than an A in her life. This accomplishment was all the more impressive, as she attended a small private academy school; so much more difficult than the high school that I had struggled to complete. Today, she would be giving a speech that she had written with great care and rehearsed many times. Proud did not begin to describe my feelings for my daughter, this day. On top of this, my affection and pride were also there for Cody, for Alexis, for Josh, and others; young soon-to-be graduates who, over the years, had spent nights and dinners in our home, who had worked hard on sports teams that I had coached, who had striven through life's challenges and acquired graduating status from this difficult school; wonderful young people who held deep loving places in my heart.

Proud relatives of our family had driven in from as far as two hundred miles away to see Lydia graduate. My brother, Shanon, was there. This was Lydia's day. We were there to honor her.

My right kidney spoke up. "I'm still here. Don't forget about me," it seemed to shout, as a sharp pain shot deeply, working its way around from back to front.

I didn't know if this pacing back and forth was helping, but, every time I tried to sit down at the back of the auditorium to watch the program, I found myself quickly getting back up, only to pace the carpeted entry hall again, just outside the open double doors of the large main room.

I had just returned from another of my many top-speed sprints out the building's side door to heave and retch in the privacy of the soccer field, and I resumed my pacing, trying hard to hear what was going on inside, my body slightly hunched forward, hands pressed against my lower back, elbows out. Silently, she watched me, I would later learn. One of my favorite young people that I have ever coached, she was a lovely, tall, front-row middle-hitter on the Varsity Volleyball team of this tiny school, and one of the hardest working players I have ever known. An underclassman, she was there today as a candleholder; a volunteer job wherein younger students could come and pay their respects to the graduating seniors, lighting the way as they walked down the aisle in their caps and gowns.

She had been watching me throughout the ordeal. She stayed a respectful distance away, observing with confusion and concern; wondering why her coach was acting the way that he was.

It was long past time to leave, and I knew it. As this was my tenth stone, I knew the drill. I was familiar with the progression. At this point in the process, I should not have been here. I should already have gone to the hospital. I chose to stay, knowing that every minute I delayed I would pay for later, in suffering. Pain or not, though, I was not going to miss my little girl's graduation, so help me!

"It isn't going to happen! You hear me?" I mentally shouted at my swollen kidney; my eyes creased in a fiery expression of determination. I banged one fist into the other palm as I angrily affirmed in my heart, "I can do this! I am going to hear that speech! Lord, God, please help me! Please, give me just a few more minutes."

The lights dimmed as the slideshow began. Poignant music played as baby photos, and childhood sports portraits, and preteen slumber party pictures faded in and out of the screen, accompanied by soft fond laughter from the audience. I loved these kids. My eyes watered as I tried not to squirm in my padded seat at the back of the room. Somehow, I made it through the slideshow and returned to my pacing place in the hall, sentimentally wiping my proud eyes as I limped.

I returned from another heaving session in the soccer field just in time to hear my daughter's name announced. How many of those soccer field trips had I made today, I wondered. It was speech time. I watched from the hall as Lydia ascended the stage and took the microphone. It was a lovely speech, delivered with smiles and poise; and Lydia's Daddy was there to hear it. She had found the right words; words that congratulated and encouraged her classmates without being cliché; words that tastefully expressed gratitude to her teachers, her parents, her classmates and her God; words that challenged all in the room, from youngest to oldest, to boldly be the man or woman that God intended us to be. I stood, hunched over, unable to fully stand, in the open doorway at the back of the great room with tears of pride on my cheeks, as sharp stinging kidney pain sliced my mind to pieces. I was getting worse, fast. It was time to leave.

A few minutes later, having run only one red light, my reliable brother, Shanon, with whom I have been through so much over the decades, had me at the hospital. I would not get to see the presenting of the diplomas.

"How would you rate your pain right now, Mister Ford, on a scale of one to ten…"

Short pause…

"Umm… eight!" *Heavy breath… heavy breath.* "Nine, maybe."

I can think of only two times in my life that I have experienced that level of physical pain. They were at kidney stone number one and kidney stone number ten. At the time of this writing, I have had twelve. All were bad; very bad, in fact. Those two, however, were special.

When I lay on the hospital bed that warm May Graduation Day, a grown man struggling not to sob like a child, a lot of things were forgotten. Forgotten were the deadlines and challenges of my projects at work. Forgotten was the driver who had cut me off in traffic earlier that day. Forgotten was the comment that had offended me earlier in the week. Gone, completely, from my mind were the mortgage payment and the lawn that needed mowing; the car that needed washed.

As far away as East is from West, were any painful memories of my past or worries about my future. Absent from my mind were any insecurities about self-worth, or thoughts of inadequacy as a man. Nor were there any aspirations of greatness; wealth, fame, respect. A swollen bank account. A beautiful home. A solid retirement plan.

In place of all these things, my hope, my priority, my singular focus was on my next breath; on staying conscious; on surviving without falling into madness. An acute kidney stone attack is not something that I would wish on my worst enemy. But I would wish it for my best friend. Never before have I had so great an opportunity to truly press my spiritual reboot button as I did that day. Though it was the hardest, most unpleasant thing I had ever endured physically, it was one of my greatest moments of victory. I came out of that experience changed.

My focus, now, was much more on my wife and my children; my friends and my community; on forgiveness, patience, compassion. I am not sorry that it happened; not at all. I had just traveled through a rare opportunity to absolutely come to terms with my own helplessness. I had been humbled to a point where I had cried out to God, and surrendered the illusion that I had ever been in control; to rely on Him completely. What a release. What a freedom. What a lesson.

It was an experience that I am so glad to have had; a lesson so good to have learned. But, I have to be honest. I sure do hope that it's a lesson I won't ever need to learn again.

"*Embracing the spirit of everyday adventure requires living in the present moment and waking up to the spontaneous wonders always going on around us.*
                                                                      Anjula Razdan

All men die. Not all men truly live.
                                                              William Wallace,
                                                              Braveheart

30

An Ocelot in an Underwear Drawer

"Where have you been, in a hole somewhere?" he asked me with a smile.

It was our second day in "the big crack," and I was almost bug-eyed with surprise and awe. He looked at me, amused. I laughed at my brother's joke, knowing that he was just as dumfounded as I was. "Can you believe this?" I asked him, gesturing all around me.

He shook his head with a smile and said, "No. I can't."

As our light blue Winnebago-sized raft made its way slowly across the river, powered by a large outboard motor attached at its transom, Dad pointed at the massive rock that was directly south of us. "If that thing was anywhere else, it would be a national monument."

He was right. All three of us, Shanon Dad and I, stared up at the glorious monster that loomed above us, hundreds of feet tall. The sun lit its bright desert colors, and created stark contrasts that dappled its surface of cracks and cliffs and vertical flutes of stone. It was huge. It was beautiful.

If we had turned around and looked upriver there was another one, almost as big. To our left and to our right rose huge picturesque cliffs of red rock. We had been drinking-in unreasonable amounts of breath-taking beauty for almost two days, but this place beat anything that we had yet seen. What made it even more exciting to us was the knowledge that this was just day number two. Relatively speaking, we had barely poked our noses into this place. There was a lot of Grand Canyon yet to be seen; a lot of Colorado River yet to be rafted.

We had just finished setting up our camp on the west side of the river. It was too warm to need tents, so we would be sleeping under the stars again, on cots. The hot Arizona sun had beaten down on the exposed rock cliffs all day long. By this hour, we were not only dealing with the ambient heat and lack of breeze that one might expect in the Grand Canyon, late afternoon in early June, but the warmth was added to by waves of convection heat coming from the sun-heated rocks; and they were everywhere, hundreds of feet high. It was an efficient solar oven that we were vacationing in.

One might think that, in those hot conditions, there would be a very convenient remedy within arm's reach. After all, we were traveling on a river. Cool river water ought to feel great in the Arizona heat. The problem with that, we discovered just after arriving, is that the Colorado River does not run with cool water. Just a little upstream from where we put in, the river pours out of the giant concrete Glen Canyon Dam, where it flows through numerous generators, providing electricity to much of the West. The water that flows into the dam is not surface water. It is water from deep in Lake Powell; cold water that likely hasn't seen daylight for a very long time.

At the point where this river trip began, a historic site called "Lee's Ferry," the water temperature is a frigid forty-two degrees Fahrenheit. This is not the kind of water that is pleasant to swim in. It's not even something that you'll want to have splashed on you, no matter how hot it is outside. In fact, of the forty-four intrepid souls on this voyage, only one braved the waters for his evening bath at our first night's camp. Only one.

So cold was the river that a small crowd had gathered to watch the fool, pointing and laughing good-naturedly. Using words like "crazy man" and "masochist," they watched him lathering his body and hair with his environmentally-friendly eco-soap, wearing only his swim trunks, and dunking himself over and over in the frigid river, each time emerging with a more pathetic, and therefore funnier, expression of frozen agony. Eventually, sufficiently bathed, he clumsily ran out of the river, uttering strange high-pitched noises, where he was greeted by his small grinning audience of strangers who welcomed him with wisecracks that may have held a tinge of admiration.

My skin was blue for the next half hour.

The next afternoon, as the raft slowly puttered across the river, from right to left, I was still staring up at the massive beautiful rock, when our tour guide said something fascinating.

"Back in 1956, two large passenger airplanes collided during a storm and crashed down into the Grand Canyon. At that time, it was the worst air disaster in history. It happened right here." Ryley, our trip leader, two days into his ninety-third trip down this river, pointed to the giant rock straight ahead of us, the very rock that we had been admiring moments before, and continued. "One of them smashed into that rock and came to rest way up there. The other," he said, as he turned and pointed to the steep hills and cliffs to our left, on the Eastern slope, "ended up over there. Everyone died."

With a faraway look in his eye, Dad said quietly, "I remember that. I was a teenager. I remember hearing about it on the radio. It was a big news story. That happened right here?" After that, we looked at the scenic beauty around us with a little bit more reverence.

Ryley told us that, though the large pieces of the wreckage had been removed decades ago, there are still some things up there; remnants of the crash. It's illegal to take them, so quite a few of the pieces remain there to this day. He told us that it's a big hike, but he had seen a piece of an airplane seat, some twisted metal and a few other things. Worst of all, he told us, was the wristwatch that he had seen; forever frozen on the minute and second of the disaster. He told us of how seeing that watch had made everything so much more personal to him.

"Well, enough of that!" he suddenly announced, after a respectful quiet moment had passed. "Who wants to see something amazing and beautiful?" A lot of smiles and a lot of hands. "You're about to leave the freezing clear water of the Colorado River, where you will suddenly find yourself in the warm blue water of the Little Colorado. This is the confluence of the two rivers, and one of my favorite places in the Grand Canyon."

He explained that we would soon be seeing something that we will probably never see again. "Look down into the water, as deep as you can, as we cross from one river to the other. You'll know when it happens."

I looked down, as Ryley had said to, and, once again, I was impressed by the beauty and the clarity of the Colorado River. It was like looking through a slightly green-tinted window, deep deep into the depths, all the way to bottom. I had rarely seen water so clear. Then it happened, as Ryley had promised it would. I was dumbstruck. Stretching from surface to river's floor stood a light blue wall. Where the cold clear green water of the Colorado met the warm, milky light blue of the Little Colorado, the waters did not mix. They stayed aloof from each other, as if there was an invisible cellophane membrane separating the two rivers; a membrane that went all the way to the bottom.

The water of the Little Colorado, I would later learn, contains a mineral that the Colorado River does not have, nor had any river I had ever seen. Ground to the finest powder, this mineral hangs in the water without any weight of its own, in such quantity that the river looks almost like it is flowing with light blue milk.

It was so bright that it seemed to glow. It almost looked artificial. It could not be seen through. So great was the contrast between the two rivers, I almost expected to feel a bump in the surface, as we rafted over the vivid dividing line. There was no doubt about where it was that we had changed rivers. We were now in the Little Colorado.

I reached down and, instead of the forty-two degrees that I had so painfully bathed in the night before, I felt something more like a backyard swimming pool. I turned and looked at my dad with my jaw hanging open. I was beyond awestruck.

We spent several hours at the Little Colorado. All forty of us, from the youngest, a fifteen-year-old girl, to the oldest, an eighty-four-year-old World War II veteran, played and splashed and floated in the soothing cool waters of the Little Colorado.

The best way to enjoy the Little Colorado is to hike up the long riverside trail, and then to float back down, through the gentle pools, around the rocks, and over its many small natural water slides, using our rafting life vests as float toys. Ryley showed us how to reverse the polarity of our vests, putting them on upside-down like pants. We all looked like we were wearing giant caution-orange diapers. In that orientation, the life vests held our bodies in exactly the right angle and at exactly the right height for optimum river drifting. It also brought on a lot of laughter and a lot of Kodak Moments.

As we hiked up the trail that snaked along beside the river in a constant uphill slope, Shanon, Dad and I became separated. I had been at it for a few hundred yards, taking it slow, happily humming to myself as I looked all around me, contentedly drinking in the glory of my surroundings, when I came upon Vivian, sitting beside the path on a large rock. Having spent two days in some fairly close company, I was getting to know everyone. This was especially true of the twenty who were on my boat, like Vivian. Our trip consisted of forty people and four boatmen, distributed over two massive rubber rafts.

I wasn't sure how old Vivian was but I had heard her talking, earlier, about her daughter's grandkids. Vivian, like her daughter who was on the trip with her, was a very short woman. I'm not sure of the best way to complete her description kindly, so I'll just say it. She wasn't a thin girl. Is that alright?

We made eye contact as I walked up to her. I smiled at her and I happily boomed, "Hey! How's Vivian today?"

She squinted and looked at me silently. Then, after a long pause, she spoke in short loud bursts, like little rifle shots, with long pauses between them, "I don't... I just... I... I can't..." and she started to softly cry.

"Okay, come here Vivian." I smiled at her as affectionately as I could, and I reached for her hand. "Let's stand up... that's the way... come with me, Sweetie." Slowly, I led her toward a calm milky blue pool, just a few yards away. I helped her into the refreshing cool water. It felt really good after hiking in the canyon heat.

"Do you remember my name, Vivian?" Her only reply was a faint vocal exhale, like one might make when they're scared, or not feeling well. In this case, I think it was both. "Sit here, on this rock," I told her.

She obeyed, sitting in water that reached to about her underarms. I knelt in front of her in the pool. There was no river current here. I could hear the sounds of people splashing and laughing nearby. I could see that the cool water was helping her almost immediately, as her eyes were focusing and her demeanor was becoming more coherent. "Vivian, did you bring your canteen?... No?... That's alright. Here's mine. Take a big ol' drink. Let's get a few ounces into you nice and quick… That's the way… Vivian, I'm going to take your hat for a moment, okay… feeling any better?… Now, I've dunked your hat in the water, go ahead and put it back on. We're going to get your core temperature down a little, alright?… Good… That's the way."

She sat still for several minutes in the refreshing coolness. Water trickled down from her wet hat and ran between her eyes. She looked at me and smiled. "Thank you," she whispered. Smiling at her, I pointed at my bright orange Nalgene water bottle, still in her hand, whom I affectionately referred to throughout the trip as, "My little orange friend." She took another big swallow or two..

"I'm feeling a lot better now," she sighed. "I guess I got a little overheated."

"It's a hundred and five degrees, Vivian. I'll bet you're not the only one."

"I didn't know what to do. I was so confused. What if you hadn't come?" She handed me the orange friend. "This is little embarrassing… you know why?" I shook my head, smiling. "I'm a nurse!" she said. We both laughed out loud. I guess we LOL'd.

Once Vivian was back on her feet and reunited with her searching daughter, I was on the trail again, working my way upriver.

My pit stop with Vivian had taken a fair bit of time, so I knew that Dad and Shanon would be well ahead of me. No sooner had I completed that thought, when I was proven wrong. Up the trail, fifty yards or so, I saw my brother. He was at the top of a sloping rock. It was about fifteen feet high and there was no way around it. The trail continued on the other side. Anyone who wanted to keep going, would have to get over this rock. The stony ascent sloped upward at about thirty degrees. It was smooth and it looked slippery. There at the top stood my brother. I proudly watched him in action as I hiked toward him. He was reaching down and helping people up the rock slope, one at a time, taking their outstretched hands, pulling them to the top.

As we were both in our mid-thirties, most of the people on this trip were older than we were, and Shanon, it seemed, had given himself the task of helping them get past this otherwise difficult obstacle. I wondered how long he had been at it.

The last hand that he reached down for was mine. He pulled me to the top and we stood there, watching his appreciative group of satisfied customers waddling up the path ahead of us. We both smiled over them with fondness. It was strange to feel that way about people we had met only a day earlier, but, we couldn't help it.

I was just so doggone happy; so full of... I don't know... joy, I guess.

"What took ya?" He asked me, smiling, still gazing up the trail. In his face, I read the same contented feelings that I was enjoying.

"Took a little break with a new friend," I replied. He didn't ask for an explanation.

We eventually hooked up with Dad, donned our bright orange diapers and happily floated and bobbed our way down that beautiful baby blue river.

Shanon and I were both married to wonderful wives, raising young families of our own, back in the world; families that always had our full attention. Today, though, it was the old Ford crew, like old times. We laughed a lot, we three Fords. I wished that Mom could have been there with us to round it out. Today went a long way toward filling a very old need that I had forgotten.

Later that evening, forty of us crowded onto a single raft, we were on our way back up and across the river, back to camp. Three of the four Boatmen had taken raft number one back to camp early so they could start making our dinner.

I sat on the floor of raft number two, way out at the front, facing backward, as we slowly motored our way against the current. The temperature had gone down quite a bit from the late afternoon heat that had so sidelined Vivian a couple of hours earlier. As I was scanning the hills and cliffs, trying to take mental photographs of everything, my eyes happened across Ray. He was the oldest member of the expedition, at eighty-four. His son, earlier, had proudly announced that Ray was a veteran of the Battle of the Bulge. Having done some reading about that harrowing conflict, I was immediately moved with admiration and patriotism when I'd heard that.

Ray was sitting alone, near me at the raft's forward area, staring straight ahead, seeming not to focus on anything. He was shaking;

shivering in a way that seemed extreme to me. I'm not sure that I have ever shivered as badly as Ray was doing.

Shanon sat about seven feet behind and to the left of where Ray sat, one of the many crowded together for the short trip. As my brother's eyes drifted by, I caught and held them with mine. Once I had his attention, I pointedly fired my eyes over at Ray, then I looked back. I watched as Shanon then looked over. I saw his eyes travel down the length of Ray's quivering frame. Soon he looked back at me and wordlessly gave me the tiniest of head nods. Our silent conversation complete, we simultaneously looked away and resumed our happy sightseeing. We had no idea that our short exchange had been noticed and watched with curiosity.

With our raft held fast to a nearby tree by a rope that sported a huge impressive sailor's knot, we all lined up to step off of the raft's bow, one by one, into the warm beach sand below. I nonchalantly stepped into line so I would be climbing off of the raft right in front of Ray. I didn't need to look back to know that Shanon would be in line directly behind him. Once on the sand, I reached up and offered Ray my hand. He took the hand and silently stepped down and started to walk away. The beach here was unusually steep, causing us to make a bit of a climb to get up to the main level where all the people were. Shanon and I quietly fell in, walking about two steps behind the shivering little man as he climbed the beach, I on the left; Shanon on the right.

About halfway up the dune, it happened, just as we'd feared it would. Down he went. Ray's busy day had caught up to him, and, into my arms he fell. Shanon, without a word, rushed away and returned almost immediately with Ray's muscular son, who took him by the hand and led him away. "You alright, Dad?" I heard him ask as they left us.

Shanon and I silently looked at each other for a full two seconds. I smiled, he nodded. No words needed, we went off to find our own dad and start getting ready for another surprisingly fantastic dinner. But our private brother-moment had not gone unnoticed. It had, as a matter of fact, sparked a certain fascination with which a fellow river-goer would privately watch and study my brother and me for the remainder of the trip, I would later learn.

"Childhood!" Shanon replied. "Probably around eight to ten years old. Those were great years. Especially while we were living in California. How about you?"

We'd been at this for a while. The three of us sat on our cots, in the shade of the towering cliffs. Bellies full, beds made, warm June evening in a beautiful setting, we felt like we had it made. We had already been through "what's your favorite food, what's your favorite game to play, what's your favorite cartoon," and a number of other silly but surprisingly interesting conversation seeds. Favorite sounds had seeded a far more interesting discussion than I would have guessed: the smack of a billiard ball, the kerplunk-splash of a cannon-ball dive into a pool, ocean waves with seabirds, a supe'd-up V8 engine, ten bowling pins being blown into the pit from a solid pocket shot, skis on snow, a gently flowing stream, bacon frying in a pan, laughter - especially from a child. Lots of great sounds had been discussed.

"Me? I'd have to say my early thirties," I replied. "I've loved being a husband and raising my small kids, teaching them to ride bikes, carving pumpkins, taking them swimming, camping, praying with them at bedtime, helping them do homework, coaching their sports teams… Yeah, I think my thirties have been my favorite so far, though I'm not done with them yet.

"Dad?" I asked him. "Your turn. What was your favorite time of life?"

He paused a moment, and looked at each of us, one at a time. "Right now."

"Right now?" Shanon asked.

He smiled and replied, "I'm rafting the Grand Canyon. I'm in this beautiful place and I'm with both of my boys. My favorite time of my life?" He paused for a short while, and then he smiled again. "Right now."

Wow… best answer all night.

I suddenly felt a little tightness in my throat. None of us could talk for a few seconds.

The rafting trip went on, day after glorious day. We admired the scenery, we took hikes up slot canyons, we slept under an ocean of stars, we swam through warm waterfalls, we ate like kings, and we smashed our way through the biggest baddest river rapids I have ever seen.

"Hakatai!" I burst out in a high-pitched scream.

"Hakatai! Yah Yah Yah Yah!" I heard yelled from somewhere else on the boat.

When you're riding a rubber raft, even a giant motorized one, over massive violent class nine or class ten Grand Canyon river rapids, with freezing water smacking you in the face, there's something very satisfying about screaming some kind of crazy war cry. It just feels right, almost primal. "Hakatai" was as good a war cry as any other. We had learned the word a day or two earlier from one of our river guides. Hakatai is a geological term for a certain kind of shale that is commonly seen on the rocky talus slopes at the bases of many Grand Canyon cliffs. Originally, it was a Havasupai word. The Havasupai were an ancient civilization of native people who once lived in the canyon.

Upon learning of them from Boatman Ben, it struck me as to how different our modern lives are compared to the old Havasupai, who were born, raised families, hunted deer and harvested crops, grew old and died, all within the confines of this canyon.

Along the way, Boatman Ben taught us several Havasupai words. I wish I could remember them all now. My favorite was Matkatamiba, which was pronounced mat-cat-a-meeba. "This next rapid," Boatman Ben had announced, just after telling us to get ready for a great ride, "is called Matkatamiba. It's a Havasupai word meaning 'girl with a face like a bat.'"

When we could be, Shanon and I were usually up on the very front tip of the boat when we headed into the nasty rapids. That's where the ride was always the best - or the worst, depending on your perspective. After emerging from such a rapid, the people on the back half of the boat were rarely wet at all. In the next area forward of there, a few people were often about half wet. But those of us who had ridden through the bubbling churning monsters up front were always completely drenched. That's why we would armor up in rain clothes, before we hit the big ones. Ryley called that *"Full Battle Gear."*

"Hakatai! Wooooooooo!" Sometimes it was a fist-pumping victory scream after the rapid. Yeah, I know. It's just a type of rock. It's not a battle word. But it worked! Some words are just fun to yell. After a day or so, I had a bunch of other people on that boat screaming "Hakatai" with me.

Eventually, we, the riders of boat number two, were even using it as a greeting. "Hakatai." It worked a lot like "Aloha" or "Yo." It was a versatile word.

It came as a complete surprise to me, discovering the beautiful sandy beaches of the Grand Canyon. From the South Rim, where most pictures are taken, or from aerial photos in books, the Grand Canyon looks like a majestic but dry and barren place. I had seen those pictures my entire life. I was shocked to learn that there are lush tree-filled spots with golden sandy beaches and warm blue swimming holes. There's a secret Garden of Eden in the bottom of that big hole.

So beautiful is it, in places, that some of the tropical island paradise scenes in the 1980 Brooke Shields movie, *The Blue Lagoon*, were actually filmed in the Grand Canyon, on a beautiful tree-lined tributary with waterfalls and cliffs and tiny pools. We visited that spot. It was hard to leave.

"Who wants to play a game of Rocks?" Shanon yelled happily, one evening. We were midway, or so, through the canyon and camp was all set up. We had some time to kill while the boatmen were making our dinner. They had told us that we would be eating something special that night.

The two of us walked around in the sand, holding up volleyball-sized rocks.

"Come on! Come play Rocks with us!" I yelled just as loudly.

"It's those crazy brothers. At it again," said an older man with a smile. A large circle of folks were sitting on their tiny three-legged camp chairs, in one of the few shaded areas. They all looked up at us with amused grins, like we were some kind of oddity.

"Don't you two ever wind down?" asked a woman in the group. "Do you know how hot it is?"

"Yup!" said Shanon happily. "It's a hundred and eight! Come on, who's in?" We knew the temperature because Shanon always had his handy thermometer with him.

"But, it's a Dry Heat!" I announced, holding my index finger in the air, like a salesman giving a pitch.

"Aren't you dying, like we are?" asked another man.

"Of course we are." I replied, "A hundred and eight is tough to ignore! Man, it's hot out!... Wanna play?" I grinned.

We couldn't get any takers for a game of Rocks. Even the teenagers were wiped out. But that was alright. It had been a fun conversation.

Boatman Ben had been right about us getting something special for dinner that night. We ate some kind of fish; trout, I think, served Almandine. I don't know what that means but it was amazing; and then, for dessert, Banana Flambe, with ice cream. It was actually flaming. Yum! This river guide company is so good, we had ice cold vanilla ice cream four days in, on a hundred-degree river trip. We had dessert in the desert. Hah! Never thought I would get to use those two words together.

"Just wait 'til our last night," said Boatman Jonathan, "if you think this dinner was good."

There was a young boatman on the trip. His name was Kip. He was Ryley's Swamper, over on boat number one, so we didn't see as much of him as we did Boatmen Ben and Jonathan - respectively our own Boat Number Two Pilot and Swamper. Jonathan was training to be a Pilot, so Ben had been giving him the tiller through several of the rapids. But, this was Kip's very first trip. He had just been picked up by the guide company. He was the perfect choice. He was friendly and helpful. He was also extremely handsome. The older ladies on the expedition loved that young man!

My favorite thing about Kip was that he just about always had his guitar out. Any time he had a break he was sawing that axe, and singing another song.

We had just stopped rafting for a midday lunch break. We were on another of those golden sandy beaches. Kip was sitting on a rock, plucking his scratched well-worn guitar and humming to himself. Suddenly, as a large group of us was going by, he broke into song. "My grandpa, he's ninety-five, he keeps on dancing, he's still alive…"

It was clear to me that Judy was not a student of The Steve Miller Band when she laughed sardonically at Kip's lyrics and shook her head. As my momentum took me directly by Kip, at exactly the opportune time of the song, I quickly stood beside the seated guitar man, threw an arm around his shoulder, and joined in without missing a beat.

Together, in bad two-part harmony (the bad part was me, not Kip), we belted out the next line, loud and proud, "My grandma she's ninety-two, she loves to dance and sing some too." Kip looked up at me and grinned. On we crooned, speeding up the cadence, just like Steve Miller would have wanted, had he been there, "I don't know but I've been told, if you keep on dancin' you'll never grow old. So, come on Darlin' put a pretty dress on, we're gonna go out tonight. (strum strum strum) Dance, dance, dance… Dance, dance, dance… Dance, dance, dance, all night long…"

"Hakatai!" I heard from someone in the small crowd walking by.

"You know that lady, Judy? The doctor's wife?" Dad asked us a little later, looking over his sandwich at us. "Today she told me that I must be a great dad, because I have two of the best boys!" He grinned at us proudly. "She said that you two guys have just made this trip for her and her family. She said you're like having two more river guides on the boat, because you're so helpful and fun."

Really? Not meaning to be. Just having a good time.

"Well, she's right. You are a great dad!"

Another day, we were deep up Havasu Canyon. This might very well have been the prettiest spot of the whole trip. Hard to say, I haven't even told you about Deer Creek, or Elves' Chasm, or Shinumo Falls, or "The Patio."

Havasu Canyon was a long, winding, high-walled slot canyon that we had all hiked up. Down the middle ran the beautiful warm blue Havasu River, almost as blue as the Little Colorado. We had been here for a couple of hours and our forty-person party was spread out, up and down the canyon's length. Farther than anyone, way up the Canyon, exploring and playing, heedless of the blistering heat, was a pair of brothers. Any guess who they might have been? Tall, mid-thirties?

Finally, our explorer curiosities far from satisfied, we decided to turn around and head back downstream to where everyone else was, due to the time. We figured that Ryley would be rounding everyone up soon. At this point, we decided to part ways. I opted for a slow meander back down the trail. A salameander, I decided to call it. I saw this moment as a rare opportunity to enjoy a little quiet solitude in the lap of nature; a chance to talk with God and listen for his reply.

Shanon, on the other hand, made his way back at top speed. I laughed as I watched him descending down the steep winding trail ahead of me, leaping from rock to rock, recklessly pounding his way down the trail at an adrenaline-pumping full sprint, leaving a dust cloud in his wake. Mr. Extreme! Such a fun guy!

I had strolled and shuffled my way along, all alone, for some time, taking in the majesty around me and appreciating that I might never see something like this again. Praising God and being thankful for the many blessings in my life, I came across Beth, sitting alone in the shade.

"Did you see the gazelle?" she asked me.

"Gazelle?"

"Yes! A crazy two-legged gazelle just flew through here at a hundred miles an hour," she said, laughing. "Startled the dickin's out of me! See that gap up there?" She was pointing to a space about seven feet wide, between two big rocks, a good eighteen feet above us. "That brother of yours flew across that gap! It was crazy! But it was so cool!" she said laughing. "I screamed, and he yelled 'sorry', while he was in midair! And he just kept going." Beth shook her head, laughing, as she told the story about the two-legged gazelle. "You two guys are a lot of fun, you know that?"

"Hakatai," I said as my reply, which made her laugh a little.

We walked together down the trail, slowly. Beth was a nice lady with short reddish hair. My guess was that she was in her mid-to-late-forties, so about ten or twelve years older than I was.

After a time of walking together, she said, "I saw you, you know."

"You did?" I didn't know what she was talking about.

"I was watching. You and your brother, with that older gentleman, Roy."

"Ray."

"Right, Ray." There was a long pause, which I didn't interrupt. "At the Little Colorado, three days ago. He was shaking really bad. I was concerned about him. Then I saw you watching him. You were looking at him hard, like you were thinking. So, I watched you, wondering what you were going to do. I saw you look at your brother. It was… strange. You guys had a whole conversation, and made a plan, without ever saying a word. Then I saw you guys save him when he fell. You and Shanon were protecting him, and he never even knew about it. No one asked you to. You just did it.

"I've been watching you two ever since then. You guys are different.

"And, I know what you did for Vivian. She told me. You saved her from getting heat stroke. You didn't even think about it, you just did it. You really care about people, don't you? You're always helping. You carry people's luggage for them. You usually get into the food line last. I've noticed. And you always have a joke handy, or a big friendly 'Good Morning' for someone.

"And you two are both so full of... I don't know, life! Even when it's so hot. It's all a big adventure to you, isn't it? You made me laugh, that first night, when you were the only one who got into the cold water. I couldn't figure out why you did that. I didn't understand. Now, I think I do. It was part of the adventure, wasn't it? You find the adventure where you can, and when it's not there, you just invent some."

I smiled.

"There's something different about you. You're content, even when you're last; even when you're hot and tired."

I wasn't sure what to say, or even if I should say something. We strolled along quietly for a few seconds. I had the feeling that she had more to say, and that, if I just stayed quiet, it would come. I was right.

"You live life." She emphasized the word "live." "I've just been doing life," she said sadly.

There it was. I was a little surprised to have a person that I hardly knew open up like this.

"What does that feel like, Chris?"

"It's good... Most of the time, I'm as happy as an ocelot in an underwear drawer."

"A what?"

"An ocelot," I drew it out more slowly this time, "in an underwear drawer." I saw her brow furl. She was trying to get it. This was important to her.

"Have a cat?"

"Yes, I do," she replied.

"Walk away and leave your underwear drawer open sometime. Where will you eventually find your cat? When we were kids, Shanon and I shared a bedroom. We used to, sometimes, leave our drawer open for Kitty, on purpose. We'd find her in there later, loudly purring like a little chainsaw. It was up off the ground, it was soft and protected. Super comfy. It was her happy place. She had kittens in there once. Pretty gross." Beth giggled.

"You want to see contentment? True happy? Leave your underwear drawer open."

"Okay, but why an ocelot?" she asked.

"Ever seen one?" I replied. "They're cool. Not huge and scary like a tiger or a lion. They're sleek and colorful. Mysterious and wild. That's the adventure part. See, I want to be happy; content, like a cat in an underwear drawer, but, I'm not interested in seeing myself as a house cat. I want to live a life of adventure, Beth. I believe I'm called to do just that. The life of the wildcat, willing to take risks; finding the adventure. But I want the peace of the underwear drawer. Plus, 'ocelot' is a really fun word - more fun to say than 'cat,' which makes it just that much better." I gave her a big toothy grin.

"But," she paused, still walking, wheels turning in her head. "The underwear drawer is a place of safety and comfort. That's why the cat is so content there. But you speak of adventure; of risk. That doesn't sound very safe. Isn't that a contradiction?"

I smiled, happy that she was getting it; that she was interested enough to ask. "That's right. It's a delightful contradiction. It's a sense of peace, in the face of risk. Adventure is risky, but adventure is the only way to live, even if your adventures are tiny, and private, as most of mine are. Living without adventure, without a little risk, means living without victories. That kind of life won't bring growth. It may be safe, but it doesn't bring real contentment.

"Beth, what if you lived in a place where, for the sake of adventure, you made it a lifestyle to find the fun, and to allow yourself to risk some things, like embarrassment, gossip or even mild physical injury, knowing that, along with your cherished victories there will be some failures; and what if you were just fine with those odds, knowing that they come with the gig? Could you live there? Some people will think you're weird. Some will even say that you're wrong. You've got to be okay with that. Others will envy you for your freedom and your sense of adventure. Most won't even notice.

"When you do even tiny little adventures, simple things like eating your M&Ms without looking, trying to predict what color will be the last one in your hand, just to make an enjoyable thing even more enjoyable, or lifting your feet so you don't trip, whenever you drive over a state line, laughing at your own joke, and your friends see you doing it and they call you weird; you've got to be okay with that. Those are some of the risks that come with a life of adventure."

"Like bathing in an ice cold river, even when you don't have to, while strangers laugh at you?" she asked smiling.

"That's right. That bath was painful, and I did get laughed at, but I came out of it laughing, didn't I? I also came out of it with a great story to tell. Or... how about sprinting down a canyon trail, soaring over a potentially leg-breaking chasm, just because you can?

"But, yes, it is a contradiction, risk with peace; a very nice contradiction, in my mind. A fun way to live. A risky, yet happy, life of adventure. It's far easier to sit still, in your underwear drawer, basking in the peace, with recent memories of victory and accomplishment, than it is without those recent victories. Victories provide satisfaction, and growth provides strength and wisdom. Do you know that nervous, almost sick feeling you get in your stomach, just before you try something new and scary? If you can get through life without ever feeling that feeling, have you really lived?

And what about the thrill of accomplishment that comes when your scary task is done? It's those experiences that help to make it possible, later, in your quieter moments, to truly enjoy the fulfilled, satisfied underwear drawer. Does this make sense?"

"Yeah! It does." she said thoughtfully. There was a long pause. "But how?" How do you do that?"

"Choose it," I replied. "Then, pursue it." I paused for a second or two. "Beth, there's this one thing that you have to carry with you everywhere you go, every day, all day, no matter what."

"What is it?" she asked with great interest, still walking slowly.

"Your attitude. You have to take that thing around with you everywhere you go. Now, if you've got to always have a thing, shouldn't that thing be a good thing? Some people take a big, ugly, loud thing with them everywhere they go. But, they don't have to. Isn't it better, if you have to carry a thing around with you everywhere, for it to be a light thing that's easy to carry? One that looks nice, sounds nice, smells nice and goes well with all of your outfits?"

"Ha ha ha. You have a funny way of putting things," she said. She was quiet for a few dusty steps on the trail. "But, what does that look like? How can I pursue it?"

"Hmmm… I'll give you an example. Ever get cut off in traffic? You know, when you're driving on a freeway or someplace, and someone just blasts right in front of you, making you slam on your breaks to avoid an accident?"

"Oh! Yes! Man, don't you just hate people who do that?"

I nodded my head up and down, smiling. "No." I replied nonchalantly, still nodding, "I don't."

"Ha ha, you just nodded, and… said no… heh… okay, I'll bite. Why not? Why don't you hate people who you cut you off in traffic?"

"That's easy," I replied. "It's because the other driver is a surgeon, and he's on his way to save someone's life. He had to cut me off to get there in time."

"What?"

"Yeah. It's that easy. If you'll let yourself assume that the driver of that car is about to save a life, all kinds of patience and forgiveness come easily." I walked a few steps. "Ok, let's say he's not a surgeon. That guy that cut me off in traffic has his very pregnant wife in the passenger seat. She's in labor. I can't see inside his car. How do I know there isn't a pregnant little wifey in there?"

Beth was smiling at me. "Come on…"

"Alright," I said, laughing. "That guy who just cut me off is late for a super important job interview. It's the job he's always dreamed of, but he's running late because of traffic. This new job could change his life. That's why he had to cut me off. So, no. I don't hate him."

We walked a few steps, she was looking up at me with a confused smile.

"Ever watch romantic comedies?" I asked her. "You know, chick flicks? Something with Meg Ryan or Hugh Grant. At the end, there's usually some great coming-to-his-senses moment, when he realizes that he can't let her walk out of his life. So, there's this mad drive to get to the airport in the nick of time, to tell her that he was wrong, and that he loves her and he would die without her. All the ladies in the theater go, 'Awww'."

Beth was laughing again.

"We're all on the edges of our theater seats, clutching our popcorn bags, hoping that he gets there in time to stop her, before she gets on that airplane and flies out of his life forever, right?... Well, that was the guy that cut me off in traffic. He had to do it!" I exclaimed smiling.

We walked a little farther, silently, both of our minds doing aerobics.

"Okay, okay. I know what you're gonna say," I said. "So, I'll go there for you. Let's say that none of those things are true. There's no surgeon, or pregnant wife, or job interview, or romantic rendezvous. Okay. Let's say that he doesn't have some big reason, and that he just cut me off. Beth, what if he's a good man, who just made a mistake? He cut me off because he messed up." I picked up a rock and threw it into the river. I wanted her to chew that one for a moment.

"Should I hate? I mess up all the time. In fact, none of us are perfect, right? We live in a fallen world. We all make mistakes. So, it's a mathematical certainty that I will make a mistake sooner or later, right? So, why should I hate when another fallen imperfect person makes the very mistake that I'm liable to make at any minute? Maybe, I should treat that person the way I hope to be treated, when I inevitably make my next big mistake.

"Alright. Let's take it one step farther, Beth. Let's say that the guy who just cut me off in traffic isn't a good man at all. Let's say he's a putz; an absolute jerkweed, who cut me off because he couldn't care less about me or my feelings."

"Now you're talking!" she said loudly.

"Now THAT is a different subject." I announced with a smile.

"Oh, so then it's okay?" she asked.

"No. But it is a different subject."

She laughed again.

"Beth, in that case, when I've been cut off in traffic by a real jack-wagon, would it do me any good to hate? Who does it help? Will my hate make him a better person? Will it make me a better person? And, what will it do for that thing that I have to carry around with me everywhere?

"Hate, resentment, bitterness... they're the rifle that backfires, Beth.

They're a weapon that we shoot at others and wound ourselves. You know, there's only been one perfect person who ever lived, right? And they killed Him. Who am I to expect perfection from anyone?"

We walked along a little farther. We were almost to the crowded swimming area. We could hear laughter and splashing a short distance away.

"Would you get mad if a blind person stepped on your toe as they were walking by?" I asked her.

"No," she replied.

"Why? Because it was just a mistake?" I asked.

"Aaaahh… I see what you mean," she exclaimed. "In our own ways, we're all a little blind, aren't we?" I smiled. We walked several steps.

"Forgiveness and patience aren't natural talents," I continued. "In fact, it's the opposite of those that come naturally, isn't it? Forgiveness and patience are a skill; a skill that needs practiced, over and over, until we become good at them. It's a skill that requires strength. It's a skill that needs to be chosen. Pursued. Hate and resentment are easy. They don't take any effort at all. Weak people choose the easy way.

"You can be The Ocelot, Beth. In the immortal words of the great philosopher, Steven Tyler… 'Walk This Way.'" My timing was perfect, as she was sipping from her water bottle right at that moment. Her abrupt laugh launched a mouthful of water onto the trail.

"You can choose to see life this way and be happier," I continued, as she wiped her lip, still chuckling quietly. "You can choose a life of adventure, and you can pursue it. That means finding the adventure, even when it's not obvious. I find that loving others, serving them, sometimes even denying my own wants, is a great adventure. Making people happy, seeing them smile and knowing that it was I who helped to give them that smile, is adventure. It's something that I fail at far too often, but I want to keep trying.

"You want to be strong? Use your strength to serve and protect others. Even if they don't know you've done it for them, serving and protecting others is a big part of the wild life.

"I don't want to be a happy, contented sloth in an underwear drawer, Beth. Where's the adventure in that? But I don't want to be just a wildcat either. Not without the peace. I want to find both… as often as I can. The ocelot AND the underwear drawer - both!

"Beth, I fall short every day. I struggle with ego, with insecurities, with laziness, with envy. I do. You should have seen me about ten years ago, before I made these changes. I was aggressive and impatient, selfish. Sometimes, I still am.

"In the book of Matthew, in the Bible, The Lord said, 'If you do anything for even the least of these, you've done it for me.' So, when you serve others, you serve Him. You want adventure? Man, there's nothing more stimulating and exciting than serving The King! Nothing more rewarding. The underwear drawer can't be your goal, Beth. The underwear drawer is the result. Love is the goal.

"And, when I say love, I don't mean love as a noun. Love has to be a verb. Serving and forgiving are parts of that verb. Don't just have love. Do love. Fire that rifle instead."

The next morning, I sat down for a little alone time. Ryley had trained us all that the best way to go pee, on this trip, was to just walk out into the water, about waist-high – preferably in one of the warmer side rivers – and stand there. He called it taking a "smile break." Well, as you can imagine, when you're on a six-day trip, everyone's going to need to do more, a time or two each day, than just smile.

For those more serious moments, there were two porta-potties on this trip. One was kept in a small yellow tent that served as a portable outhouse. The other was always set out well away from the camp, behind a bush or a big rock, so it couldn't be seen from camp. It was not in a tent, but free to the breeze. This one Ryley called, "Poo with a View." This is where I was, that next morning after the Havasu Canyon excursion. I couldn't see camp from my open-air alone-time place, due to the giant boulder between us, but I did have a great view of the River and the cliffs beyond.

I sat there, remembering my chat with Beth from the day before, as I enjoyed the awesome scenery around me, and I thanked God for setting up that meeting. "This has to be the prettiest setting for a poo in my entire life," I thought, and I laughed. "Poo with a view" took on a whole different meaning, a moment later, when a large crowded river raft motored by, filled with people that I didn't know. With my pants around my ankles and absolutely no way to hide what I was doing, I looked out at them with a big smile and I waved. A raft full of Grand Canyon adventurers smiled and waved back. When they were gone, I went right back to enjoying my scenic alone time.

Just as happy as an ocelot in and underwear drawer.

An Afterword, A Farewell,
An Invitation

In a few of these chapters, I have lightly alluded to my Christian faith. However, most of the chapters do not, as I have purposely tried to avoid being preachy. I want this book to be entertaining and – occasionally - thought provoking for anyone, Christian or not. But I refuse to avoid that Christian side of me entirely. To do so would be to deny a big part of who I am. And that is why you probably caught a few glimpses of *Chris, the friend of God*, in chapters like Firewind; My Own War; A Life Well Lived; West of Bliss; Sideways; A Momentary Lapse of Raisin; It's Like A Whole Other Country; Forty Feet Down, Fifty Years to Go; When It's Ten; and An Ocelot In An Underwear Drawer.

Though I would be delighted to see this book in a Christian shop, I would also really love to see it categorized on *Amazon* or set in a mall bookstore shelf, in sections for Memoirs or Inspirational Humor. I'm hoping that I have been able to inspire a smile or two somewhere along the way.

The next chapter, here at book's end, will be the one where I will break the mold, so to speak. So, if you will indulge me, I will unapologetically touch, a bit more, on the spiritual. With that in mind, if you would rather not hear the God Stuff, please feel free to close the book at this point, or skip straight to the Notes section (which I think you will enjoy - much cooler than your ordinary End Notes). Of course, you've always had that option. But, if you want to dive deeper into the underwear drawer; or if you would just like for us to spend a little bit more time together, I invite you to keep reading. You just might like this last one. The Epilogue is pretty cool too.

If you should choose to end your reading now, I would like to thank you for the time that we've spent together. It has been an honor to have you turn my pages and hear of my adventures. I wish I could know you as well as you now know me. I have had a ton of fun writing the stories that you've just finished reading and it is my hope that you have enjoyed them as well. It is, further, my hope that you will always strive to be The Ocelot, wherever you can and as often as you can. I would love to hear from you sometime. Farewell, my friend.

Hey! You're still here. I am so glad. Thanks for sticking around. Let's do one more together, shall we? Just you and me? I'd like that. And, before we get started, thanks.

Now, take my hand, dear friend, and come with me. Let me whisper in your ear.

"God has called you to live a life of adventure"

Donnie Thompson

31

Being The Ocelot

It's here, my friend, at book's end, that I would like to talk with you more directly and personally; me to you; no stories this time. No, this isn't going to be some long-winded lecture about how ol' Chris thinks he's got it all figured out, 'cause I don't. I do know a lot more than I used to, but I have so much still to learn. I would love, however, to introduce you, a little bit more, to my friend The Ocelot. This chapter is just as much a message for me as for you; perhaps more so. This is something that I have been in great need of learning, and God is taking me through a number of experiences, to get me to a place where I am finally grasping it. I'm finally getting what He's been trying to tell me, and I'm so excited to learn more. Just as importantly, I am excited to share it. It is with that sense of excitement that I come to you now.

I meant every word that I told my raft-mate, Beth, on that dusty Grand Canyon river trail, years ago. You read about her in chapter 30. She was unhappy. She confessed to me that she had been just "doing" life. What she wanted was to really "live" life, as she perceived that I was doing. She had bought into a trap, as so many have; a trap set by our enemy. She was comfortable, but not truly content; experiencing, but not really pursuing; doing, but not fully living. She was stuck in the slime. Do you know what she was feeling? Have you been there? I sure have.

Are you there now?

On the cover of this book, you will find the quirky and memorable, intentionally cryptic and proudly tacky main title, "An Ocelot in an Underwear Drawer." Just beneath it, you should see a less cryptic, but hopefully just as provocative, subtitle; "Adventures of a Profoundly Imperfect and Intensely Happy Man." As you have no doubt discerned, having read this far, I am he. And, yes, I am. I truly am both profoundly imperfect and intensely happy; foiling, for the most part, the enemy's slimy trap.

Do you think that the enemy (and we do have one) wants you happily living the bold life of a wildcat? He certainly doesn't want you enjoying the peaceful sanctuary of the underwear drawer. Let's walk past his slimy trap. In fact, let's take a stick of dynamite to it. I came up with a personal slogan, a couple of years ago, that I am a little reluctant to share here. It's a very unconventional thing to hear from a Christian; a bit more edgy than the standard ecclesiastical line, but who ever said that I have to be a conventional Christian? Though my friends have heard me say it plenty, I actually hadn't planned on sharing it here. But, as I sit typing today, and though I have been trying to fight it, it keeps wanting to come out. So, here we go. "I want to kick the devil's hide" (see notes!). Seriously. Let's do what I said a couple of sentences back, and take some dynamite to his slimy trap. Let's do a little hide kickin'. Hah! How's that for wildcat thinking?

Let's get out of the slime. That's not where we belong. Stuck-in-the-slime thinking can so easily become a way of life. It's so easy to allow ourselves to slip into that mode, and to stay there without realizing it.

We have a loving Father who created us, and he has a plan for our lives. The details of those plans differ from person to person, but there is a common hope that he has for everyone; a number of things that we all have in common. First off, He wants us all to succeed; to survive; even to thrive. In his own words, "...the Lord is...not willing that any should perish..." That's an excerpt from the book of Second Peter, chapter three, verse nine, as rendered in the King James Version. I'll come back to it in a moment to discuss it in more detail. Did you catch what the excerpt said; "not willing that 'any' should perish?" Yes, that includes you. He wants you, my friend, to live.

The King of the world and Architect of the universe knows you, and cares about you. But He doesn't only want you to *not perish*. There's more.

He wants you to thrive! What do I mean by that? He doesn't want you stuck in the slime. He doesn't want you to just do life. He wants you to step out of the slime and pursue a bold life of adventure.

The enemy's slime trap steals from us. Our stuck-in-the-slime thinking robs us of adventure, of contentedness, of joy, as surely as a thief would rob us. In fact, let's hear what our generous Father has to say about that thief. "The thief comes only to steal and kill and destroy, I have come that they may have life, and have it to the full" (John 10:10 NIV). That's the way one modern translation renders the Greek; "...have it to the full." Another translates it, "...a rich and satisfying life" (NLT), while another says, "...in all its fullness" (BSB). I love the way the translators of the King James Bible chose to put it, "...that they might have life, and that they might have it more abundantly."

It's time to choose an abundant life, my friend. Our God, who created all of this for us, wants you to live your life abundantly. Look that word up, sometime. How many meanings can you find for abundantly; how many synonyms? As many as you can find, that's how many *abundantlies* our King wants for you. It is His will for you not to perish but to have a life of adventure, a life full of *abundantlies*. Your thief, your enemy, the one who hates you, wants you happily stuck in the slime. He wants you comfortable in your lack of abundance. He wants you believing that you're not worthy of a happy, satisfying, bold life of abundance.

So, whose plan should you follow? Whose vision; whose hope for your life will you pursue? With which Grand Canyon hiker did you better identify in chapter 30, Beth or Chris? When you read that conversation, which of those two life attitudes most accurately reflected the life that you are living right now, Beth's or Chris'? Which lifestyle would you select, if given the choice; comfortable in the slime, or Ocelot in an Underwear Drawer?

Our Bible is so full of great advice regarding this subject, and an almost infinite number of others. But, if you will indulge me, I'll explain the Bible-based method that works for me. Why am I so content? Why, while profoundly imperfect, am I intensely happy? How do I, a pretty normal guy, have the audacity to liken myself to a wildcat?

I'll give you the program, step by step. There's more to it than just this, but here's the greatest-hits version. It's pretty simple to explain and it doesn't take a lot of talent to pull it off, or I would be in big trouble. So, here we go…

We'll start with Flesh. We'll call that *part one*. Flesh can mean meat and bone, but, in Scripture, it is often used metaphorically for the things of the world, or the things that distract. To be more specific, Flesh refers to our own weakness as we, in our humanness, indulge in varying unfortunate responses to those distractions. For example; I moved too many times from town to town and from school to school when I was growing up. You read about that in chapters 6 and 7. As a result, I lacked stability, or opportunity to build lasting relationships. I learned, right or wrong, that good things don't last. Also, I was bullied too much in my early teens. As a result, I lacked self-worth; leaving me with a wormy, unconfident feeling that lingered for decades. A long list of personal failures and mistakes had taken their toll as well. I had that list of mistakes stapled to my frontal lobes, and it was a tough obstacle to see past. I also, at one time, had to extricate myself from beneath a pile of empty booze bottles, and the sticky self-condemnation that drips out of them. There were other impacts; other *Flesh*.

For too long I allowed myself to focus, not on what I could be, but on what I was. Without realizing that I was doing it, I was focusing on The Flesh; the things that distract. Said in a different way, my weak Flesh was causing me to focus on those distractions. I had allowed my past, or at least my interpretation of it, and the way that it had wired my mind, to dictate my present. Again, like we did with the question of what The Father wants for us, let's look at another of His promises. Let's look at how He feels about those distractions, about us allowing The Flesh to derail our abundance. In His written word, He says, "…the mind set on the flesh is death, but the mind set on the spirit is life and peace." That was Romans 8:6, as rendered in the New American Standard Bible translation.

Will we allow our stuck-in-the-slime thinking, the distractions of our unworthiness, or our fatalistic acceptance of our mediocre lot, to rob us of, or bring death to, our abundance? Should we permit The Flesh - the memories and perspectives that weigh us down - to steal away our promise of abundant life? Romans 8:6 promises that the mind set on the spirit is life and peace. That sure sounds better. But, peace? What does that mean? What is *peace*?

Philippians 4:7 refers to a peace that only God can provide. He calls it, "...the peace of God, which transcends all understanding..." (NIV). I call it *the Underwear Drawer*. You might wonder; *how can I have peace after all that I've seen; the things that I've been through?* You might even think something like, '*You don't know the terrible things that I've done! Why would God want to give me peace?*' To that, I can only answer, "I don't know." I don't know how, and I certainly can't imagine why, He would want to love a wretch like me, or you. But that's the cool part. I don't need to understand how or why, and neither do you. In fact, we can't! He called it a peace that "transcends all understanding." No one can understand it. Can you be okay with that?

"The mind set on the flesh is death, but the mind set on the spirit is life and peace." Okay, that sounds pretty good. I admit that I want that. But how does one set their mind on "the spirit?" What does that look like? How do I do it? Great questions. Let's talk about that.

This is a fun one. Can you, right now, imagine yourself as a wildcat? Can you picture yourself as a man, or a woman, that is ready to accept hardships, embrace challenges, endure a few failures, and have a great time doing it? Do you want adventure? Are you ready to see beauty and even fun, in almost every direction you look? Are you ready for some *happy*? Are you ready to feel affection and empathy for strangers, even the unlovable ones; the least of these? Do you want to be that person? Friend, you are that person, already. You only need to break out of your stuck-in-the-slime mentality and embrace who you really are, as you embrace the adventure. First you will need to accept the truth of what I've just spoken over you, then you will need to act on it. I will explain how to do both, or, rather, I will ask God to explain.

First, though you're full of imperfections; moles, warts and bad breath; mistakes, disappointments and failures; you can be seen, by the eyes of God Himself, as a conqueror. Can you think of a stronger word than "conqueror?" Wouldn't "challenger," or "winner," or "all-around-great-guy" be good enough? No! He's not compromising when it comes to you! He uses the word "conqueror." Let's talk about being a conqueror! You can add up all of those things that are holding you back; all of the reasons that you're just an average ordinary guy, or gal, and you can list them alphabetically, in your favorite font, and God simply says, "No." Here's another huge promise from the One who created you. This is the part where you can slap yourself for ever having believed yourself to be worth less than anyone else, or unworthy of abundance. In my favorite chapter in the Bible, Romans, chapter eight, there is an answer to your list of reasons; your distractions of the flesh. It says, "Who shall separate us from the love of Christ? Shall trouble or hardship or persecution or famine or nakedness or danger or sword? *No*, in all these things we are *more than conquerors* through Him who loved us" (Romans 8:35-37 NIV).

Did you catch that big "No?" He says "No!" to your distractions of the flesh. A mind, set on the flesh, is death. No! Don't go there. We are more than conquerors! You, my friend, are more than a wildcat! More than an Ocelot. It's what He is calling you to be. This is how He already sees you, and He is the maker of all; the One whose opinion of you really matters. Be a wildcat! Be more than a conqueror!

Next on our list is, how. I promised you I'd get there. You might ask, "Is there something that I need to do first? Do I need to earn this?" The answer is no… and yes. No, you don't need to earn it. It's a free gift. But there is something that you need to do. You need to accept the gift. When you're handed a birthday present, it's a free gift from someone who cares about you. But you still need to accept it from their hands, and unwrap it. Am I right?

How do I unwrap the gift of conquerorness (I made a word up!)? How do I install the batteries and turn it on? Here's how. "Seek first His Kingdom and His Righteousness, and *all these things* will be added to you…" (NASB). That was Matthew 6:33. That's it. It's that simple. It's not always easy, but it is a simple concept. What does "all these things" mean? What things is this verse talking about? The answer is simple. They're the things that He wants you to have. And what things are those? They're the things that we have been talking about.

Do you want freedom, strength, purpose? Compassion, forgiveness, courage? Fun, fulfillment, abundance? Intense Happiness? Seek Him. Trust and serve Him, and these things will be yours.

"Intensely Happy," it says, on the front of this book. You might be wondering, *can you really get there, all the way to "Intensely Happy," simply by seeking His Righteousness?*

Do yourself a favor sometime, and read Matthew, chapters five through seven. Read it a few times. Let it sink in. These chapters tell the remarkable story of how Jesus, one day, looked out over the huge crowds that were flocking to hear His amazing words, and He loved them. He went up onto a hill, from which they could see and hear Him and He taught them. This speech is generally referred to as His "Sermon on the Mount." Over and over, that day, He provided teaching about how to be "blessed." Over and over, His instructions started with terms like *"blessed are those who…"* and *"blessed are you when…"*

We can read and act upon those instructions and get "blessed." Great! So what does "blessed" mean? It means happy! Do you want to be "Intensely Happy?" Get blessed. "Blessed" is a term whose meaning has evolved. Currently, the word "blessed," according to *Dictionary.com*, means a number of things, including, "consecrated, sacred and holy," or "divinely or supremely favored, fortunate," and other things. Those are all good meanings and, for the most part, they all fit nicely with the Sermon on the Mount. But, the word originally used in these Bible passages, in the place of "blessed," is the Greek word *makarios*, which, literally defined, means "happy." It can even mean "blissful."

Now, read those nine instructions again, from Matthew 5, and use the word "happy," wherever it says "blessed." "Happy are those who…" "Happy are you when…" This understanding of the correct translation does two wonderful and amazing things for us. First, it provides us some very good and understandable instructions on how to be more happy. Second, and more important, I think; it shows us that He wants us to be happy. Happy is the goal with which the Creator of the Universe began His profound and momentous speech on that hill. So, when He tells us, a little bit later in that same sermon, to "seek first His Kingdom and His Righteousness, and all these things will be added to you," *Happy* is one of those things being promised.

There's a common misconception out there that a good follower of God should be long-faced and sorrowful; humbly enduring, selflessly sacrificing. If that were true, why would He say that it's His will for us to "live life abundantly?" If that were true, why would he provide so many "happy are those who…" instructions? Why would he, in the book of James, spend so much time explaining to us that we can even be happy, or joyful, when we experience suffering? It's because He loves us and He wants us to be happy!

He wants to do this for you!

You're a skeptic, right? Maybe just a little? Maybe a lot? I know a man who once told me something like, "Sure! That sounds great! It all sounds fantastic, and I envy you, Chris. I would love to believe all that stuff. But I don't." Are you there, my friend? Do you want what I've described, but you just can't get your mind wrapped around believing it? That's alright. There's a lot of that going around. I was there once, myself. In fact, God even has something to say about that; something specifically for you. Mark 9:24 tells the story of just such a guy. He wanted to believe. So, he humbled himself and cried out, through his reluctance and skepticism, "I do believe! Help me overcome my unbelief!" (NIV). He recognized that this was something that he needed. He forced his desire for God to overcome his fear, pride, skepticism, and, though he still felt the doubts, he cried out for help to believe.

It's right there in print, in the written words of the One who loves you and wants to do so much for you; the One who yearns to give you abundance. He provided the example, in Mark 9:24, of the self-humbling skeptic, for you. You do your part, and He will do His.

That's almost it! There are a million other things that you can read and study and put into practice, but, for the basic foundation for living the life of abundance, for being The Ocelot, you've got what you need, right here, in this chapter.

There is one last thing, more important than all of the others combined; more important than anything else written in this book. And what is that? It's the Ultimate Ocelot; the King of Conquerors; the Giver of Abundance; the Remover of Slime. It's Jesus Christ.

He is the glue in every Scripture that I've quoted here. When, in step one, we learned that "…the mind set on the flesh is death, but the mind set on the spirit is life and peace," the "spirit" mentioned in this verse is Jesus Christ. The mind set on Him is "life and peace."

In step two, "…the peace of God, which transcends all understanding…" is what? Remember that? It's a free gift of undeserved peace that's so true and wonderful that it's not understandable, right? Do you know what the very next line is, in that scripture? It says this, His peace "will guard your hearts and minds *as you live in Christ Jesus*." (Philippians 4:7 NLT)

What about step three; the "more than conquerors" step? Do you suppose He's there too? He's more than just *there*! The very next lines say, "For I am convinced that neither death nor life, neither angels nor demons, neither the present nor the future, nor any powers, neither height nor depth, nor anything else in all creation, will be able to separate us from *the love of God that is in Christ Jesus our Lord*" (Romans 8:38-39 NIV). Now that's some kind of love!

It's all about Him. Step four; "Seek first *His* Kingdom and *His* Righteousness, and *all these things* will be given to you..." Whose kingdom do you think we mean, here? Here's a hint; he was born in a manger - his initials are JC.

When the self-humbled skeptic cried out, "I believe! Help me to overcome my unbelief," to whom do you think he was speaking? The fact is, when he said this line, he was physically standing right in front of the man, Yeshua; Jesus Christ himself. And why did he say these things? Because he needed a miracle; a solution to his current problem. Jesus had just asked him, in a sense, "Do you believe that I can do this?" "I believe!" the man replied. "Help me to overcome my unbelief."

Where do you find yourself, right now. Do you need Him to do something for you? Do you want to ask Him for help? Would you like to take His strong outstretched hand and allow Him to pull you from the slime? But, are you struggling to believe? Here is where the boot hits the ground, dear one. You can do this. Ask Him. Tell Him that you want to believe. Ask Him to help you overcome your unbelief. Ask Him to help you accept that there is a place for you beyond the slime.

Just understand, and believe, that He wants you to live, to *not perish*. And, despite your past failures and beyond all troubling voices of doubt, He wants you to live "more abundantly," with a peace that "transcends understanding!" Can you see yourself as "more than a conqueror?" He already knows you to be. Doesn't that give you some confidence to step out of the slime?

You can take your mind off of your limiting slime, and grasp hold of life. "The mind set on the flesh is death but the mind set on the spirit is life and peace." You can take your mind off of the things that have been bringing death to your abundance, and slime to your peace. And the way that we get there is through Him. Our job is not to seek happiness, or to strive for abundance. It's not our job to make loving others our priority. We are not expected to just change everything, turn on a dime, and walk, under our own power, away from bondage and slavery to our past. No! None of those things work. They sound like noble endeavors, but they fail. Instead, "...seek first His Kingdom and His Righteousness, and *all these things* will be added to you."

It's that easy. You can free yourself from the slime trap, by seeking Him first; by making Him first in your life.

I am so tired of seeing unhappy Christians. We should be the happiest, boldest, most empowered, adventurous people on the planet. I'm tired of seeing sons and daughters of The King, comfortably accepting a life of non-abundance; non-conqueror; non-Ocelot. I'm tired of seeing the enemy robbing my friends.

Let's seek first The King; Jesus Christ, and His Righteousness; and together, let's kick the devil's hide.

Epilogue

I looked out over a room full of teenagers, all sitting quietly, facing forward. They ranged from seventh to twelfth grade. In many of their faces, I thought I could already see a mild glazing over, as they quietly settled into their padded church pews, preparing themselves for their weekly forty minutes. It was Friday; Chapel Day. Every Friday, the students of this private Christian school filed into this room and then, later, filed back out.

"Don't worry if they look bored, or if you see some of them whispering to each other; not paying attention," I was warned by a friend who had spoken here in the past. "Happens all the time. They're teenagers. Attention span problems. Some might even fall asleep on you," he said with a laugh. "But, some of them will listen. You'll do fine."

I recognized many of them. Some were friends of my kids, and had been in my home. Some had been members of athletic teams that I had coached. Those were the kids who looked forward, now, with respectful attention. Most of the faces, though, were new to me, especially the younger ones.

"I'm not going to talk down to you." I started. "I'm going to try very hard not to treat you like just a bunch of kids today. You get enough of that already. Am I right?" I paused and looked out over the room like I expected an answer; and I saw a few heads cautiously nodding. "And... I'm going to ask you to return the favor. You might hear some edgier stuff today. Can you deal with that - maturely? Be more than just a bunch of kids today.

"Right now, I figure there are four different kinds of students in this room. Listen for a moment, and answer silently to yourself; which group are you in?

"Group one. Some of you have a close personal relationship with God. You've accepted Jesus Christ as your Savior." I took a moment and looked around, making eye contact with as many as I could. "You like feeling His love and you enjoy learning more about Him.

There's a second group. Good chance there are some in this room who believe in God; you've said the prayer of salvation... several times, maybe. Maybe you've been baptized. But... somehow... you don't have that intimate relationship with Him that you hear others talking about. You want it... but you don't even really understand what it means. And... you wonder, 'Is there something wrong with me, God?'

"Then there's group three. I believe that there are some here who think something like, 'I'd love to believe. Really. I would. I'd like to have what all those other people have... but, I guess I don't. I don't know, maybe there's a God. I hope there is. But, something's just holding me back from believing."

I moved my attention to more new faces, taking a moment. "And... there's group four. In a crowd this size, even at a Christian School, I'll bet there's someone here thinking, 'Yep, this is the school my parents have put me in, so I have to look the part. I hear all about God almost every day. And on Fridays, I have to go listen to some preacher or guest speaker tell me about a benevolent *Man upstairs* who knows my birthday... If my parents knew half of what I really believe, it would probably really disappoint them. So, I'll play the game a little bit longer, and, when I'm eighteen, I'll make my own decisions."

I paused a moment. "Which of those four groups are you in? If you are in group one, please listen today. And I pray that you will be edified and your faith will be strengthened. If you are in groups two or three, I've been there. I know what you mean. Please listen, and I hope that you will find a piece of what you're looking for.

"Group Four People; I am so glad that you're here. To you, I want to say, thanks. Thanks for coming, and thanks for sitting there and enduring another chapel service quietly and respectfully, like you have so many others. But you, Group Four Person... I have a challenge for you. Today, while I'm here, I challenge you to not just look and listen. I dare you to really hear me." I emphasized the word "hear." "And, when it's all said and done, you can privately let me know how it went. If you still feel just the same, or if you feel something new happening inside. Come tell me. But, I challenge you. Hear me today. Give me a fair shake... And, know that I was once a member of group four."

At this point, I introduced myself, and I provided a very short explanation of my background. Then I said, "I would like to tell you a story. A story about a kid, a boy... a teenager. Not a real special kid. Not very popular, but not a dork either. Pretty smart, but no honor student. He wasn't a jock or a preppy. Not a bookworm, a teacher's pet or a class clown. He wasn't goth or emo. Not a stoner. Definitely not a chick magnet. No one hated him, but no one voted him class president either. He had a few friends, but most people didn't know him. He was... just a guy. You know the type? Just an average teenage guy.

"Then something happened... kind of accidentally... a little at a time. His life became less average. More... fun. Exciting. And, this is his story... my story. Yeah, this is a story about me.

"It really wasn't that long ago. I remember it like it was yesterday. I can vividly remember the day that I got drunk for the first time. And I mean drunk. Falling down drunk... and, I liked it!" I smiled as I nodded my head, trying to give my attention more toward the back of the room, where the older students sat. "I liked it a lot! From then on, my buddies and I worked to find ways to get a hold of booze, and none of those ways were legal. Sometimes it was beer, sometimes hard alcohol, which we would usually pour into a Big Gulp.

"I was thirteen years old." I saw heads rise up, and surprised eyes were meeting mine all over the room.

With a serious countenance, I continued. "Nearly every weekend, my friends and I were drinking... something. Slowly, I met other people... guys and girls... that also had this same... hobby. Eventually, I realized that I wasn't so ordinary anymore. Instead of picking on me, as I was used to people doing, they wanted to drink with me. I was finally being included. I belonged.

"On weekends, I was at big keg parties, sometimes. Other times, I drank in small groups. Often, it was just my best friend and me.

"I liked it! I liked how it made me feel. I liked the way I was being treated by other kids. I kind of even liked the fact that I had a secret that my parents knew nothing about. And… I just enjoyed the warm pleasant feeling of being drunk.

"At one time, I was the chug-a-lug champ. I could drink a can of Coors beer in nine seconds. Budweiser was too bubbly to do that. It hurt my throat. This gained me a small measure of fame. Other kids thought that was cool. I guess that chug-a-lug talent meant that I was a really good drinker. I was kinda proud of that.

"It went on for years. The partying got more and more serious. Soon, we were smoking pot as well as drinking. This opened up a whole new group of friends to me, the dope smokers. I knew that I was breaking rules, but I was okay with that. After all, it's not like I was killing anyone. I was okay with it, so… what's the big deal?"

"Well," I continued. "I wasn't getting good grades. I was becoming more and more interested in my hobby, and less interested in other things. 'Where was the next party? Where would my next drink come from?' I was stealing from my parents. My party buddies were stealing from their parents. But, we were okay with that. In our minds, we were just fine with what we were doing.

"I had a few close calls along the way, including one high speed ambulance trip to the hospital. I sat up front with the driver, as my friend lay bleeding from his head, on a stretcher in the back. I was even arrested once, and charged with 'Minor in Possession.' But those things didn't make me stop. I liked it too much. Looking back on it now, I probably should have noticed that something might be out of whack, when, one day before school, around 7:30 in the morning, I was alone, hiding by the railroad tracks, drinking straight vodka from a 7-Up can… in ninth grade."

I stopped talking for a moment, and I moved my eyes from face to face, giving them a couple of seconds to picture that last image in their minds.

"On it went, through high school. So, what do you think eventually happened to me? Do you think I was able to just quit one day? Put it all behind me and just start a new life, no problem?" I saw a few heads slowly shake side-to-side, as if to answer "no" to my question. "Yeah! That's exactly what I did. Just like that.

"I met a girl. She wasn't into that scene. And, since I liked her a lot, I changed. Right there. It seems that I wanted a girlfriend more than I wanted alcohol. Normally, that doesn't work. Normally, that quick turnaround isn't possible. So, why did it work for me? I have a natural gift that I did nothing to deserve. It seems that I am resistant to that kind of addiction. I, for whatever reason, after all of those years, after all of those drinks, never got addicted. In fact, all of those times my friends and I smoked marijuana together, and they all got so baked, I had sat there wondering why it wasn't working on me. I, apparently, have a resistance to that too. Even the good stuff, the expensive stuff, the one-hit-bud; it didn't work. So, I was able to just walk away.

"You, my drinking teenage friend, might be looking up here at me right now and thinking, he drank like I do, and he seems to have it all together. If he can do it, I can do it.'" I shook my head. "No! It won't work for you, like it did for me! Not if you keep it up for too long. Walk away now, while you can! Let me tell you a little about my drinking friends from those years. Three of them are dead, one from an alcohol-related suicide, and one from a drunken drowning. A third from the cumulative effects of a life of bad choices. You see, those guys never made it out of that party life the way I did.

"A couple other old drinking buddies are still alive. I haven't stayed real close with them, but we do keep in touch. For years, after high school, one of them, every time I saw him, had a beer in his hand, for years and years. Beer has been his constant companion. He's divorced now.

"Another party buddy, one night, long ago, while clearly not in his right mind, thanks to one mood-altering substance or another, fell off of a moving car that he was, for some reason, riding on, and hit his head. He needed emergency brain surgery to survive. The effects of a traumatic brain injury, like that one, can last a lifetime. He is lucky to be alive.

"If you'll read any article about addiction and alcohol; if you ask an expert about teen substance abuse, you will learn that a quick happy exit from that lifestyle, like I did, is not common at all, and that, far more often, the results are long lasting and painful, very often leading to adult alcoholism or worse addictions.

"Guys, I made it out; easy as can be. It's almost like I got a special one-of-a-kind exit pass. Why was I spared? Certainly not because I deserved to be! I was no more important than those other guys. Call me lucky, blessed, chosen. It certainly wasn't because of any brilliance on my part.

"Those pleasures that had come from partying… my feelings of belonging… the adventure of it all… the excitement… they were lies! That warm physical feeling that I liked so much when I was drunk, was a lie. It was a lie that sucked me in and got me to follow the wrong road.

"The Bible tells us that the devil is the father of lies. His lies about teenage drinking; about belonging… about excitement… about thrills, took out several of my friends. He did a good job! The devil really did it to us!" I was talking more loudly now; not shouting, but everyone in the room could hear me very well. No one was whispering or sleeping.

"Remember what I told you? I had thought that we were okay! I was convinced that what we were doing wasn't going to hurt anyone. But, like it says in Proverbs 14:12, '…there is a way that seems right to a man… *or a teen*… but its end is the way to death.'" (NASB)

I quietly took a few breaths, and sipped from my bottle of water.

"Several years ago, I was eating my lunch in a big crowded cafeteria, and I noticed that there were some birds inside the room. They were flying around in the room, and a lot of us were watching them. There were three of them. They were small and cute and they were flying around, doing some real acrobatics, entertaining a lot of bored sandwich-eating cafeteria customers. I was one of many smiling upturned faces, heads moving together as we watched the little cuties and all of their comic antics.

"After a few minutes, I looked more closely, and what I saw made me look at them very differently. This wasn't cute at all! The lead bird, the one in front, had a french-fry in his mouth. The other two birds wanted it! Those birds weren't playing. This was high speed pursuit, and that french-fry had their undivided attention. One was trying all he could to keep his french-fry, while two others were giving it all they had to steal that same french-fry. This was war.

"They missed the point!" I did shout this time. "They were stuck in a building! They might never see the sky again! They might all be dying of thirst sometime very soon! If they had looked around some, I'm willing to bet that there were plenty of other french-fries and bread pieces and cracker crumbs to be found. They were expending huge amounts of energy on something that, in the big picture, didn't matter, but something that would be real good right now. Where should their efforts have been focused? They might never see the sun again! They were stuck in a place where they didn't belong, with their attention on the wrong goal."

Raising my voice again, I cried out slowly; annunciating each word carefully, "I don't want to chase the french-fry anymore!

"The french-fry might be good for a moment... maybe real good; but then what? It doesn't last! That french-fry can be what takes your heart away and leads it toward death! I told you about my french-fry. Drinking was my french-fry! I chased it... I pursued it... enjoyed it... expended great amounts of energy on it, and I completely missed the big picture. I followed its lies. And I helped friends do the same thing, leading to ruin for some of them!"

I took a short moment to pierce a few teenage eyes with my own. Then I looked in a different direction, and started the next thought with a much more gentle voice.

"Have you ever been noticed? You know... noticed... by someone of the opposite gender? What does it feel like to be a teenage girl and have that one boy... you know the one... what does it feel like to have him notice you? To have him smile at you? To have him... touch you?

"There was this girl. When she smiled at me, or better yet, touched me... oh, my heart rate surged, and I got goosebumps. Now, don't worry. I'm not going down the trail that you might think I am. I'm not expecting you girls to be nuns; or you guys to be priests or monks or something. You're not little kids anymore. You're supposed to be noticing each other. It's normal. And it's normal to feel good when someone notices you.

"But what is it that they're noticing about you? Is it your smile? Your eyes? Your laugh? Your personality?" I inserted another pause here. "Or, is it your body? Is it the way you're dressing that's getting you noticed?

"Girls! God thinks you're beautiful; just the way you are! You are beautiful! You don't need to dress that way... to show your curves and your skin, to be beautiful. You already are.

"You don't need a boy to notice you... to walk all over you with his eyes... to touch you. Yes! It feels good! It feels good right then... maybe real good. But it's another of those french-fries, there for a moment and then gone. That wonderful feeling… is a lie! It's a lie designed to take you down; to pull you from the right road.

"There's a thirst that a lot of us have. Since puberty… it's there. We're thirsty to be wanted; we're thirsty for affection. We're thirsty for that feeling of acceptance… of being attractive to someone…. Yes, the thirst is real. But, just because you're thirsty, that's no reason to drink from a toilet. There are other, better ways of satisfying your thirst.

"The Bible says, in First Peter 5:8, '…your enemy, the devil, prowls around like a roaring lion, looking for someone to devour' (NIV). Interesting word picture, isn't it? Like a lion? Well… lions are cool. I like lions. That's not so bad, is it?

"Have you ever seen a lion killing its prey? Have you seen the speed, the power, the ferociousness that a lion has? Sometimes, he goes for the throat, and rips it out with his teeth, while his victim is still alive and breathing. Other times, it's much worse. Sometimes a lion will get a hold of his victim with his front claws and his teeth, sinking them in an inch deep, and more. Then, he uses his razor-sharp hind claws to tear at his victim's belly, digging his way deeper and deeper, little by little, shredding flesh, disemboweling his prisoner. Then, as the victim lays there, awake but dying a little with every second that passes, the lion stands in the middle of the blood and the guts and the gore, and roars with triumph. No mercy! Just massive amounts of power, focused on destroying his opponent."

I saw some students cringe as they sat there. Some stared up at me unblinking. Some looked sideways at each other, their mouths open in shock.

"This…" I shot out loudly, pointing at the audience, "…is how the devil feels about you! This is how much he hates you! This is NOT cool! You really do have an enemy. A real enemy. God says that your enemy is like a lion. He's that kind of enemy. He'll rip you apart! He blew my classmate's brain all over a wall. He ripped my other friend's marriage apart.

"He will use the lies that he's a master of, to take you down. He'll use that warm feeling you get inside every time you get drunk, if you're into that. He'll use that special feeling you get every time that certain boy shows you affection. He'll use that heart-quickening sensation that happens with certain Internet websites. He'll use that welcome feeling that you get from others who are doing the same things that you are doing, that feeling of belonging. Do you have something else in mind right now? A different french fry?

"Ruin wrapped in pretty ribbons and bows. That is what they are, these french fries. Rat poison, dipped in chocolate.

"When I think about the mistakes that we allow ourselves to get into as we pursue these attractive, appetizing lies, I get a picture in my mind, of a runaway train, zooming down a mountain. There's a sharp turn at the bottom. Doom - death - loss… are moments away. But all we care about, as we ride that train, is how fun it is to go that fast.

"When a teenager dies in a partying death, like some of my classmates did; when a marriage collapses, tearing a family apart; when someone gives up on their beautiful dream, to follow an ugly path; when a young person gives away the only thing that she really owns, to a boy who then walks away and forgets her; the devil… your enemy, wears a smile.

"Did you know that you have an enemy? A deadly enemy? Not good news! Did you know that you have another enemy? The Bible says, in Jeremiah 17:9, '…the heart is deceitful… who can know it?' (KJV). Yeah, sometimes we can be our own worst enemy. Remember what I said earlier about my drinking? My friends and I thought that what we were doing was just fine. So we were okay with it. It was truly just fine with me. Yes, I knew I was breaking rules, but, in my heart, I wasn't hurting anyone so, what's the big deal? But, was I hurting anyone? I was a leader. I had a certain amount of influence. And I influenced others, my good friends, with my behavior. My example was laid before them, and some of their lives were impacted by that poor example, to my lasting shame.

"'There is a way that seems right to a man but its end is the way to death.' I mentioned that verse before. And it means the same thing that Jeremiah meant about the heart being deceitful. So, you can't even trust your own heart, or the way that seems right. You can't do what Jiminy Cricket sang, in Pinocchio, and 'Always Let Your Conscience Be Your Guide.' Your 'Conscience' is corrupt. Then, what's the answer? If we have this terrible devil guy after us, trying to destroy us all the time… and, if we have a heart that's so deceitful that we can't trust ourselves… how can we make it?

"The truth is we can't! That's right… we can't make it. We are all doomed. No one can survive that kind of world." I took another drink of water, letting that last statement dangle out there for a moment. "Well, there is one who can. In all the world, there's only been one who ever could. His name? Jesus Christ. He can do it for you. Without Him… you're done. You're lion food. You don't even have a chance. With Him, though… with Jesus, you can!

"It won't always be easy. You'll still have to fight these things… these lies of the enemy, for the rest of your life. But, with Jesus… you can. You can fight, and you can win.

"Philippians 4:13 says, 'I can do all things through Him who gives me strength" (NASB). You can even fight the prowling lion.

"So, what does this look like… in a practical way? How is it done? Start with Jesus. Make Him your priority. Make Him a way of life. Spend time in your Bible. Go to church. And, when you're there, really pay attention to what's being taught. Hang out with other Christians. Try to eliminate the things in your life that you know are pulling you away from Him. Get rid of the french-fries.

"How many of you know what you had for dinner, last November third? No one? How about the day after that? Or, the day after that? No? But, you did eat dinner those nights, right? We need food to survive, and we eat every day. It's okay if not every meal is life-changing or memorable. It's okay if some meals are downright boring. Sure, we all remember a few great dinners. Maybe some barbecued ribs with watermelon and lemonade, last summer in the back yard? Or, a particularly good lasagna a few weeks ago. An unusually great bratwurst dog, at a ball game? Most meals aren't things that rock our worlds, right? But, they're important, aren't they? They keep us alive. They're nourishment. Church, Sunday school, and youth group, are a lot like that. Listen to what your teachers and guest speakers have to say during these Friday Chapel times… yes, even the boring ones. It's all nourishment. It's good food for the soul. We need Godly nourishment.

"A few of those teachings and nourishing experiences will be so amazing that you will remember them the rest of your lives. Most won't be like that. But all of them, all of the sermons, youth meetings, bible studies, worship times, hymnal pages… all of it… they're what you need. Stay nourished. Eat, and stay alive. Choose Him.

"I have a quick story that I'd like to tell. I wish I could remember who I first heard it from, so I could give him credit for it. I know that I heard it on Christian radio." I had, long ago, heard a tiny short word picture used during a radio interview. It may have only been twenty or thirty seconds long, and I had, ever since then, hoped that I could someday develop that idea into an inspiring longer story; an adventure story of sorts. So, that is what I did.

"Long ago, here in our own part of the continent, a boy of roughly sixteen was about to become a man. His tribe had a ritual, as many tribes did; a rite of passage that formally ushered a boy into manhood. If he could make it through tonight's test of courage, tomorrow he would attend a special ceremony, where he would be given his manhood name. He hoped that it would be a strong name that he could carry proudly through his life.

"A sound surprised him and he startled. 'What was that?' he wondered, as a frightened yelp sound escaped his lips. 'Be brave. Just sit. Stay still.'

"The blindfold was tight across his face, and it hurt a little bit. But he would take the pain with bold endurance. He could tell, from the chill in the air and from the sounds of the forest, that night had fallen. He had never felt so alone. He had never been so afraid.

"The air became colder as the hours grew on. His body shook softly and the skin on his bare arms felt bumpy like the skin of the ducks from his father's traps, after they had been plucked clean of their feathers. This, too, he would endure with courage and strength. Sounds were all around him; night sounds; sounds that he had heard all his life, though he had never known that they could be this loud. Frogs, crickets, birds of the night. These did not bother the boy. But there were other sounds; deeper, larger sounds; sounds that he could not give a name to. Some were far away. Some were so near that he wanted to cry out - to rip the blindfold from his face and run to his village. He stayed. 'I will earn a strong manhood name this night.'

"It was the longest night of his life. Long frightening mysterious hours went by. He didn't know how many. Cold. So cold. So dark. So alone. So afraid.

"After an eternity, he noticed the forest sounds changing. Now, he heard different animals, different birds. He remembered his violent shivers of a few hours before; shivers of both cold and fear, and he welcomed a new warmth in the air. He sat still, his bare back pressed against the bark of the great fir tree beneath which he had spent the night.

"'Almost done,' the boy thought. 'Just a little while longer.' He knew that these early hours were hunting times for many of the beasts of these mountains. It was now, so close to the finish, that his fear was at its greatest. Terror tried to seize him. His heart pounded in his chest. Monsters. Giant creatures tormented his mind. Spiders. Snakes. Strange creatures with unfamiliar shapes. New sounds; terrifying sounds, came out of the air all around him. A scream rose in his chest, and he fought it for control. Tears soaked into the cloth that held his eyes closed, as he covered his head with his arms. 'How can I go on?'

"Then, almost as if a veil had been lifted from before him, he felt heat splash across his face, and, at that very moment, despite the blindfold, light could be seen through his closed eyelids. Oh, what a glorious feeling. It was over. He had faced the terrors of the night, and he had prevailed. He stood and walked two or three steps toward the warmth, away from the rough-skinned tree that had been his only companion, and he reached for the blindfold.

"The world was a murky blur as his eyes tried to adjust. Trees were thin fuzzy shapes at first. He looked around him, trying to focus. Leaves. Bushes. Rocks. A thin fog lay low on the land. And there was something else. Fifty paces away, he saw a shape. It was out of place, here, and it was large. It didn't move at all, but the boy knew that it was no tree. He reached up and wiped his bleary eyes, trying to focus on the strange thing. Slowly, it solidified before him, far away, and he could see that it was a man. A bolt of fear shot through the boy, but he did not run. The man held a bow, and he had an arrow strung, ready to pull. Then, out of the mist that had partially hidden him, the boy's father strode forward, a serious expression on his face. He came to the boy and placed one hand on the boy's shoulder. The boy looked upward, into his father's eyes, trying to read his expression. Then, the corners of the great man's mouth turned upward slightly. Deep in his body, the boy's heart launched like an eagle taking flight, and he too smiled.

"As they silently walked together, toward the village, the boy started thinking. 'My father was there when I finished. How did he know exactly where I was or when I would emerge? Perhaps he had been there a long time.' Then, realization smashed into his brain. 'He was there the whole time! My father was there, watching over me, the entire night, ready for anything, with his bow and his war club. I need never have feared. He had been there all along, watching over me. He had seen me shivering, and he had heard my soft cries, yet, when it was over, he had been pleased with me; even proud.' And suddenly, the boy's heart was full of a new kind of warmth, as he looked up at the father who walked beside him."

As I looked out over the chapel full of junior high and high schoolers, I noticed not one sleeping student. All eyes were solidly attached to mine. I paused from speaking as I looked around the room, quickly making eye contact with as many as I could. I let the pause linger several seconds.

"Young people, this is the way it works with The Holy Spirit. He will always be there for you, even when you don't see Him or feel Him. Even when you feel utterly alone, he's there. And, He loves you. He tells us, in Hebrews 13:5, 'Never will I leave you; never will I forsake you' (NIV).

Would you like to know God this way? You can, you know. In a moment I'm going to lead you in a prayer. It's a prayer very much like ones that you've heard before. We call it the 'Prayer of Salvation,' or sometimes, 'The Sinner's Prayer.' You can follow after me, if you'd like to. If you've already prayed this prayer, and you know that you're good with God, that's okay. You can pray it again. I've done it dozens of times. But, if you're feeling something new today, and you want to get right with God, please join me. If you aren't ready, that's okay. No one's going to make you do this. I just ask that, if that's you, you close your eyes respectfully along with everyone else and wait it out.

"For those who would like to, please repeat after me, and please remember that he really does love you…

"Lord Jesus, I am lost without you." I heard students repeating. It was such a beautiful sound; so many of them were speaking. "Without you, I don't have a chance… I ask you to save me from the enemy that hates me… from the french-fries that pull me away from you… and from

the deceit of my own heart... I ask you to be my Lord and my Savior...
my guide and my friend... my King and my God."

I knew that I had gone over on my time allotment. I hoped that the
teachers of their next classes wouldn't mind too badly. Late as it was, I
was surprised when a line of students formed before me. One by one, they
thanked me for coming, for what I had said, for how it had made them
feel. Beyond the others, standing away from the line, she waited; cheeks
wet with tears. She paced back and forth and wiped her face over and
over. I watched her from the corner of my eye, as I greeted and thanked
each student in line, and I hoped that she would not leave. No matter
how she fought them, her tears came and came, and she repeatedly wiped
her palms across her cheeks.

"I've never seen this group pay attention like that in any chapel
service, Mr. Ford. That was great." Thanks, Josh. I shook his hand and
watched him walk out the side door. Aside from their Chapel teacher,
who, noticing what was happening up front, astutely kept himself busy
in the chapel's sound booth, cleverly finding knobs that needed turned
and buttons that needed pressed, only she remained.

She came to me and lost whatever semblance of control had
remained. I waited patiently as she cried. The Daddy in me wanted to
take her into my arms and hold her close, but that's not something that
a guest speaker can do with a seventeen year old girl. So, I waited, with
a gentle smile on my face. I moved to my side and sat on the front pew
and I pointed to the place beside me.

She sat. Finally, words came. Insecurities. Fears. Yearnings. Struggles.
Confessions. Requests for prayer. Gratitude. It was heart-wrenching for
me to see the pain being worked out right in front of me, but rewarding
to know that growth might be happening, right now, and that victory
might be working itself out. That God would use me today! What joy. I
replied. We spoke softly. We prayed together. Her grateful tear-streaked
smile, at the end, was one of the most precious things ever given to me.

Notes

Unlike the Notes section of most books, you will not find this one boring or text bookish. In fact, some of this book's best things are in these Notes. I hope that you won't skip this portion. There's some cool stuff here.

Also, I've decided to do my End Notes a little bit differently than those found in most books. This is not a textbook. In fact, I think it reads more like a novel. As such, I didn't want distracting little numbers at the ends of sentences. Instead, I am providing the sentences at the beginning of each End Note.

Chapter 1: Almond Or Raspberry

1. "Adrenaline surge to the gut!" It was very purposeful that I started this book with this incomplete sentence fragment. My daughter, Lydia, and I have made a game of identifying and texting each other our favorite opening sentences (or sentence fragments) from the books that we read. Some are long, like the opening line in Charles Dickens' classic, *A Tale Of Two Cities*, which starts, "It was the best of times, it was the worst of times…" and then continues in a lovely way, for another half of a page. Emmuska Orczy's *The Scarlet Pimpernel* also starts with a very poetic and very long, beautiful sentence, as does *The Red Badge of* Courage, by Stephen Crane. On the flip side of the coin, there are some wonderfully evocative, yet delightfully short first sentences, like Peter Benchley's opening to *Jaws*, "The great fish swam slowly." Or, Tolkien's masterpiece, *The Hobbit*, "In a hole in the ground, there lived a Hobbit."

Then there are some special first sentences that, right when I read them, I wanted to know more. One of the best of those was from John Wyndham's provocative 1951 future-shock Sci-Fi thriller, *The Day of the Triffids*, "When a day that you happen to know is Wednesday starts off by sounding like Sunday, there is something seriously wrong somewhere." *What is it? What's seriously wrong? Why does it sound like a Sunday? What does that even mean? I need to keep reading!*

Another of my favorite reach-out-of-the-book-and-grab-the-reader's-throat opening sentences can be found in Louis L'Amour's extremely entertaining western adventure, *Sackett*, where he started the whole thing off with, "It wasn't as if he hadn't been warned." That's a good one! Don't you just want to keep reading to find out why, and what it was he was warned about, and what's going to happen, now that he's ignored the warning… whoever "he" is? *Tell me more!*

Then there's the wonderfully quirky first sentences. In John Kennedy Toole's Pulitzer winning novel, *A Confederacy of Dunces*, this was how it started, "A green hunting cap squeezed the top of the fleshy balloon of a head." I chuckled out loud, just one sentence into that book.

I would never compare myself to Dickens or Benchley, or any of those others, but, like they all did, I wanted my book to start well, and it was after the L'Amour example that I most followed. It didn't bother me at all that I would start the book with a sentence that doesn't contain a proper subject and predicate, like we all learned from our sixth grade teachers is absolutely necessary. After all, my sixth grade teacher is not here, with her red corrections pen. My book; my rules! Hah!

2. "Her name was Chelea." Using Facebook, I was able to get in touch with Chelea while I was writing this chapter. Facebook, with all of its good aspects and bad, is an amazingly effective way of keeping in touch with people. I wanted to tell this story of young infatuation and unrequited love, and I really wanted the name of the girl to be special, as she had been special, even if I have to change the name to protect her privacy. I thought about using the name Jasmine as her

fictitious appellation. That's a pretty name, for a pretty girl. I was delighted, though, when Chelea, to whom I had nervously sent an early draft of this chapter, contacted me back and told me that she would be glad to let me use her real name. Thanks Chelea.

3. "Maybe she didn't have Kimberly's eyes or Dianne's hair or Lexie's bod." I hesitated to write this sentence. First off, those are all invented names. They are code names for specific real-life individuals that sort of ran in that same beautiful circle of girls in my graduating class. I'm not going to contact the actual "Lexie" and ask her if I can, in a published book, write a general reference about her spectacular high school figure. How would that be for awkward?

    I also hesitated, because I don't want to give the impression that Chelea, herself, didn't also score well in all three of these categories. She was, and is, a very attractive lady. But I did have a reason for keeping that line in there, and that reason was contrast. The lines that follow, which describe her "intangibles," are made all the more important. I wanted to show that she was, to my eleventh grade sensibilities, so much more than a pretty face. If all I had been looking for was gorgeous hair, or eyes or curves, there would have been plenty to choose from. Our high school was famously wealthy in those departments.

Chapter 2: To Be An Astronaut

1. "Miss Livingston was a good teacher..." "I want to be the best Kindergarten teacher that I can be..." Here, as we move from chapter 1 to chapter 2, we experience the first of many timeline adjustments. A few pages earlier, you had been reading the story of an infatuated sixteen-year-old, and now that same main character is only six. Remember, as I said in the Author's Note, this book is not a biography. It is a series of short stories that each stand alone, while, when looked at together, tell a greater story.

    In life, her name was not "Miss Livingston." I can't remember her name, so I gave her another name. I thought of pulling a name out of the air, but that could have resulted in anything from "Smith" to "Schmuckatelli." I do, however, remember the name of the Kindergarten teacher under whom I had worked at the end of the previous year. Her last name was Livingston. So, you can see what I did there.

Chapter 4: Sequins and Safety Pins

1. "<u>It was our very own high school classmate Lisa Elliott</u>!" I am pleased to say that I did not have to change Lisa's name. I was delighted, and a little bit surprised to be honest, when she put her stamp of approval on this chapter. Lisa plays a pretty major role in this story – a potentially embarrassing one. After I nervously emailed her a draft of this chapter she immediately fired back an enthusiastic letter wherein she said that I had not only made her laugh until she cried, but that I had, if anything, been too kind.

2. "<u>She and Ken, her handsome 'friend zone' prom date</u>…"
   …and we're still using real names. I was able to get a hold of the real "Ken" Just before publishing, to ask him for permission to use his first name. Again, I was super jazzed when he agreed. None of what happened that night was his fault. In fact, I believe that he was an absolute gentleman whose behavior was beyond reproach. A very good guy.

3. "<u>His family ran the local hardware store there in Snohomish. Through the years, my dad had bought a lot of nails and paint, a lot of thinga-ma-jigs and whatz-its from Brad's dad, Bob.</u>" The reigns of the family business were turned over to Brad some time ago and that wonderful hardware store has been run by his trusty leadership ever since. Years later, when he and I were both dads, I bought a lot of thinga-ma-jigs and whatz-its from Brad.

4. "<u>She (Lisa) was very sweet and I respected her a lot.</u>" She still is and I still do.

5. "…<u>she and I had the same favorite teacher in Mr. Mike Jenson.</u>" I did change the name on this one. This particular guy may have been my favorite teacher of my entire life. Laura now tells me that she felt the same way. But his real name was not Mike Jenson.

Chapter 6: The New Kid: Boy You're Gonna Carry That Weight

1. Cool chapter title, huh? I've liked the Beatles as long as I can remember. One of my favorite pieces that they ever did is the big medley on side two of Abbey Road, which includes the song "Carry That Weight." If you string all of those Side Two songs together as one song, which was obviously their intent, it's arguably the best thing that they ever did. Ol' McCartney's line, "Boy, you're gonna carry that weight, carry that weight a long time..." was certainly not written about a young boy who moved from state to state, and school to school, always feeling like an outsider; but it sure does apply to how it felt to be that boy.

   When it was all said and done, if you include the apartment to which I was brought right after I was born, I moved into my seventeenth home just a little after I turned seventeen.

2. "Mrs. Swanson" wasn't the real name of my second kindergarten teacher. The real teacher's last name did start with an "S," though. In fact, I gave different names to my kindergarten classmates in this chapter as well, though most of them did keep their first initials.

3. "We all walked the same direction." Can you imagine kindergartners walking home without adult supervision now? Gasp!

4. "...having moved there recently from New Mexico." Prior to moving to Washington, we had lived in three different homes, in three different neighborhoods, in New Mexico; all in the greater Albuquerque area.

5. "...shouted and yelled words like, "Cool!" and "Whoa, man!" This story takes place right between the "groovy" and "totally awesome" days. "Whoa!" was pretty much the best of what we had to work with. "Far out," though a little stale, was still getting some traction around then.

6. "...Will I still be in first grade when we get there?" Starting brand new at a strange school is tough. But, it's especially hard if the school year has already started. You're never more *The New Kid* than when the school year is already underway. By then, routines have been established, and cliques are already formed and are rapidly

solidifying. There is much more of a spotlight on you. Several of my school changes, through the years, happened this way.

Chapter 7: The New Kid: Mighty Mouse and his Reign of Terror

1. Quote, "<u>And forgive us our trespasses as we forgive those who trespass against us</u>." (quote on inset) This is a fascinating reference. Well, I think it's fascinating. You might not. I can be a little geeky about this kind of stuff. I would love to credit this version of Matthew 6:12, and tell you the Bible translation from which it comes and give proper credit to those who currently own the rights to that translation. But, I can't. No one owns this version – because it's not real. The King James Bible and nearly every other version since then, renders it, "...forgive us our debts..." not "trespasses." But I'll bet you've heard "trespasses" in this phrase all of your life, as I have. We have to go all the way back to the Tyndale Bible of 1549 to find where the "trespasses" thing happened. That was prior to the King James, which only goes as far back as 1611. And, though Tyndale's said "trespasses," the rest of Matthew 6:12 was worded very differently there than I have shown it. The way that I have written it is a misquote, but one so common that it's almost come to be canonical. If required to credit this quote, one could only write *Traditional*. The thing is; I really like it the way that I've written it here – the way that I have heard it misquoted my whole life - and this version fits best with the Ocelot chapter that it immediately precedes – so I'm going with it. If, Dear Reader, you take exception with me propagating this common misquote, please forgive my trespass.

2. "<u>...the record number of hangings that took place there, due to claim jumping, theft and murder.</u>" Nowadays, I sort of frown and laugh at the same time when I drive by our local shopping mall. Right next to the mall, there's a very nice restaurant called Claim Jumper. In fact, there's a successful chain of these restaurants. Great food, great atmosphere, bad name. Claim jumping was a terrible crime at one time. Hmmmm...

3. "<u>Mrs. Charles was a very different character...</u>" Once again, I have changed the name, though, if my arm was twisted, I'd probably

eventually admit that the name, Mrs. Charles, is very close to what her real name was. But, you'd have to twist my arm for me to admit that.

4. "...but without Howdy's ubiquitous smile." Hah! I got to use *ubiquitous* in a sentence!

5. "I did have a couple of English teachers later in high school, that made a valiant run for that title, but, in the final analysis, Mrs. Charles was the worst." As I look back on the many teachers that I had, in the many cities and states of my Education-Across-America odyssey, I really did, all in all, have a great bunch. Other than a handful of spectacular stand-outs (bleh!), most were quite good.

6. "Then a miracle happened, a bright blonde miracle named Mike Vogan." I can happily say that I did NOT change the name in this case. Mike has graciously allowed me to use his real name in this book. I believe that, were we not separated by six hundred miles and almost four decades, we would be best buddies right now. Mike Vogan, you rock!

7. "The second was about a young boy who dealt with troubles worse than mine..." *A Day No Pigs Would Die* was the first book written by author Robert Newton Peck. In his career, he would write sixty-five. A lot of them were about young boys dealing with circumstances. As an author, Mr. Peck was expert at creating characters that I was able to get a hold of and identify with. This was especially true of that first one. Robert, the main character of *A Day No Pigs Would Die*, helped me get through some tough times.

While I was writing this chapter, specifically this portion about hiding from Mighty Mouse in the library, it occurred to me how much this book had meant to me. I don't know if I've ever fully realized the book's impact until I wrote about it in this chapter. After I whispered a silent, "Thank you, Mr. Peck," to myself, I stared straight ahead for a moment and came to a realization. "I really should thank him."

Taking a break from Ocelot, I searched for Robert Newton Peck on the Internet. I found plenty of information about his work, but nothing about how to find him. I wasn't even sure if he was still alive. Coming from a generation that's often not real nuts about *that fangled Interweb thing*, he didn't own a personal website or fan page. It took a few days of detective work, which I won't bore you with, but I finally found an address on the East Coast.

I then sent a fan letter to Mr. Robert Newton Peck. I apologized to him for using his home address, and I thanked him for his influence. I told him, generally, about my teen struggles, and of how his characters, especially young Robert, had inspired me to battle on; of how his books ignited in me a love of reading, and of how I was now, in my own small way, trying to do the same; to entertain, and maybe even inspire, with my own printed words. I didn't expect him to write back, but he did. He sent me a quirky, hand-written letter with giant colorful print and a funny cartoon drawing of himself. The author asked me to call him, and he provided his home phone number. He signed the letter, "Your pal, Rob."

I was simultaneously excited and scared when I heard the phone pick up on the other end. I called at exactly the time of day that his letter had asked me to, so as not to interrupt his afternoon nap. I was greeted by his wife, who was a delight to chat with.

"Who?" I heard a male voice shout in the background, as I pictured Mrs. Peck holding the phone out to him. "Chris Ford, in Oregon?" he continued, still shouting, sounding like he was several feet from the phone. "Chris Ford! Well, if that isn't one guy that I just hate!" A second later, sounding, now, like his mouth was up to the phone, "Chris! How'n the world are ya?!"

My immediate thought was that "Rob" really is just as friendly and quirky as his letter had hinted at. He had me laughing, off and on, throughout our conversation. I told him that I was honored to speak with him. He told me that the honor was his, as both he and his wife had been deeply touched by my letter, and by the knowledge that his work had made a difference in someone's life. Between his delightfully corny jokes, I think he told me three times that he was eighty seven years old. At one point, after another corny one-liner, he said, "Sorry about that. I'm kinda a smart-ass sometimes. But, you've got to be smart, to be a smart-ass. Otherwise, you're just an ass."

He was warm and welcoming and he seemed genuinely interested in me and in my well-being. I was deeply honored, when he gave me advice, quoting from Matthew, chapter twenty-four, in The Bible. He mentioned the verse where Jesus told His followers that anyone who helps even the least of these (His people), that person would be doing it for Him.

This was exciting for me, because I had recently read that same passage and I had been mulling it for a few days. In fact, I have given similar advice to others, in the past. "Chris, it's all about loving Him, and loving others," Rob confidently shared.

"Thank you, Rob," I replied. "I will remember that." I enjoyed my conversation with the great author very much.

"If, or when, I get my book done," I told him, "I'll make sure that you get an autographed copy."

"Bah! I'll be dead by then!" he replied.

I laughed out loud.

8. "That training certainly did come in handy years later. But that's a different story." Let's tell that other story now. Those Judo classes saved my bacon a couple of times! In one case, when I was a senior in high school, I decided, for whatever reason, to ride sitting on the hood of my friend's car. He was parked about a half block from the school, and I guess I thought it would be easier to hitch a ride there than to walk. Boy-brain can be a powerful force for stupidity! I sat, sort of sidesaddle, on the driver's side of the hood, just behind the front left wheel, and he took off, slowly, toward the school. Just as we neared the big tree in front of the school, where about forty students were hanging out, I decided that it was time to leap off.

I have no idea why I thought that it would be alright to step off of a moving car! The instant that my feet hit the ground, I discovered that the car had been traveling far faster than I had realized. Forward I pitched; headlong. But, instead of smashing my face into the asphalt, like most people would have done, I instinctively did a perfect judo tuck-and-roll over my left shoulder. Books and folders spread across the street, in an abundantly visible paper explosion, right in front of that herd of loitering classmates, as I shot back up onto my feet and involuntarily affected a nimble karate fighting stance. As quickly as I could, I tried to act nonchalant. Other than my pride, I had incurred no injuries at all. I did receive a lot of comments from my appreciative audience - comments that ranged from, "What in the world was that?" to "That was the coolest thing I've ever seen!"

Years later - at, I'm guessing, thirty-two years-old - I was on top of my house, pressure washing the steep-pitched cedar shake roof. Everything was wet. Suddenly, a bee of some kind, a yellow jacket I think, took a personal interest in my head. I don't know what he thought I was! I doubt that I looked or smelled much like a flower, but the little menace was on me with enthusiasm! After multiple attempts to wave him away had failed, I started shooting the pressure washer at him. Off balance, due to the awkward positions that this battle required, my feet were suddenly out from under me and I was hitting the very wet cedar roof, buns-first. Down the bumpy slip-and-slide I shot, straight as an arrow toward the backyard. Thank goodness we lived in a one-story home! As the rain gutter passed beneath me, I not only kicked effortlessly into judo mode, I even had the presence of mind to utter a confident "yee-haw!" as I flew through the air. I hit the grass feet-first and, with just the right amount of spring in my legs, I immediately executed the same left-shouldered roll-out that I had done fifteen years earlier on that high school street.

Hearing the unmistakable sounds of her husband falling off of the house, Cheryl came running out of the back door just in time to see her wet husband challenging the backyard fence in a menacing karate fight stance. I quickly adjusted my position to a hopefully-not-as-embarrassing standing posture, and I blurted, "I'm okay!" She rolled her eyes, shook her head, and went back inside. I quickly tossed up a short prayer of thanks to God for my good reflexes and for Sergeant Daly. "You've saved my skin again, Top!" Top Sergeant Dick Daly, I wish you were still alive to read this, and to hear my heartfelt 'thank you' for being one of the men who invested time and effort into me during the crazy teen years. I know that there are plenty of other 1980's teen boys - now men, a little gray around the temples - that can look back and say that too. Here's to you, Top!

9. Regarding Bullying: In, and of itself, this chapter was meant to do nothing more than to tell a story. I'm not trying to elicit sympathy

for the unfortunate victimized skinny kid of thirty-five years ago. Quite the contrary, actually. I am not at all fond of the *victim mentality*, and I don't want to have it. So many people have had, and currently do have, far worse situations than mine. In fact, it's my hope that this story, indeed the entire book, will help someone to realize that strength can come from unlikely places; even from wimpiness - even from failure.

Decades later, I got an opportunity to have a frank discussion with a young seventh grade bully. It may be that my previous exposure to it had given me a perspective that I might not have otherwise had.

"Mike**," I told him, "You are the toughest, baddest kid in your grade." I paused for a moment. His eyes were on the ground. We stood outside of the main youth camp building, so we could have some privacy. I knew better than to single him out in front of his peers. He stood with a hand in his pocket, looking away, giving me no attention, biding his time, wondering how long he would have to stand and pretend to listen to the old dude.

"I could kill you with my bare hands, right now." That got his attention. He looked up at me and I silently held his eyes for a few seconds. "Right?... Do you doubt that?"

After a moment, he shook his head slowly. "No," he admitted quietly.

"In fact," I continued, "I might be wrong, but I'll bet that I'm the biggest, baddest guy in this whole place. There's not a student or a teacher or a kitchen staff person or any adult chaperone at this camp whose rear end I can't kick. Right?"

He nodded. He was holding my eyes now, paying attention. My unconventional ice-breaker had worked, it seemed.

"But everyone already knows that, Mike. I don't need to prove it. I don't need to make them afraid of me to have their respect. In fact, I hope that they all feel just a little bit safer, knowing that I'm here. I hope they all know that I will stand in front of them, if something scary comes through the door.

"It might be that no one in there has even noticed me, or knows that I'm here. That's alright with me too, because, whether they know it or not, I am that guy, and I know it. I will stand in front of them, if something scary comes through the door. Would you?"

I paused, to let him think.

"Respect is important, Mike. It feels good to be respected. I get that. But respect that's forced isn't real. The respect that you get from these kids, when you push them around, is based on fear and dislike, and that is false respect. It's a poor substitute for the real thing.

"Mike, you want respect? Real respect? Give them someone who is respectable. Be the man that others will want to hide behind, not the man that others want to hide from.*

"Mike, you're the dude. You're the honcho here. That's a cool thing. Use that. Use it to serve others, to protect others. Show your strength, not with anger or meanness, but with courage, and authentic manhood. The man that protects and helps them will get a lot more respect from them than the man who hurts them ever will. That takes real strength! Do you know why?" He slowly shook his head. "Because it's tough. It's hard to be strong, selfless and courageous. It's hard to be a leader. It's hard to put others first, and to stand up for what's right. It's easy to be mean and cruel. Weak people take the easy way, Mike. Bullies are weak. Is this making sense?"

"No one's ever told me this before," he replied very quietly.

"That's okay. No one told me either. Just think about it." I touched his shoulder and turned him toward the door. "Let's go back in there," I said with a smile. "Let's be the two men that they'll want to stand behind."

**I don't know how things turned out for Mike. As you could probably predict, Mike wasn't his real name.

*I placed a star (*) beside the sentence: "Be the man that others will want to hide behind, not the man that others want to hide from." I really like that. In my lifelong quest for authentic manhood, I think that this was one of my top five revelations. I like to quote great things that others have said and written. I believe that this is the only thing that I have written that I consider truly quotable. So, this is my quotable quote of the day. You're welcome.

10. "I wandered into the huge lunch room and sat alone in the middle of a long straight table." I've got to tell you a story about that table.

I need to place it here, in the Notes section, because it didn't fit the theme of chapter 7. Roughly a year prior to the events described at the end of chapter 7, an epic event happened while I sat in that same place; an event that is still talked about today. I'm not kidding. There was a big recent Facebook string about this, thirty-five years later. No one has forgotten.

It was Spring, 1981. I was still in seventh grade. I was sitting alone at the long table that I described in the subject sentence of this Notes entry, the one with the imitation wood grain. Suddenly I saw a pair of girls, two tables away from me, in the row closest to the stage, stand up and start throwing food. I didn't know them. They were eighth graders, and they were pretty; two excellent reasons why they wouldn't have known that I existed. They were grabbing large handfuls of spaghetti from their trays and hurling them at people sitting across from them. It was Spaghetti Day at Snohomish Junior High. They couldn't have chosen a better day!

Our vice principal, Mr. D, shouted from atop the stage for them to stop what they were doing. They ignored him, and threw their lunches as fast as they could, using both hands. It seemed to me, at the time, that what happened next must have been part of a large plan - a plan with many conspiring participants. The actions of the two mystery girls must have been the signal, for, at the next moment, chaos broke loose.

Movement drew my eyes to the right, where I saw a high wall of food coming toward us from a long distance. Like a missile attack in a low budget Armageddon movie, a massive barrage of innumerable foodstuffs arced across the lunchroom. I don't know why I find it so funny, but I will never forget the half-pint carton of milk that led the attack. It flew bottom first, spinning like a spiraling football, but slower. From the carton's opening, a long white line of fresh milk trailed behind it like the flaming tail of a rocket.

Once that first barrage of food hit their marks, a free-for-all began. I laughed as I slid under my table, and I watched as spaghetti and green beans and foods of all kinds flew in every direction. An uneaten bologna sandwich on wheat bread spun through the room like a Frisbee, and then, at the apex of its flight, came apart into

309

its individual mayonnaise-coated components, flying in different directions. Like a multi-warhead ballistic missile, it deployed, hitting multiple targets. One mayo-covered bread slice hit a girl in the back, slimy-side-down, and stuck there, right between her shoulder blades. I shook with laughter. Mr. D had stopped shouting and was frantically trying to take cover, as he seemed to be one of the main target objectives. His white dress shirt and his brown polyester pants, holdouts from the previous decade, were covered in marinara-coated noodles, like dozens of little bloody worms.

Our school was overpopulated in 1981, (Valley View Junior High was still being built), so the lunchroom was very full. A crowd of startled diners, mostly seventh graders, screamed and rumbled into each other like a herd of confused cattle.

Unable to make it to a door or a suitable hiding place, a group of victims were pinned against a long wall. Those poor youngsters were sitting ducks, like targets at a shooting range. I watched as they seemed to all get hit at once, some of them dropping to the floor as if hit by a real firing squad.

It was a food hurricane. So great was the battle, and so complete the carnage, that we made the famous food fight scene in *Animal House* look tame by comparison. I was one of the few to make it out clean. I'm sitting here, laughing quietly to myself, as I type this during my lunchbreak, almost thirty-five years later. Cleanup must have been horrible. I've always wondered what consequences came from that, for those most involved. If you were there, get on my website and tell me what you remember. Who knows – your memories might make it into a future printing of this book, should I be that fortunate. Oh, what I'd give for some film footage of that day!

Chapter 8: Firewind

1. "Quite the romantic at ten years old, I often loved imagining that I was seeing and hearing and smelling the very same things that long-dead colorful characters of the past had seen, heard and smelled. Okay, I still like to do that."

I really do, almost everywhere I go! For instance, almost every time I drive my family through the majestic Columbia River Gorge, where the massive and beautiful Columbia River separates Oregon from Washington, I tell them something about how Lewis and Clark came through this very gorge, and canoed this very river, and gazed up in awe at these same majestic cliffs and at the monolithic monstrous form of Mount Hood, very likely the first eleven thousand foot snow-covered volcano that any of them had ever seen.

"We know, Dad," (yawn…)

2. "We fancied ourselves much like treasure-hunting archeologists, but we were garbeologists." Around that same time, I went through a brief fascination with Archeology, especially as it dealt with ancient Egypt. In school libraries, I enjoyed looking through the books about Egyptian kings and tombs and the great archeological finds at exotic and mysterious places like Karnak, Luxor, the Valley of the Kings, and other exotic places. The traveling King Tut exhibit had recently come through nearby Sacramento, and the hype generated by that show probably added to my interest.

So, the word archeologist was very fresh to me. It seemed only fitting, to me, to invent the word garbeologist, as we did our own version of treasure hunting. Plus, it was a funny word that was fun to say, and it got a few laughs. I'm all about that!

Chapter 9: My Own War

1. "My mind would not come to rest, but it raced – wound up like a two-dollar watch." I have no idea what a two-dollar watch is. I included this simile just because I love the quaint, quirky, sometimes almost-unintelligible, idioms of the grandpa generation of men, like this one. "Wound up like a two-dollar watch." "It was colder than a well digger's belt buckle!" "I've known that since Moby Dick was a guppy." "He's nuttier than a squirrel turd." I love that stuff!

Chapter 11: The Goodness

1. "<u>Yes, there were times when the game took a diabolical and downright reprehensible direction as we played, (gasp!) 'Cowboys and Indians.' Oh the horror!</u>" I wonder what a Millennial mommy or, better yet, a twenty-first century public school administrator would say if their little Jimmy came home from a friend's house and said, "We played Cowboys and Indians!" Would they outlaw that friend's house, or just make them change the name of the game? Maybe they could call it, "Cowpersons and Indigenous Peoples." Or, how about, "Native Americans and Trespassing Aggressors?" I won't even mention our favorite game that used a football. I think it was called "Smear the..."

2. "<u>I had never seen one before. It was a Mountain Bar.</u>" They're still sold today, in the candy aisle of most grocery stores. They're made by a company called Brown & Haley, the same folks that bring us Almond Roca. So good!

3. "<u>...more healing than any prescription</u>." Results may vary.

Chapter 12: Always on Friday

1. "<u>...though they both had names that began with 'O'.</u>" Oley and Oria.
   "<u>Six-foot-Four? Yeah. Something like that. Maybe six-three.</u>" In the 1960s, and decades prior, six-foot-four was huge. It could be easy, reading this book now, to miss the significance. When I was a boy, in the '70s, I sometimes felt, in my odd little boy mind, almost like I had special status because my dad was six-four. It didn't matter where we went. My dad would almost always be the tallest person in the room. Comments were often made. "How's the weather up there?" It always made me a little proud.

   Just one generation later, six-four, while still pretty neat, is nowhere near as unusual. My father tells the story of the evening he dropped in to see my younger brother, Shanon, at his fraternity, at the University of Washington. Dad entered through the open front door to find an occasion of some sort in full swing. To find Shanon, Dad tried scanning about the crowded room for the tallest head. When that failed, he was required to make a more careful search. Finally, he found the six-foot, three-and-a-half-inch Shanon, chatting with a group of his Fraternity brothers. Dad was surprised to see that his son was one of the smaller guys in the group.

I topped out at a bit under 6'2". The runt of the litter.

Chapter 16: West Of Bliss

1. "It never failed to get some sort of exasperation out of Mom, which somehow made everything better." It's a teenage boy thing. If you are a mom of teen boys, you're probably smiling and nodding your head right now.
2. *"There are old chipmunks and there are bold chipmunks, but there are no old bold chipmunks."* This is a very old saying, though I might be the first to apply it to woodland rodents. I first heard this saying as it described airplane pilots. *There are old pilots, and there are bold pilots, but there are no old bold pilots.* I've heard this phrase used for mushroom hunters as well. I think its meaning is plain enough. And, like it does with pilots and mushroom hunters, I think it applies well with chipmunks bold or foolish enough to trust a dumb teenage boy.

   This was one of those memories that deserves *the sad smile.* Hmmmm... I think I need to write a story called "The Sad Smile" someday. That's a great title.
3. "...the Coronet's driver knew that ..." I am choosing to refer to him in impersonal terms, like this one. However, I do know the man's name. I have the newspaper article. But I will not use his name in this book. His prison sentence, from the events described in this chapter, is over. I am a believer in debts paid and in second chances. I am a believer in forgiveness. The black marks on his name caused by the mistakes of his youth will, no doubt, follow him throughout his life, in various ways - but not in these pages. As far as I am concerned, this person paid his debt to society when he complied with the orders of the court and served his time. He would be in his late fifties now, and I hope that he is living a happy life. Should I be fortunate enough to find my way into his book collection, I hope that he will reach out to me and say hello.

4. "Me? I'll go west." I love that William A. Shedd quote, "A ship in harbor is safe, but that is not what ships are built for." I've seen hurt and tragedy. I've had friends die. They could have avoided those deaths and heartbreaks if they had stayed home. But I can't live my life that way. No, I'm no daredevil. I like to think things through and weigh the risks. But, I like to live a life of adventure - even if, when I say "adventure," I use my own definition. You'll see a better explanation in the chapters called, "The Thread from Which We Hang," and "An Ocelot in an Underwear Drawer."

Chapter 18: Sideways

1. "When you're rafting that river..." This is the one story that is, technically, the least accurate, though it's not false by any means. In this story, I combined a number of elements from various real life events. Everything written in this story really did happen. It just didn't all happen the same day. I've been on a lot of rafting trips on a lot of rivers, and they've all been eventful. Though I described him accurately, I can't remember the real name of the river guide that led us around the great obstacle, which I have fancifully called, "The Meat Grinder," though it was called something else in real life. I've named him "Marty," because I like the name, and it was something close to that – Gordy, maybe. This is why I didn't identify the river by name.

Chapter 20: A Momentary Lapse of Raisin

1. "Sitting Looking out the Window, How Lucky the Birds..." From the poem "Birds," Copyright Betty Sampson, 2016. Previously unpublished. Used with permission. Betty makes amazing peanut brittle!

Chapter 23: It's Like a Whole Other Country!

1. "Texas has the best city names in the world!" Not intended to be a factual statement.

2. "I thought that, at any minute, he might break right into one of those wonderful old Country/Western ballads that tell the stories of young men meeting up with old men..." How many of those songs are there? I've referred to two here, in the wonderful old songs, "Old Dogs, Children and Watermelon Wine," by the great story teller Tom T. Hall, and "The Gambler," by Kenny Rogers. Kenny Chesney did a very poignant old-man wisdom song called "Don't Blink." Phil Vassar's, "Don't Miss Your Life," has some well-aged wisdom that'll just about make the toughest daddy and husband cry a little. "Chiseled in Stone," by Vern Gosdin will sure put a proud young man in his place.

I love John Mellencamp's great song, "Minutes to Memories," where a young song narrator tells of his bus ride with an elderly stranger, and of his advice that sounds almost word for word the same as Ol' Prospector John gave me in the Texline Café, as the song says things like, " you are young and you are the future, so suck it up and tough it out, and be the best you can." I especially like the part where the old traveler in the song contentedly falls asleep with his head against a cold bus window just after telling the younger man sitting beside him, "an honest man's pillow is his peace of mind." Man, I love stuff like that!

Chapter 24: Dining with Greatness

1. "My head pounded, my belly screamed, and I wondered if I was going to make it." It wasn't until I reread the book that I noticed what might look a little like a theme forming. Several of my stories sort of revolve around physical discomfort. Pain is memorable, I guess.

2. "On the wall, immediately beside the men's room door, there hung an oval picture, an elegant profile likeness of an ancient first century Roman man on the wall." I've tried internet searching to learn the identity of the handsome ancient man-of-stone hanging by those hundreds of identical restroom doors across America. No luck. The courteous young employees that I've spoken to all seem to think it's

Julius Caesar. Who would that make the pretty young stony lady by the door on the other side of the room? Greer Garson?

3. "Into the men's room I hurried, wishing I could have James Doohan transport me to Planet Exo III, or to the Motara Nebula, - anywhere but here!" Trekkies! I added these real Star Trek place names for you. *"Bonk Bonk on the head!"*

Chapter 26: Perspectives From Behind Bars

1. "It was Little League District All-Stars." Everything that I've written in this chapter is true, except the team names. At Little League District All-Stars, at least in our district, the team names are called by the names of the Little Leagues that they represent, which are often named after towns or neighborhoods. So, a typical All-Star match-up might be something like; Clackamas Little League versus Mount Hood Little League. I chose to simply give them generic baseball team names (Rangers and Mariners) so as not to reflect in any way on actual existing Little League programs. It isn't important who the characters were in the story. What's important is what they did, how they did it, and what the impacts of those actions were.

2. "In walked my umpire hero; the boss, Greg Handley." About two weeks after that All-Star tournament, Greg put me to work at another; the Seniors Division (sixteen year-olds) Oregon State All-Star Tournament, of which he was Umpire in Chief. At one particular game, I worked first base, and my umpire mentor worked the plate. Over at third base worked Brad, an excellent young umpire who calls me his 'Mentor.' Greg told us of what an honor it was to umpire that game with us, seeing first-hand the benefits of his own leadership efforts being handed down. I know what he meant, as I have, since then, had the honor to work a game with Brad and an excellent young umpire who now calls Brad 'Mentor.'

A few weeks later, Greg Handley got to realize his umpire dream as he officiated at the 2014 Little League World Series, Intermediate Division (thirteen-year-olds), in Livermore, California. He did a great job and had a wonderful time, but, while he was there, he wasn't feeling great. He wasn't sure why.

Shortly after returning from the World Series, still feeling less than well, Greg went to see a doctor. He was diagnosed with cancer. He was gone within a few months.

Without knowing that his days would be few, Greg Handley, in the cramped wooden shack of chapter 26, was helping me to move one step closer to being the man that I am today. The effects of his encouragement and his leadership will be with me forever.

At chapter 26's second game, the game in which one can, hopefully, recognize my 'lesson painfully learned,' I umpired wearing a shirt that said "In Loving Memory, GJH." I wear it often.

Before publication, I sent a rough draft of this chapter to Greg's beloved wife Leanne. I was delighted when she told me, in her very warm email response, that she enjoyed the chapter and she gave me permission to use Greg's name. She was happy that I would want to honor him this way.

At the end of one of her letters, she said something that has stuck with me. She wrote, "Thank you for honoring my beloved Greggie. I wish you all the best in your life. And remember to kiss and hug your wife. Love her like she won't be here tomorrow, because you never know what tomorrow will bring." A great reminder for all of us; and who would know better than she? God bless you, Leanne.

3. "Had I been wrong about my epic amounts of stinkitude?" Coining a word. How about 'Stinkage?' 'Stinkosity?' 'Stinkness?' 'Stinkality?'

4. "What ever happened to baseball being fun?"

I said, at the end of chapter 20, "A Momentary Lapse of Raisin," the following line, "A little suffering is worth it, if it'll make a good story." I have a short baseball adventure to illustrate that point. Though it has very little to do with Big Dave's question, "What ever happened to baseball being fun?" I give you a story from a different baseball game, where I was, for a moment in time, the only person having fun.

It was 2015 District Little League All-Stars, about a year after the events of chapter 26. The weather was hot that afternoon in Southeast Portland, but not unbearable. The crowd was huge. The grandstands were filled to overflowing, and there was an impressive number of lawn chairs and picnic blankets everywhere else. Hundreds of enthusiastic sweaty baseball fans completely surrounded the ballfield. I was the umpire behind home plate.

Well into a very exciting game, suddenly there came a new sound, ringing out over crowd - a loud high-pitched "beep-beep-beep." When I finally had an opportunity to, I looked toward the sound. Slowly rolling toward me down the sidewalk, just outside the ballfield on the first base side, was a truck with a big shiny white tank. The baseball spectators seated in that area split before it like the Red Sea, picking up their ice chests and camp chairs as the truck slowly lumbered deeper and deeper into the crowd, the truck's driver seemingly undaunted by the fact that there was a big event going on at the park today.

The schedule on his clipboard said that this was the correct time to empty the portable outhouses, and he was going to follow his schedule, by gum! Never mind the patriotic colorful banners and the barbecued chicken vendor and the throngs of children. Today is sani-can emptying day.

Unfazed by the dozens of angry glares around him, our cover-all-clad interloper opened the plastic door and went inside the first of the two portable restrooms, big flexible hose in hand.

Amused at this unusual bit of side entertainment, I returned my attention to the ballfield. The home team had just made an out, had run into their dugout, and were donning their batting helmets. The other team was taking their defensive positions on the field. A pitcher threw a warm-up pitch to his catcher.

Behind me, coaches stood talking through the backstop, reporting their player substitutions to the officials in the score booth. I moved myself into position between the catcher and the coach's defenseless turned backs with my mask in my hand, ready to use it as a shield, should a wild practice pitch come our way. I have blocked more than one would-be coach slayer this way.

I glanced toward the septic man to my right. The sound of the truck's sucker pump had just come on. It was at this point that I witnessed something fascinating. It came like a wave. I couldn't see it. It was invisible, but its effects were not. Like a sea of dominoes falling in order, baseball spectators moved as if choreographed.

Dozens of heads fell forward, hands covered faces, mouths fell open, and muffled grunt-and-heave sounds burped forth. As the stink wave came, I knew exactly where its leading edge was, as every single person that it hit changed immediately from the body language of pleasant conversations to that of near-vomit misery. Observing its advance, I knew the exact moment that it would hit me. When it did, I wasn't caught unaware. I was the only person in that stadium who was ready, though I must say that I had not quite prepared myself for just how bad it would be.

Freeze-frame! Stop your mind movie here for a moment, Dear Reader, and take in the still mental photograph. A beautiful early summer day in Oregon, flowers in bloom, trees in leaf, a crowded park in All-Star glory. Exactly half of a baseball crowd, the half on the first base side, is nauseously doubled over, eyeballs bulging, hands on mouths; while the other half looks normal - happy even. In your still frame, you can see smiles over on the third base side, conversations in midsentence. A hot dog is raised in front of an open mouth. Directly between these two disparate factions, at home plate stands a man in gray slacks and a blue shirt, with district and state patches sewn to the sleeves. In his hand, a shiny black umpire's mask; on his face, a wry and mischievous grin. You can't tell from your mind photo, but he is holding his breath.

Now, Reader, start your mind movie up again, but at half speed. The people of the third base grandstands' bottom row all react simultaneously as the stink wave reaches that far. Eyes open wide. Bodies flinch as if struck. "Bleh!" a few of them shout. Now spectator row two... now three. On it goes, like a wave, straight uphill. Row four, then five. Now six. On it rolls. Myriad ball cap wearing Americans, for the most part strangers, unwittingly perform a harmonized heave-and-retch dance, in near-perfect synchronicity.

At this point, as I stand there on the infield dirt, I don't even mind the bad smell. Trying not to grin, I am reminded, once again, as my nostrils burn and my eyes water, "A little suffering is worth it, if it'll make a good story."

5. A very appreciative *Shout-Out* to the excellent Little League officiating volunteers of chapter 26; Greg and Leanne Handley,

Corey Tobias, Frank Cantino, Rob Crawley and Brad Parker, as well as all of my brothers and sisters in blue out there – the third team on the ballfield. Keep up the good work, Blue!

Chapter 27: The Thread From Which We Hang

1. "<u>But, we didn't wear them (bicycle helmets) back then. It wasn't even something that we thought about.</u>" No one that I knew of was wearing bicycle helmets in 1979. When my brother and I would jump our Redline BMX Bikes, our parents required that we wear our motorcycle helmets. But only when we were jumping.

Chapter 28: Forty Feet down, Fifty Years To Go

1. "<u>There we found a long picturesque beach; Makena Beach it was called, we would later learn.</u>" I also learned, later on, that the locals simply refer to it as "Big Beach."
2. "<u>Well done Pierre!</u>" I actually have no idea what his name was. That is why I have referred to him with multiple names; Pierre, Monsieur Lady-Slayer, Flippered Felipe, and others. They're all the same guy. He was very handsome and very confident, but I got the feeling that the young bikini beauties in my class didn't like him nearly as much as he thought they did.
3. "<u>...getting our Metro stuck in beach sand from following its bumper too well...</u>" I've never been a burly muscular guy. This was especially true when I was younger. But those Metros are so small, I learned, on a secluded beach in Maalaea Bay, that it is possible to pick up the car's rear end and lift it out of the sand. So, feel free to try that.
4. "<u>...the all-time greatest icky-icky dance after walking through the thickest spider web I've ever felt.</u>" Truly, this was the thickest web I have ever encountered, still to this day. Fat. Tough. I looked down and saw a massive, bright green spider on my left thigh. Oh, did I freak! "Nice moves," my new bride said with a laugh. I would later learn that Hawaii does not have any venomous spiders. Had I known that at the time, I doubt that my dance moves would have been any less goofy.

Chapter 29: When It's Ten

1. "<u>At that moment, though I hadn't even laid eyes on my doctor, I loved him; in a strange disembodied way.</u>" Have you ever been there? You might understand this feeling. When the body is in distress, sometimes the mind and emotions can be a bit raw as well. I placed this sentence into the story for those of you who have experienced this strange sensation; love, or something like it - and extreme gratitude.

   Having felt it, myself, I almost sobbed during the medical scene in the movie *Captain Phillips*, expertly portrayed by Tom Hanks. I was sitting in a darkened theater beside my wife, trying not to lose it, as Captain Phillips cried and struggled to control his emotional breathing, the whole while saying, over and over, "Thank you... thank you" to the nurses and doctors that helped him. Memories of emergency rooms and kidney stones and expert medical care hit me and I empathized with the movie character. Tears poured down my face.

   It's a weird feeling.

2. "<u>Silently, she watched me, I would later learn. One of my favorite young people that I have ever coached...</u>" Her name is Christine. She would tell me, years later, about three weeks after her wedding - one of the loveliest brides I have ever seen - that those high school years had been "a tough, tough time for me in a lot of ways." She told me that she was grateful to me because her time spent under my coaching had been a great encouragement for her. Christine, I am the one who is grateful. Thanks for trusting me, for working hard for me, and for allowing me to be your coach. It was an honor that I cannot describe. That goes for you too, Michelle, Debra, Lydia, Alexis, Haley, Alina, Emily, Mary, Amanda, Talida, Heather, Roxana, Elona, Ashley and all of the rest of you! Go Huskies!

Chapter 30: An Ocelot in an Underwear Drawer

1. <u>Ryley, our trip leader, two days into his ninety-third trip down this river...</u>" Like with other chapters of this book, real life people

have been accurately portrayed, but with fictional names. The story character that I call "Ryley" was not actually named Ryley. His real name was pretty close to that, though. There's another boatman in this chapter whose name I have been creative with, as well. Regardless of their printed names, they are real men, and I enjoyed getting to know them very much.

Similarly, the very real Ray, Vivian, Judy and Beth characters, in this story, have been renamed, as well.

2. <u>When you're riding a rubber raft, even a giant motorized one, over massive violent class nine or class ten Grand Canyon river rapids…"</u>

Whitewater Rapids are generally graded on a five-point scale, with class three and four being the standard super fun ones. Class five is a rating for an advanced rapid, based on size, speed, technicality and danger. It is the highest rating for navigable rapids. Class five rapids should be rafted with great care.

The Rapids of the Grand Canyon Colorado River are graded on a scale of ten. This may be the only place where river rapids are scored this way. Rapids with a score of eight, nine or ten are advanced rapids that are huge, fast and dangerous, each of which have recorded fatalities – the best rapids I have ever seen – indeed, the best rafting trip I have ever taken.

Chapter 31: Being The Ocelot

1. <u>"Just beneath it, you should also see a… subtitle; Adventures of a Profoundly Imperfect and Intensely Happy Man.</u>" Often, an author will consider and argue and fuss over a single word. This is especially true as it applies to a book's title. "And" or "But?" That was my conundrum, in this case. "…a Profoundly Imperfect *but* Intensely Happy Man." "*But*" works pretty well there. In fact, this was the book's working title almost throughout the project. "*But*," though, connotes a certain amount of concession, or compromise, don't you think? Whereas "*And*", in this case, provides inclusion, acceptance. I'm not Intensely Happy in spite of my Profound Imperfection; no, I'm actually Intensely Happy WITH and IN my Profound Imperfection! Through it, and alongside of it! In concert with it. This

is why I eventually decided on the word "And." It's more accurate, and, I think, more inspiring than "But." Though, I reluctantly have to admit that "But" sounds better.

Seriously! Authors do this! The ones who care, anyway.

2. "I want to kick the devil's hide." My friends who are reading this book are probably saying to themselves, "Hide? That's not the way Chris usually says it." They'd be right. No, I generally put it a bit more bluntly and strongly, with a different word at the end – one that has only three letters. As it says in the text of this chapter, "How's that for wildcat thinking?" This really is the message of this chapter. Be a wildcat! Be Strong. Get out there with boldness. Remember that Our Lord, when he was walking here on Earth, sat and ate with sinners. I don't think that He was so easily offended when He heard the odd off-color word or remark. I, in fact, wonder how we can be of any relevance or of any real help to a lost world that's hurting and in need of our message if we're so easily offended at something like a *colorful metaphor*. In this book, I have changed the word to "hide," because I know that not all share my belief on this matter. Hang out with me much, though, and you'll probably hear it said the other way.

3. "First off, He wants…" In books and other printed media, it's a fairly common thing to see words like "He" and "Him" and "His" capitalized, when referring to God. That is what I have done. To me, regardless of the reasons that other writers have done it, I do this out of utmost respect. If I followed the normal rules of prose, and wrote "he," instead of "He," I'm fairly certain that God wouldn't mind. I do this for me. I love Him and I hold Him high. In my writings, He will be capitalized. I'm not sure that I could do it any other way.

4. "…the Lord is…not willing that any should perish…" 2Peter 3:9, KJV

5. "…a rich and satisfying life." John 10:10, NLT

6. "…in all its fullness." John 10:10, BSB

7. "…that they might have life, and that they might have it more abundantly." John 10:10, KJV

8. "…the mind set on the flesh is death, but the mind set on the spirit is life and peace." Romans 8:6, NASB

9. "<u>Who shall separate us from the love of Christ? Shall trouble or hardship...</u>" Romans 8:35-37 (emphasis mine) NIV
10. "<u>Seek first His Kingdom and His Righteousness, and *all these things* will be added to you...</u>" Matthew 6:33 (emphasis mine), NASB
11. "<u>will guard your hearts and minds *as you live in Christ Jesus.*</u>" Philippians 4:7 (emphasis mine), NLT
12. "<u>For I am convinced that neither death nor life, neither angels nor demons...</u>" Romans 8:38-39 (emphasis mine) NIV

Epilogue

1. "...there is a way that seems right to a man...(or a teen)...but its end is the way of death." Proverbs 14:12 (parentheses mine) NASB
2. "...the heart is deceitful...who can know it?" Jeremiah 17:9 KJV
3. "...I can do all things through Him who gives me strength." Philippians 4:13 NASB

Acknowledgements

The first person that I want to acknowledge is you. And I don't mean that in some trite, cutesy way. I am very serious. This is my first book, and maybe my last. As such, it is very personal to me. It has been, quite literally, a labor of love. If you took the time to read this mess, then I am surprised, touched, humbled, and deeply honored - all at once. Thank you.

If it hadn't been for Lisa Dobbins, I probably would never have done this project. She's my sister-in-law: my wife's brother's wife. It is she who patiently prodded, cajoled, and encouraged me for years (decades) to start writing again. And it is she whom I have referred to as "a very good friend of mine" in the chapters called "A Rich Man," and "Walk Tall." Thanks, Lisa.

Nick Wusz was my *Real-time Beta Reader*. Each time I finished a chapter, I printed it off and walked it over to Nick, who read, considered and commented in mid-project. This was super helpful to me, as during much of this process, I wasn't even sure whether or not I was writing a book at all. Nick! You awesome, fun, genuine Dude! Thanks for the encouragement, the ideas and the constructive criticism.

Lydia Ford was my other *Beta Reader*. The book was done and off to the editor when Lydia did most of her work. As a senior in college with plenty of Writing and English teaching fresh in her mind, and as a voracious reader and an unusually insightful individual, her inputs were fantastic.

My editor was Emilie Ratcliff. Picture the sweetest person you can, Reader Friend. Now stir in an additional teaspoon of honey and you'll have Emilie Ratcliff. Thank you Emilie for the hard work, and a job expertly done! And, sorry, about, all, those, extra, commas,.

Rebecca Gillock is the artist who created the cool cover image. Thanks Beckles for the hours that you put in while creating this beautiful picture, and for your patience as you endured and indulged an author who, at times, wasn't even sure what he wanted. Your flexibility and your insightful inputs were so valuable.

Brad Glover, at the Boise Library in Boise, Idaho, went beyond the call of duty, as he did a lot of archive searching to help me find the old newspaper stories about the 1984 Idaho Olympic Torch relay, and the police chase described in Chapter 16. This info was very helpful in the writing of that chapter. I think it was just as fun to read the car and clothing sales ads in that newspaper as it was the story about me.

Big 'Thank You's' go out to Greg Hopp, Chelea (Dunbar) Hoffman, Laura (Cruger) Whitlock, Lisa (Elliott) Sylvia, Ken Roberts, Brad McDaniel, Mike Vogan, Robert Newton Peck, and Leanne Handley for allowing me to mention them in my stories. All of you played a part and had an impact on my life. And thanks, Betty Sampson, for your picturesque poem at the beginning of chapter 20.

To my family, I owe so much. To my dad, Troy; my mom, Dixie; and my brother, Shanon - the first Ford Crew - I say thank you. You played massive parts in helping me to become the man that I am today. You showed me what Family means. I love you all so much!

For my current Ford Crew, my own dear family: my wife, Cheryl; my daughter, Lydia; and my son, Mitch; words fail me. Thank you Bre, for allowing me the privilege of stepping into your life as Daddy. Love beyond containment. Thankfulness for a wife so good and a marriage so blessed. Pride in the lives of my children, now fine adults. I have so much to be thankful for. Which brings me to my final - most important - acknowledgement.

A life as blessed and happy as mine doesn't just happen. I publicly acknowledge my thankfulness for, and dependence on, a great God and Savior who sees me through - who loves me so much - who paid such a high price. Jesus Christ is His name.

Peace to you, Dear Reader. May you have the strength to forgive quickly, the faith to look upward thankfully, and the vision to look ahead expectantly. May you always strive to be The Ocelot. May you enjoy the peace of the Underwear Drawer. Be *blessed*. Be happy. And remember…

God has called you to live a life of adventure.

Makarios, my friend.
Chris

Find me out there in Cyber World and let me know how you're doing. And whether you're reaching me electronically, or you're passing me on the street, say "Hakatai!" and I'll know you've read my book.

Good night, Flash.

About the Author

Christopher Scott Ford is a profoundly imperfect and intensely happy man who loves the art of good storytelling. Having been a sports coach, teenage alcoholic, stand-up comic, baseball umpire, aerospace designer, camp counselor, church deacon, surrogate dad, amateur teacher, preacher and lover of the open road, he has a few stories to tell. He currently lives in Gresham, Oregon, where he designs cab components for big trucks and where he loves his wife, Cheryl, and his two grown children, Lydia and Mitch, as well as a handful of others who, though not legally his, lovingly call him "Dad" anyway, which he couldn't be happier about.

Printed in the United States
By Bookmasters